THIS IS ALL I CHOOSE TO TELL

In the series ASIAN AMERICAN HISTORY AND CULTURE
edited by Sucheng Chan, David Palumbo-Liu,
Michael Omi, K. Scott Wong, and Linda Trinh Võ

(Additional titles in this series can be found at the back of this book.)

THIS IS ALL I CHOOSE TO TELL

History and Hybridity in
Vietnamese American Literature

ISABELLE THUY PELAUD

Temple University Press

PHILADELPHIA

Temple University Press
Philadelphia, Pennsylvania 19122
www.temple.edu/tempress

♾ The paper used in this publication meets the requirements of the
American National Standard for Information Sciences—Permanence
of Paper for Printed Library Materials, ANSI Z39.48-1992

LIBRARY OF CONGRESS CATALOGING-IN-PUBLICATION DATA

Pelaud, Isabelle Thuy, 1965–
  This is all I choose to tell : history and hybridity in Vietnamese American
literature / Isabelle Thuy Pelaud.
    p.   cm. — (Asian American history and culture)
Includes bibliographical references and index.
ISBN 978-1-4399-0216-5 (cloth : alk. paper)
ISBN 978-1-4399-0217-2 (pbk. : alk. paper)
ISBN 978-1-4399-0218-9 (electronic)
  1. American literature—Vietnamese American authors—History
and criticism.   2. Vietnamese Americans in literature.   3. Cultural
fusion in literature.   4. Multiculturalism in literature.   5. Race in
literature.   6. Vietnamese Americans—Ethnic identity.   7. History in
literature.   8. Vietnam War, 1961–1975—Literature and the war.   I. Title.
PS153.V54P45   2010
810.9'895922073—dc22

                                                2010018210

    2 4 6 8 9 7 5 3 1

THE
AMERICAN
LITERATURES
INITIATIVE
A book in the American Literatures Initiative (ALI), a
collaborative publishing project of NYU Press, Fordham
University Press, Rutgers University Press, Temple University
Press, and the University of Virginia Press. The Initiative is
supported by The Andrew W. Mellon Foundation. For more
information, please visit www.americanliteratures.org.

Contents

PREFACE

*Once upon a time there were three blind men strolling down
a path. They came to an elephant standing in the middle of a
road. "Watch out for the elephant!" someone nearby yelled. The
first blind man approached the elephant, touched its trunk, and
said: "I know what an elephant looks like. It looks like a tree!"
The second blind man walked up to the elephant's ear, touched
it, and said: "No, no, you are wrong. I know what an elephant
looks like. It resembles a giant cabbage leaf!" Finally, the third
blind man caught the elephant's tail and exclaimed: "What are
you two talking about? An elephant is like a broomstick!"*

STORY HEARD AT A BUDDHIST TEMPLE, 1984

As with all researchers and literary critics, the questions I ask
and my analysis are shaped by my academic training and personal background. My personal upbringing differs from that of
many of my peers. I was born in France to a Vietnamese mother
and a French father, and neither one has a college education. I
attended a public high school near a small village in the south of
France. In 1984, at the age of nineteen, I immigrated by myself
to the United States, where I first lived in Gardena near Los Angeles with my Vietnamese American aunt, uncle, and their children. I did not speak English and knew nothing of the academic
world. I worked in a nail salon near Orange County, home of
the largest Vietnamese American community in California, and
as a horse trainer, before moving to San Jose some years later. I
then attended ESL classes, adult school, community college, and
finally the University of California at Berkeley. There I studied
cultural and visual anthropology, film, and francophone literature, and eventually focused on Asian American literature. I
received the help of many along the way. Because of my unique
background, whatever critiques I may have of American society

are mitigated by the experience of America as a land of rebirth. This book includes observations made on a long and uncharted path, and was born out of my personal commitment to work at the intersection of academia, activism, and art.[1] Behind *This Is All I Choose to Tell* lies the desire to inform, include, understand, and create.

Acknowledgments

I owe my perseverance to my son, sixteen years old at the time of this writing, as his smile and his trust gave me the strength to keep going on this academic, activist, and creative path. I also owe some of this drive to my mother, her energy and sense of sacrifice; my discipline I owe to my father. I am most grateful to my husband Antoine, who during the last ten years has given me the tenderness and steadiness that I need to hold still, and a little bit of editing along the way. I can focus thanks to his gentle and patient companionship.

I am profoundly indebted to David Palumbo-Liu for believing in me, a faith that has carried me during the last seven years as I pursued what I thought was impossible. I thank Kathy Nguyen not only for her diligence but also for caring about this project. It could not have been completed without her careful editing, which she did as if the manuscript were her own. I thank my students for motivating me and providing relevance to this work. Their questions and comments over the years have greatly contributed to the shaping of this book. It is designed for them and others like them.

My continued involvement in Asian American studies is a

testament to the field's diversity and inclusion of mixed-race perspectives. I am grateful to my academic mentors, some of whom have deeply influenced my thinking and ways of being. I am grateful to Elaine Kim for serving as my dissertation chair and role model. I am thankful to the late Ronald Takaki for introducing me to Asian American history and race inequalities in the United States and for inspiring me with stories. I thank Khatharya Um, with whom I studied Vietnamese American scholarship, and Trinh T. Minh-Ha for always asking hard questions. I thank Karl Britto for introducing me to postcolonial literature, for his encouragement, and for reading and thoughtfully commenting on early versions of some chapters in this book. I also thank Peter Zinoman for reading and commenting on my analysis of *Fake House*, and Lisa Lowe, who without knowing me personally, provided generous and meaningful support for the last five years. Much of my work, analysis, and reflections can be thought of as a distillation of these scholars' respective approaches and intellectual visions.

I am blessed with the love of old friends who kept encouraging me throughout the development of this book. I thank Anh Bui, Emily Payne, Ulla Reinitzer, Michelle Tellez, and Loan Tran for always being there, happy when I am happy and mad when I am mad. I also thank Anh, along with Rebekah Linh Collins, Eithne Luibheid, and Viet Nguyen for generously reading, editing, and commenting on early drafts of this manuscript. I thank Viet for helping me brainstorm and come up with the title, and Dan Duffy for helping with references. My friends Lexine Alpert, Nerissa Balce, Mia Ong, Mimi Nguyen, Thuy Linh Tran, and Diep Vuong made graduate school a warm and memorable experience. I thank Mariam Beevi Lam, Lan Duong, and Thu-Huong Nguyen-Vo for their warm support. I thank Gilles Marin for helping me be aware of the links between body and emotions.

I am also grateful to all my colleagues at San Francisco State University, whose dedication to students is admirable. I am particularly thankful to Chris Chekuri, Madeline Hsu, Ben Kobashigawa, and Amy Sueyoshi for their friendship, as well as for providing productive and generous feedback on drafts of this manuscript. I thank Russell Jeung and Wei-Ming Dariotis for their good advice. I thank Department Chair Lorraine Dong and College Dean Ken Monteiro for their fairness and encouragement. I thank students Daisy Isarraras, Yuki Obayashi, and Danny Nguyen for their contribution to this project.

I want to acknowledge the substantial help from the Asian American Studies Department and College of Ethnic Studies, as well the offices of Provost John Gemello and President Robert A. Corrigan at San Francisco State University, who awarded me various grants, release time, and two semester sabbatical leaves, without which this book would not have been completed. I thank Janet Francendese at Temple University Press for working with me so kindly and patiently. I also thank the William Joiner Center for the Study of War and Social Consequences for its support.

I have high appreciation for those with whom I engage in community organizing, and many of them have become my friends through the years. I respect and admire their spirit of volunteerism. Working with them brings me meaning as well as valuable insights. I thank Nguyen Qui Duc, whose leadership brought me to enjoy community organizing and with whom I share the pleasures of a glass of wine in the company of friends. I am grateful to Khanh Mai, David Nguyen, Marguerite Nguyen, and Minh Tsai for their dedication over the years. I also thank the Vietnamese American writers and poets I have met, who do not cease to elevate my spirits and whose work and life keep on expanding my understanding of human resiliency and creativity.

I thank Binh Danh for creating an art piece especially for the cover of this book, Andrew Pham for letting us use a handwritten letter to his aunt in Viet Nam for it, and Viet Le for the design.

I am grateful to my parents, who sent me to the United States, a country with many flaws but where I was able to build a life beyond their dreams. Thanks to the welcoming treatment I re-

XII / ACKNOWLEDGMENTS

ceived from my Vietnamese American family, from my aunt Kim Lai Pham in particular, and the tolerance for difference that I found in northern California, I was able to reinvent myself and serve causes beyond myself. And not least, I thank my recently found brother Gerard Pelaud for accepting my love.

THIS IS ALL I CHOOSE TO TELL

Introduction

This Is All I Choose to Tell offers an analytical introduction to Vietnamese American literature, and delineates the historical, social, and cultural terrains from which the writings emerge and critics read and interpret them. It addresses the debates, themes, and issues that surround the production of that literature, foregrounding the concept of hybridity, and closely examining a few texts that students are likely to read in university settings. *This Is All I Choose to Tell* views many Vietnamese American literary texts as discrete steps in the process of articulating new identities that cannot be fixed in time. As it generalizes strategically about Vietnamese American identity and experiences, this work simultaneously examines these identities in terms of subjectivities that are always in flux and vary greatly, depending, for instance, on the individual's time of arrival, class, race, gender, sexuality, and exposure to trauma.

Although Vietnamese Americans established a presence in America more than thirty-five years ago, this is the first book-length study of their literature. It considers such questions as who Vietnamese Americans are and what are the main themes and markers of the literature they have created. What can we learn from Vietnamese American texts? And what is the place of this literature in Asian American studies, and why? From a more theoretical standpoint, I ask how one can study the external forces that shape Vietnamese American identity and articulate this identity while acknowledging the impossibility of fully encapsulating it, and while recognizing the imperfect nature of generalizations. Also, can the term "Vietnamese American," so freighted with memories of the Viet Nam War and national guilt, be disassociated from the systems of representation and history of that event without eradicating its legacy? And finally, can a Vietnamese American narrator's memory of the past be analyzed without replicating a problematic law of origin as arbiter of both content and form?

As it addresses these questions, *This Is All I Choose to Tell* engages with the material, political, and historical production of differences that stands in stark contrast to a multiculturalism that asserts representationality for all. Rather than regarding the texts as narratives of progress and assimilation, it detects forces of exclusion and directives that work both for and against Vietnamese American literary production.[1] Race is understood here as politically, socially, historically, and culturally constructed. Vietnamese Americans writers, because of their connection to the Viet Nam War and because they are people of color, encounter stronger pressure of representation than other Asian American immigrants.

The book is divided in two parts. The first, which includes three chapters, speaks toward the "inclusion" of Vietnamese American literary studies in academia and of Vietnamese American literature in American culture. Because students know so little about the Vietnamese American history that is often woven into the narratives themselves, the first chapter provides an introduction to social and historical contexts of postcolonial, refugee, immigrant, minority, and transnational Vietnamese American experiences; it also looks at what it means to be largely absent from the narrative of the nation. To further situate the texts selected for discussion, chapter 2 surveys Vietnamese American literature from the 1960s to 2010, pointing to themes like home politics, nostalgia, history, return, and identity. The chapter considers how and why novels, autobiographies, memoirs, collaborative projects, translations, and anthologies have changed over this half century. In chapter 3, I locate Vietnamese American literature within the field from which this book is produced, namely, Asian American studies. It asks why no book on Vietnamese American literature has been published until now in that field, and it identifies key frameworks within which one might read that literature, stressing the importance of those that account for hybridity. This chapter challenges the ubiquitous images of the Viet Nam War that tend to color the perception of Vietnamese Americans and addresses concerns about the depoliticization and dehistorization of Asian American literary criticism.

After setting the larger context in which Vietnamese American literature is produced, Part Two, "Interpretation," deepens the analysis. Chapter 4 explores strategies of survival in Andrew Pham's creative nonfiction memoir *Catfish and Mandala: A Two-Wheeled Voyage through the Landscape and Memory of Vietnam*[2] and Lan Cao's novel *Monkey Bridge*[3] while taking in consideration issues of race, class, gender and trauma. It looks at the narrators' memories and emotional responses to resettlement, and finds them central to the identities articulated in the texts, sometimes also constructed as protective shields. The narrators' trauma-induced and heightened sense of vulnerability has called for a borrowing of cultural nationalist observations. Even in the first decade of the twenty-first century, as relatively new immigrants they still wrestle with issues of self-hatred and lack of entitlement. In contrast to cultural nationalists, I do not frame the stories, however, solely in terms of resistance or accommodation.

The fifth chapter examines two books from different genres that expressly work against audience expectations, though they arrive at opposite points of view, one emphasizing hope and the other despair. Truong Tran's prose poetry *dust and conscience* (2002) argues that Vietnamese American identity is elusive, intangible, and in the process of formation, and thus cannot be captured in linear narratives. It examines instead the void created by the absence of home. The narrator remains hopeful for a stable and recognizable identity by inventing new words and ways of communicating the marginal self. Linh Dinh's collection of short stories, *Fake House* (2000), on the other hand, emphasizes despair, provoking the audience with raw and crude language. It explores the dysfunction produced by conditions across lines of class, race, gender, sexuality, and geography; it suggests that poor Vietnamese and Vietnamese American women are located near the bottom of a food chain impacted by wars, globalization, and patriarchy.

The four books analyzed in those two chapters explicitly or implicitly address the enormous pressures of being associated with the Viet Nam War. The sixth and last chapter focuses on these pressures: reading mostly mainstream press reviews along with the texts highlights the existence of a dialectic relationship between mainstream American society and Vietnamese American cultural productions. Reviewers clearly tend to read those texts with the Viet Nam War in mind and with preconceived notions of Asian Americans; the expectations of reviewers in turn, I suggest, can influence the writing of the texts.

Inspired by those who fought hard to institute ethnic studies programs forty years ago, *This Is All I Choose to Tell* covers the issues I see as relevant to this body of work, even if they might elicit discomfort among readers. Edward Said observed that the choice facing engaged scholars is always between actively representing the truth to the best of their ability and passively allowing a patron or authority to direct them. "For the secular intellectual," Said reminds us, "*those* gods always fail."[4] I chose to serve the field of Asian American studies by honoring both the unity and diversity among us. In 2010, I do believe that we must listen to the multiple voices within communities and afford them all respect in order to imagine and make a world free from racism, sexism, classism, homophobia, and imperialism.

PART ONE

INCLUSION

1 / History

> Irretrievable, the past must be mourned and remembered and
> assimilated. To truly grieve the loss of a nation and the robbed
> history of a banished people, that old umbilical cord must
> be unearthed and, through the task of art, through the act of
> imagination, be woven into a new living tapestry.
>
> ANDREW LAM, "CHILD OF TWO WORLDS"

> At best, history is a story about power, a story about those who
> won.
>
> MICHEL-ROLPH TROUILLOT, SILENCING THE PAST

In a speech to Veterans of Foreign Wars on August 22, 2007, President George W. Bush said: "One unmistakable legacy of Vietnam is that the price of America's withdrawal was paid by millions of innocent citizens whose agonies would add to our vocabulary new terms like 'boat people,' 're-education camps,' and 'killing fields.'"[1] He went on to cite the 400,000 Vietnamese who were sent to prison camps and the tens of thousands more who perished after America's withdrawal from Viet Nam in 1975. This recollection of the past clashes with the normative memory of the conclusion to the Viet Nam War as an ignominious end to a misguided war with very few negative repercussions for the United States and its allies.[2] Vietnamese refugees' tears, losses, and blood were suddenly reinserted into the historical narrative, not to learn from these experiences but to request more funds to continue a war in Iraq. This revisionist national rhetoric appropriates human rights violations to allow America to shed itself of national responsibility and guilt, and rationalizes conquest and war.[3]

In light of this recent political context, it is thus important to keep in mind that America is a superpower. By 1914, we cannot forget, Europe held roughly 85 percent of the earth in the form of colonies, protectorates, dependencies, dominions, and commonwealths. To compete with Europe, the United States intervened abroad extensively after 1945, in more than seventy nations, and as of 2007 had 745 military bases in 120 countries.[4] Viet Nam was one such occupied nation, having been colonized by the French for one hundred years.[5]

Refugees

Vietnamese Americans came to the United States in large numbers around the time of the fall of Saigon in 1975, and their arrival represents the largest population movement to America since the immigration of Jews during and after World War II. They number over 1.5 million, constituting the fifth largest Asian American group in the United States and the most important population of Vietnamese in the diaspora.

The term "Vietnamese American" commonly refers to Vietnamese refugees who came to the United States after the victory of communist forces in Viet Nam in 1975, or what Vietnamese Americans call "The Fall of Saigon." Not all Vietnamese came to the United States as refugees, however, nor did they all come in 1975. Vietnamese came to the United States after World War II as students, scholars, and war brides.[6] Young Vietnamese were recruited to study in America by the CIA and the U.S. military to combat communism. The number of such temporary migrants increased as U.S. involvement in Viet Nam expanded.[7] The Vietnamese student population grew, for instance, from a mere two hundred between 1952 and 1959 to about three thousand between 1960 and 1969.[8]

For over twenty-five years, South Viet Nam was an ally of the American government in what was the longest war in American history. Some Vietnamese soldiers spent their entire adult lives fighting in that war. South Vietnamese fought with the Americans against the North Vietnamese, believing that Americans would continue to support them until they were victorious over the communist forces. They believed America, the strongest superpower in the world, could not lose. When the Americans left Viet Nam, Vietnamese southerners felt deeply abandoned and betrayed. They feared for their lives and for the lives of their family members. Many attempted to flee. The United States received the largest number of refugees at the end of the Viet Nam war, followed by France, Australia, and Canada.[9] Smaller numbers went to Germany, England, Japan, and later to northern European countries.[10] Most of the 700,000 Vietnamese who came to the United States as refugees did so because they feared retaliation by the communists due to their past affiliation with the Republic of Viet Nam in the south and its American allies.[11]

South Vietnamese refugees lost their land, their homes, their wealth, their social status, their neighborhoods, family members, and friends. Some had already experienced emigration in 1954, having moved from the North to the South when the country was divided at the seventeenth parallel at the Geneva Conference.[12] Those from more privileged backgrounds had received a French education under the influence of a century of French colonization, or had worked closely with Americans and spoke English.[13] Many did not. Some were traumatized by the war, their departure and journey, and their experience in refugee camps in neighboring Asian countries. Many who could not flee in 1975 and emigrated later suffered tremendously in postwar Viet Nam from unemployment, malnutrition, and oppressive government measures. Thousands were incarcerated in reeducation camps, where human rights violations were rampant.[14] It is rarely mentioned in textbooks that the American government had not prepared for the evacuation of large numbers of refugees in April 1975 when Saigon "fell." Plans for evacuation only began to be drafted in March 1975. While 130,000 were able to emigrate to the United States the following month, 60,000 ended up in refugee camps in Hong Kong and Thailand.[15]

Social scientists have divided the immigration pattern of refugees in America into waves of migration. The first wave ranges in general from 1975 to 1978, the second from 1978 to 1980, and the third from about 1980 to 1995. The notion of immigration waves is useful in accounting for the diversity of Vietnamese Americans, but it is not entirely accurate. It does not include, for instance, those who did not fit temporally into these waves nor the ethnic and class diversity of each category. There is also no full consensus among scholars as to the start and end dates of these immigration waves.

The first wave commonly refers to Vietnamese who worked for or were in close contact with U.S. military personnel. They were more likely to have experienced war directly, were more educated, wealthier, and had greater exposure to American and French culture and language than those from subsequent waves of immigration. Shadowed by the notion of the first wave are the experiences of those who migrated at the same time but were not part of the wealthy or elite class, and those who had hardly been outside the capital. First-wave departure at the end of the war for those of all classes took place in a panicked state because of fear of retaliation by the communist government. Unlike most emigrants, South Vietnamese had very little time to prepare physically or emotionally for their departure. They did not know where they were going, when or if they would ever return, and how they would adapt to life in a new land. Having had very little time to conclude personal affairs, some were left with a sense of incompleteness and at times guilt toward those who were left behind, a state referred to as "unfinished business."[16] Once in the United States, they had a very difficult time adjusting to the new culture and environment.[17] Much of the poetry written at the time expresses deep nostalgia for the past, for Vietnamese culture, and everything that was left behind. While a high level of education may have better prepared some of these refugees to be retrained and to enter the workforce, the loss of social status and the absence of ethnic enclaves in the United States made their resettlement extremely difficult.[18]

The second wave is associated with the "boat people" who left Viet Nam in large numbers between 1978 and 1980 at a time of strong anti-Chinese sentiment in Viet Nam. Invisible within this second wave are the non-ethnic Chinese who also left during that time.[19] The Vietnamese government had nationalized businesses in the South, and as a result many ethnic Chinese business owners lost their livelihood. The border clash with China in 1979 exacerbated tensions between ethnic Chinese and the Vietnamese government.[20] Pressured to leave Viet Nam, a large number of ethnic Chinese risked their lives escaping the country by boat.[21] Because this was illegal, they plotted their journey in secret for fear of being arrested and sent to prison. Most were ill equipped to face the journey. Among those who left, at least 10 percent died at sea. Arriving near the coasts of Malaysia and Thailand, an estimated one-third of the boats were attacked by pirates, and many of the women on board were raped.[22]

Little scholarly attention has been paid to the impact of the refugee camps upon Vietnamese Americans' resettlement. Vietnamese had to stay in refugee camps in neighboring countries in Southeast Asia and Hong Kong until they received approval to emigrate elsewhere. Overwhelmed by the flood of refugees, some countries became economically stretched. Malaysia and Thailand, for example, forcibly sent boats back to sea and left Vietnamese refugees to die. In the camps, refugees were caught between two worlds. Most who stayed for years in the camps developed a sense of helplessness and dependency. Violence against women and children destroyed family ties and structures. Single women, female heads of households, and young unaccompanied girls were most vulnerable. Children who were confined more than four years in the camps with very little education and parental control had an especially difficult adjustment to their country of resettlement. The longer Vietnamese stayed in the camps, the more discouraged and distrustful of others they became, and the more difficult was adjustment to a new country.[24] A man who stayed in a Thai refugee camp said in an interview: "I found myself again in a prison camp. . . . We were deprived of everything. The Thais treated us as prisoners rather than refugees. Those who violated camp regulations were beaten inhumanely."[25]

Upon their arrival in the United States, Vietnamese refugees were subject to dispersal policies. The U.S. government wanted to avoid repeating the situation in Florida, which had become the center of the Cuban immigrant community. States feared the formation of ethnic enclaves by people of color dependent on welfare assistance during a time of economic recession. The attempt to scatter Vietnamese Americans throughout the country in order to manage domestic economic and racial concerns did not work as planned, however. Secondary and tertiary migration took place, and Vietnamese enclaves were formed in such places as Orange County, San Jose, Houston, Dallas, and Washington, D.C.[23]

The third wave was defined to include everyone who came between 1979 and 1996 as refugees and immigrants under the Orderly Departure Program (ODP).[26] In 1979, undergoing "compassion fatigue" and wanting to stem the continuing flow of boat people, officials of Viet Nam's neighboring countries implemented a problematic interview process to determine whether a person was a refugee or an immigrant.[27] Those who failed the interview were not recognized as refugees and were repatriated to Viet Nam. In 1984, as part of the ODP, 10,000 former reeducation camp prisoners came to the United States. By 1995 they were joined by 85,000 other former prisoners incarcerated for at least three years in reeducation camps and who had suffered from starvation and mistreatment.[28] In addition to former prisoners, 40,000 Amerasians and their relatives entered the United States, starting in December 1987, through the Amerasian Homecoming Act. Most Amerasians had lived as social outcasts and without adequate education for years in Viet Nam.[29] Not counted in this third wave are the 1,600 out of 2,000 refugees who were still in the Philippines without residency or legal status, and who immigrated to the United States in the fall of 2005 as part of a special refugee resettlement program.[30]

The United Nations stopped recognizing Vietnamese as political refugees in 1989 and closed refugee camps throughout Asia in 1996.[31] In the mid-nineties, the Resettlement Opportunities for Vietnamese Returnees Program allowed those remaining in

Southeast Asian camps to return to Viet Nam and reapply for resettlement in the United States.[32] Since then, a very slow immigration of Vietnamese has taken place and more Vietnamese students, some of whom are the children of communist officials, are entering American universities. Today, a third generation of Vietnamese Americans is entering elementary school. For these children, the Viet Nam War and their grandparents' experience are things they know very little or nothing about.[33]

Immigrants of Color

Vietnamese Americans are not only refugees, they are also immigrants of color. We often hear Vietnamese American success stories in the mainstream media and from Vietnamese Americans themselves.[34] These stories can easily be incorporated into preconceived notions that Vietnamese Americans, because they are Asian, possess Confucian family values and innate abilities to work hard without protest. These types of success stories affirm that Vietnamese Americans are assimilating well and may be held up as a "model minority." These stories mask the experiences of those living below the poverty level, those who are subjected to violence, and those who are falling between the cracks of the system.[35] The model minority paradigm also does not address the diversity of the Vietnamese American community, in which a loose hierarchy exists between those who arrived in 1975 by plane and who as a group are largely Buddhist and tend to be more educated and financially successful, and those who came five or ten years later by boat with fewer resources and less education, and might be Catholic. Additionally, the myth enhances race tensions in poor communities.[36] In effect, it boosts America's image as a color-blind society where there is freedom to assimilate and equal opportunity for all.[37]

It is significant in this social context to remember that Vietnamese Americans were not always welcome in America. At the end of the Viet Nam War, public opinion polls showed that 54 percent of Americans opposed receiving Vietnamese refugees, and only 36 percent favored their immigration.[38] Vietnamese Americans have been attacked and at times killed because they were associated with losing the Viet Nam War.[39] When a dozen boats owned by refugees were burned in the 1980s on the Texas Gulf Coast, the attack was not only motivated by economic competition. Louis Beam, a Viet Nam War veteran and Grand Dragon of the Knights of the Ku Klux Klan, who chased Vietnamese American fisherman from the coast, made the following statement: "There are a number of Vietnam veterans like myself who might want to do some good old search and destroy right here in Texas. They don't have to ship me 12,000 miles to kill Communists. I can do it right here."[40] Beam made no distinction between America's South Vietnamese allies and North Vietnamese enemies, lumping both sides together. The idea of "destroying" Vietnamese regardless of their political affiliation echoes war rhetoric that portrays Asians as "gooks" who deserve no mercy and virtually demand extermination.[41] Confusion over the political allegiance of Vietnamese Americans has been compounded by race. In 1989, Patrick Purdy, a twenty-six-year-old "drifter with guerrilla-warfare fantasies," armed himself with an AK-47 assault rifle and opened fire on the schoolyard of the Cleveland Elementary School in Stockton, California. He killed five Vietnamese and Cambodian children and wounded twenty-nine others before killing himself. Purdy did not differentiate between Vietnamese and Cambodian Americans, seeing them all as one and the same, as foreigners and enemies.[42]

Vietnamese Americans are often grouped together with Cambodian and Laotian Americans under the category "Southeast Asian," a term used commonly during the Viet Nam War. As Southeast Asians, their representations often shift from that of the model minority to poor people dependent on welfare. As Southeast Asians, they are depicted as mostly suffering from post-traumatic stress disorder (PTSD) and plagued by social problems, such as gang-related activities.[43] These representations do not adequately depict diverse Vietnamese American communities, either. The categorization of Vietnamese Americans as welfare recipients or as a model minority overlooks the failure of the United States to take responsibility for the war in Viet Nam and the bombing of Cambodia and Laos, as well as America's reluctance to incorporate its allies into the nation and its history. It does not address, for example, why for twelve years Amerasian children of American soldiers, and their mothers, were left behind in Viet Nam to live as social outcasts with little or no access to education.[44]

But Vietnamese Americans also benefited from U.S. refugee policies, which, since the end of World War II, allowed those fleeing communist oppression to immigrate to the United States in order to support America's self-appointed position as leader of the free world.[45] In 1980, 99.7 percent of the more than one million refugees admitted under the parole system in North America came from countries with communist governments.[46] The Viet Nam War was not only about Viet Nam or its people; it was also an anticolonial struggle turned into a cold war battle in which China, the Soviet Union, and the United States were the major players.[47] By declaring, after the first war in Iraq, the death of the "Vietnam syndrome"—the impact on foreign policy of a national sense of guilt for having gone to war under false pretenses and having inflicted harm on so many civilians— President George H. W. Bush gave the signal to future admin-istrations that it is possible to continue intervening militarily, economically, and culturally in the Middle East, Latin America, Africa, and Asia.

In the United States, Vietnamese Americans have become part of "the minority." As people of color, they have joined the ranks of those who have been historically excluded, exploited, and mistreated because of the associations and stigmas attached to their race. Compounding the difficulties associated with ra-cial dynamics in America, Vietnamese American refugees ar-rived in large numbers in 1975 during a time of recession, when immigrants of color are historically blamed for national eco-nomic downturns.[48] As Asian Americans, they have entered an invisible racial and ethnic hierarchy located somewhere between whites and blacks and below Japanese and Chinese Americans.[49] In the aftermath of Hurricane Katrina, the majority of stories in newspapers and television reports of social relations in the area focused on tensions between blacks and whites. Few addressed the plight of 55,000 Vietnamese Americans living in the Gulf Coast region, 15,000 of whom were evacuated to Houston, Texas. When Vietnamese American victims of Hurricane Katrina did make the newspapers, they were described mostly as people who lost all they had earned through their hard work. Since they were seen as a model minority, journalists overlooked the fact that a significant number of the Vietnamese American population in the Gulf Coast are fishermen, and that two-thirds are living below the poverty line.[50] Very few news stories mentioned that the hurricane triggered memories of displacement(s) in Viet Nam,[51] or that some Vietnamese American fishermen had already lost their livelihood after they were run out of the Gulf Coast by angry white fishermen who saw them as an economic, political, and racial threat.

As refugees and as Asian American immigrants of color, Vietnamese Americans have continually suffered from discrimination and violence. In 1981, as mentioned earlier, Ku Klux Klan members burned the boats of Vietnamese fishermen in Texas.[52] A year later, Oklahoma residents harassed people attending a Vietnamese Buddhist temple. One white resident was quoted as saying: "We don't need these chinks around here screwing up our kids."[53] Vietnamese Americans have been killed because they were mistaken for Japanese. "Oh I killed a Jap a while ago I stabbed him to death" wrote twenty-one-year-old Gunner Lindberg, who murdered Thien Minh Ly, a Vietnamese American, in 1996.[54] In 2003, Cau Thi Bich Tran, a mother of two, was killed by a San Jose police officer who said he thought she was brandishing a weapon at him. According to the officer, she was waving a "cleaver" or "dagger" in a menacing way, so he shot her. It was later discovered that the woman was actually holding a vegetable peeler commonly used by Vietnamese for cooking.[55]

Transnationals

"Where do I belong?" asks one anonymous writer in *Once upon a Dream.* "I was born in Vietnam, but I am reborn in America. I am here to stay. And inasmuch as I want to help rebuild my homeland, I also claim a role as an American."[56] The loss of homeland is not necessarily linked to the loss of cultural and national identity. Because of the specific conditions of forced (rather than voluntary) departure, many Vietnamese Americans have, after more than thirty years, maintained strong familial and emotional ties that span national borders. Many hold transnational identities in the sense that they make decisions in the United States on the basis of their memories of Viet Nam.[57]

Racism in the United States, coupled with disillusionment and disappointment in the American Dream, America's cultural investment in materialism and individualism, and the relatively lower cost of travel to Viet Nam after the economic embargo was lifted in 1994 have contributed to fueling these transnational linkages. Those who came as refugees, especially first-generation Vietnamese Americans, have the strongest attachment to Viet Nam. During the first decade after their arrival, Vietnamese Americans sent an estimated seven hundred million to one billion dollars a year to their kin in Viet Nam. They could not visit nor communicate with relatives there due to the U.S. economic embargo imposed on the country after 1975, which had prohibited all trade and aid to Viet Nam for nineteen years.[58]

In the mid-1990s, the lure of cheap labor and mineral resources hastened the resolution of the POW/MIA issue, which was initially crafted to build public support to continue the Viet Nam War and then the continuation of the economic embargo.[59] American corporations wanting to compete in the global economy were alarmed that thirty-four countries were doing business in Viet Nam, the biggest investors being Taiwan, Hong Kong, and France. They pushed hard for the ending of the U.S. economic embargo against Viet Nam. President Bill Clinton lifted the embargo in 1994.[60] As a result, today Vietnamese Americans of all generations are traveling to Viet Nam to see family members, engage in business or humanitarian work, or to live as artists and writers.[61]

The possibility of transnational identity has been further facilitated by the strides of the civil rights movement and subsequent move toward panethnicity. Vietnamese Americans were not forced to deny their cultural heritage to the same degree that Japanese Americans were after World War II.[62] Although they relocated on their own through secondary migration, they were able to develop large ethnic enclaves with access to the Internet, Vietnamese videos and karaoke bars, and ethnic media, all of which contribute to maintaining transnational linkages.[63]

Over the years, domestic events linked to Viet Nam have continued to foster such identities. In 1999, when Tran Van Truong displayed a communist flag and a poster of Ho Chi Minh at his video store in Westminster, California, demonstrators in the Vietnamese American community numbering from several hundred to over 15,000 protested for more than two months. The demonstrators viewed Tran's action as supporting the communist government in Viet Nam, which they vehemently opposed.[64] Tran's display of the Vietnamese flag and Ho Chi Minh's picture in front of his video store triggered vivid memories about the reasons why people left Viet Nam and further solidified identities concerned with home politics.

Conclusion

In 2004, when the Oakland Museum created an exhibit entitled "What's Going On: California and the Vietnam Era" to document the impact of the Viet Nam War on Californians, members of the Vietnamese American community protested. In their grant proposals, the museum staff had promised to "ensure respect of varied points of view" and to "tell the complex and difficult story of the Vietnam War era through an intelligent, balanced, and compelling interpretation."[65] Mimi Nguyen, a staff member at the museum, challenged the curators, asking why only one or two South Vietnamese war veterans (ARVN) were interviewed, while twenty-one U.S. war veterans were represented, and why out of sixty-five oral histories collected, only eleven were from Vietnamese Americans. In response, she was told she did not understand the content of the exhibit, and her questions were dismissed. Frustrated, Nguyen expressed her concerns in a public memo, which she sent via e-mail to staff members. In the memo, she wrote:

> Fifty-eight thousand American GIs died in the war. Some four million Vietnamese perished and an entire nation collapsed. Shouldn't Vietnamese Californians have equal stake and voice in this exhibit? . . . Why hijack the loaded term Vietnam then deny the reality and legacy of war that Vietnamese Californians experienced firsthand? . . . Why exclude Vietnamese political prisoners who found refuge in California through the Humanitarian Operation? . . . Why keep on bringing up stories that treat Americans as Vietnamese saviors, such as the Operation Babylift mission and the war bride saved by [an] American GI? . . . Why should we erase the defeated allies whose people, manpower, land and resources were sacrificed and betrayed for U.S. interests and for a Cold War solution? . . . Why should the Oakland Museum not move forward to reflect the diversity and reality of change in the Vietnamese American community?[66]

A week later, Mimi Nguyen was fired. Upon Nguyen's dismissal from the museum, her memo was immediately published in Vietnamese American community newspapers and a petition was drafted. Within a few weeks, five hundred signatures were collected and a community delegation was formed to oversee the exhibit.[67] What became known as "The Oakland Museum Controversy" was covered by newspapers both in Vietnamese and English, including a piece in the *New York Times*.[68] A local reporter covering the exhibit described the Vietnamese American community "agenda" as "complicated, particular, and little understood outside that community," which he said added to "the confusion."[69] But the demands of Mimi Nguyen and of Vietnamese American activists were clear. California contains about 40 percent of the Vietnamese national population.[70] The California group that has been most impacted by the Viet Nam War is the Vietnamese Americans. The Oakland Museum staff was mostly concerned with the effects of the antiwar movement on Californians prior to the end of the war and U.S. humanitarian aid to Vietnamese after the war ended. These assumptions rooted in national history clashed with Vietnamese Americans' memories, which are central to their identities. In normative history, there is no room for Vietnamese Americans' cause of departure, their perspective about American abandonment and betrayal, or the suffering of those who were left behind after the war ended and forced to live under a communist government supported by China and the Soviet Union in a geopolitical war against America. South Vietnamese Americans are the forgotten allies erased from that history.[71]

The examination of Vietnamese American history does not support assimilation theories that assume an inevitable attraction toward Anglo-Saxon culture. Vietnamese Americans' memories represent a thorn in normative history. The forced nature of their initial immigration patterns, the inequities in refugee policies, the erasure of Vietnamese Americans from history, and the violence against them as refugees and as people of color, as well as the voluntary formation of large ethnic enclaves with strong attachments to home politics and culture contrast sharply with commonly accepted views of America as a country of freedom and what it means to be American. From the perspective of refugees, Asian American immigrants and transnational subjects absent from the normative narrative of the nation, the production of Vietnamese American literature is often deeply entangled with national dissemination of images of America as a successful multicultural society and fighter for the free world. Such representations gloss over racial inequalities and tensions and are part of a powerful national revisionist effort in America to forget and forgive itself in order to justify the occupation of other countries through military, economic, and cultural means.

Recommended Readings

Sucheng Chan, ed., *The Vietnamese American 1.5 Generation: Stories of War, Revolution, Flight, and New Beginnings*. Philadelphia: Temple University Press, 2006.

Hien Duc Do, *The Vietnamese Americans*. Westport, Conn.: Greenwood Press, 1999.

James Freeman, *Changing Identities: Vietnamese Americans 1975–1995*. Boston: Allyn & Bacon, 1995.

2 /   Overview

Tell me a story about the river.
It's not a gentle river. It will keep you awake.
Tell me anyway.
Close your eyes.

KIM-AN LIEBERMAN, BREAKING THE MAP

Experience and memory . . . are always already mediated and
this mediation in turn is always shaped by relations of power.

T. FUJITANI, GEOFFREY M. WHITE, AND
LISA YONEYAMA, EDS., PERILOUS MEMORIES

Vietnamese American writers have published more than one hundred literary books in English since 1963. This body of work is diverse and heterogeneous.[1] This chapter provides an overview of some of the major phases of that literature. Although not exhaustive, it traces its development and delineates and discusses main themes and issues.

Most Vietnamese in the United States before 1975 came as students and returned to Viet Nam. Very few wrote novels or memoirs, with the exception of a few such as Tran Van Dinh, author of *No Passenger on the River* (1965), a novel about the breakdown in the values and beliefs of a South Vietnamese colonel. The texts written by those Vietnamese sojourners tended to criticize the South Viet Nam government at the time and sought to educate Americans about Vietnamese history and culture. Those books did not receive much public attention.

First Generation

According to Elaine Kim, the distinction between Asian and Asian American that was crucial to the formation of writers in the 1960s and 1970s became increasingly blurred with time.[2] This pattern can be observed in the works of a majority of immigrant writers, but not among the first generation of post-1975 Vietnamese American writers. Their very identity was based on the articulation of such distinctions. In the first years after the 1975 fall of Saigon, the dissociation from communist Viet Nam by those living overseas was central to Vietnamese American literature.

Some authors, such as Vo Phien who came to the United States in 1975, were already writers in Viet Nam prior to immigration. Others became writers out of the intense desire to tell the public about the plight of the South Vietnamese people. The loss of country, of home, of relatives and friends, social status, and identity that came with defeat in the war were experienced initially as insurmountable obstacles. Poets Cao Tan, Nguyen Ba Trac, and Nguyen Mong Giac are prime examples of individuals who articulated the state of exile and the great sadness of losing their country. Their texts capture a deep sense of loneliness, anger, and alienation. The guilt of leaving loved ones behind in the midst of chaos and panic punctuate their narratives.[3] Most of these texts were written in Vietnamese and published in literary journals like *Van Hoc Nghe Thuat*. The few authors who wrote in English encountered difficulties finding publishers because of their lack of language proficiency, the perceived foreignness of their writing style, and their perspective on the war. Some of these writers founded their own printing presses and independently distributed their own writing, mostly in Vietnamese.

The years between 1979 and 1984 marked a transitional period. The new wave of refugees who came in 1979 by boat stimulated local literary activity in areas where Vietnamese Americans were concentrated. The work of novelist Mai Thao, for example, did not focus on sadness and guilt over leaving loved ones behind in Viet Nam. Instead, he spoke vividly about the hardships of living under communist rule, of escaping the country by boat, and of his life in a refugee camp. Having been incarcerated in reeducation camps, his primary goal in writing was to denounce the human rights violations he experienced and witnessed firsthand. These new writers benefited from the emergence of the publishing industry established by those who had arrived earlier. Tran Huynh Chau's *Prison Years in North Vietnam*, Pham Quoc Bao's *The Bloody Shackles*, Ta Ty's *At the Bottom of Hell*, Ha Thuc Sinh's *School of Blood and Tears*, and Hoang Lien's *Light and Darkness* were published during this period. Vietnamese-language literary magazines and journals soon blossomed. Notable titles include *Dat Moi* (New Land), *Van Hoc Nghe Thuat* (Art and Literature), *Van Hoc* (Literary Studies), *Viet Chien* (The Vietnamese Struggle), *Nhan Chung* (Witness), and *Thoi Tap* (The Times).[4] Like their predecessors, these writings were both heavily invested in home politics and marked by an intense longing for a lost past. The sorrow and despair caused by exile was particularly well expressed in poetry. Cao Tan writes:

> Breaking our back, we carry on the rest of our lives in exile
> While our heart is laden with tons of sorrow and
> homesickness.[5]

The raw quality of Tan's words evokes the cost in human lives that came with the loss of country. Those words carry a sense of doom about the permanent nature of exile. The narrator is clearly overwhelmed by the weight of his condition. The reference to exile as a force with the power to break his back suggests the unbearable rift that tears at the heart of a community marked by insurmountable grief.

In these early writings, emotions waver among anger toward Americans for abandoning South Viet Nam, appreciation for individual freedom in America, and deep disappointment vis-à-vis America's cold, impersonal, and workaholic culture.[6] Yet the intense desire to return and take back the country of Viet Nam dominates these texts. According to Qui-Phiet Tran, there is a clear difference between writings of men and those of women of that first generation. Men such as Hoang Lien, Tran Van Don, Nguyen Cao Ky, Do Mau, Nguyen Chanh Thi, Cao Xuan Huy, Hoang Khoi Phong, and Pham Huan, for instance, were former military officers and, according to Tran, primarily concerned with documenting the war through their personal stories. These memoirs were nationalist by nature and preoccupied with the fate of the Vietnamese people. The writers looked back at the past, taking on the task of rewriting history and imagining another outcome for the war had their advice been followed.[7] In contrast, women authors such as Tran Dieu Hang wrote about daily life, loneliness, nostalgia for home, and the processes of survival both in Viet Nam and in America.[8] When those women authors wrote about family relationships, they evoked romantic love in less sentimental ways than their male counterparts.[9] Literary writings by women paint resettlement as a source of stress and new responsibilities. For women who came from the elite class, work was not always considered a source of empowerment, as certain feminists have assumed, but rather as a crude reminder of loss of status and diminished lifestyle.

Like the Vietnamese who came to America in 1975, it was difficult for those who arrived in 1979 to find publishers outside the ethnic enclave. In addition to the lack of language proficiency and unusual writing styles, politics pushed Vietnamese American narratives further to the margins of the increasingly corporate publishing industry of the 1980s.[10] The few texts published in English had difficulty finding an audience, either among Vietnamese Americans or others, on the right or on the left. First-generation Vietnamese Americans preferred reading texts written in Vietnamese because they were more direct, expressed more anger, and did not expend as much effort explaining Vietnamese culture to non-Vietnamese audiences.[11] Other Americans on the right did not want to read books written by Vietnamese American authors that would reinforce the "Vietnam syndrome," since these works might provide vivid reminders of military loss and guilt over America's abandonment of its South Vietnamese allies. Americans on the left, on the other hand, were not particularly keen on reading about human rights abuses committed by a leftist regime. White liberal Americans tended to see the South Vietnamese as "puppets of U.S. imperi-

alism" and "lesser allies." As Thu-Huong Nguyen-Vo poignantly
stated, the voices of South Vietnamese who were responding to
the extreme conditions and complex realities of war have been
effectively dismissed and excluded from history on both sides
of the political spectrum.[12] After the Viet Nam War, Vietnamese Americans were the only Americans who did not want to
forget Viet Nam. The country was no longer of geopolitical and
economic importance to America so human rights violations
there (and also in Laos and Cambodia), while a central theme
in the Vietnamese Americans literature at the time, were mostly
ignored.[13]

   Vietnamese American literature in English began to attract
the interest of large publishing houses starting in the mid-1980s.
Ironically, this recognition came with the publication of atypi-
cal texts that offered a North Vietnamese perspective. Both the
Americans who fought in Viet Nam and those who protested
the war showed more interest in the North Vietnamese than in
the Vietnamese U.S. allies in the South. Two works that became
more popular are *A Vietcong Memoir* by Truong Nhu Tang and
When Heaven and Earth Changed Places by Le Ly Hayslip. The
Vietcong Memoir published by Vintage in 1985 is written from
the perspective of a disillusioned former communist official.
Le Ly Hayslip collaborated with Jay Wurts to publish *When
Heaven and Earth Changed Places* in 1989 at Doubleday.[14] The
book tells the story of a traditional Vietnamese young woman
who works for the communist North during the war but ends
up being raped by two soldiers there who mistake her for a
traitor. She then moves to Saigon, where she works in bars and
engages in prostitution before emigrating to the United States.
The book was highly controversial in the Vietnamese American
community. Hayslip's stance on reconciliation and possible normalization with the current Vietnamese government, her negative portrayal of South Vietnamese officials, and her depiction
of South Vietnamese women in particular, which many saw as
contributing to the stereotype of Vietnamese women as prostitutes, were seen as an affront. Mariam Beevi Lam criticizes the

book for inflicting "epistemic violence on the figures of Vietnamese women and the Vietnamese immigrant woman by using [the protagonist's body] to represent nationalist values and
endeavors."[15] Published the same year to hardly any attention,
Fallen Leaves by Nguyen Thi Thu-Lam relates the story of a Vietnamese woman who lived in communist-controlled North Viet
Nam before the 1954 exodus and later emigrated to the United
States.[16] Unlike *When Heaven and Earth Changed Places*, *Fallen
Leaves* does not emphasize reconciliation but focuses on the
narrator's longing for her native land and her harsh judgment of
both communism in Viet Nam and life in America.

A New Era

The United States lifted its economic embargo in 1994, and
Viet Nam once again made the front pages of newspapers
around the country. America's return to Viet Nam through the
market economy facilitated the entry of Vietnamese American
cultural production in the U.S. national narrative. The year 1994
marks the emergence of what would become a relatively popular
genre, the Vietnamese American memoir, with the publication
of two books: Jade Ngoc Quang Huynh's *South Wind Changing* and Nguyen Qui Duc's *Where the Ashes Are: The Odyssey
of a Vietnamese Family*. Both books document life in Viet Nam
but do not focus on the military aspects of the war. In doing
so, the two authors take on the role of spokespersons for their
community.[17]

In *South Wind Changing*, a high school student set to enter
university after the end of the war is arrested at a market, for no
apparent reason, and is sent to reeducation camp. The narrator
describes the conditions of internment and the strategies used
by prisoners to maintain order in their harsh dictatorial environment. They are isolated, malnourished, tortured, and forced
to do hard labor. The book narrates the protagonist's struggle
to survive in the camp and his subsequent attempts, eventually
successful, to escape by boat. Little is said of life in the United

States. After risking his life numerous times to escape and come to the United States, the protagonist is haunted by the desire to return to Viet Nam: "Why did I come here in the first place? I wished I could go home, to a place where at least my skin and culture, my morals and values were the same as others'. A place where I was born and spoke the language. I wished I could die there someday, coming back to my roots, to the taste of the water and the air."[18] Nostalgia gnaws at the narrator. The pain associated with the loss of his land and culture is more difficult to bear than the struggle to survive in the United States. Yet the narrator cannot go back because he fears being sent back to a reeducation camp and dying there. Because emigration was not a matter of choice for the narrator, but of life and death, the present is experienced as complete loss. "Were we just a bunch of people who betrayed our parents, especially our mother? Am I the one who left in the middle of the game? Am I the one who gave up?" Huynh's narrator asks, overwhelmed by grief and guilt over having left his loved ones behind.[19]

Where the Ashes Are presents the perspective of a young man whose father was civilian deputy of a military governor in central Viet Nam. The narrator's father, educated in the United States, was later arrested and imprisoned by the communist government for twelve years. The book weaves the father's story in jail with the journey of his son from Viet Nam to the United States and back.[20] The narration moves from the gaze of a child to that of a rebellious and idealistic young man, following his journey as a hospital volunteer in Viet Nam, the time he spent working in refugee camps, and his struggles in the United States before he returns to Viet Nam as a journalist. Like *South Wind Changing*, the narration privileges memories of Viet Nam over life in the United States. Reflecting on the difficulty of locating a "home" after living in the United States for almost two decades, the narrator also expresses deep nostalgia for Viet Nam. Although aware of the bright career opportunities in the San Francisco Bay area and the blessing of living near his relocated family, he is preoccupied with the idea of return.[21] In the United

States, his parents depend on him and do not approve of his returning to Viet Nam under the communist government. His commitment to family further deepens his sadness:

> It is important to us that when we have children, they have a chance to speak Vietnamese. Even more, I want them to absorb what I think are the central traits of the Vietnamese people. . . . As for Viet Nam—perhaps I should be content that it may one day be the home of my children. It may be they who, in the future, will welcome me back there. And they will know, they will know, to bring my ashes home.[22]

The narrator projects his hope of return onto children he does not yet have. He imagines he would be able to send them to Viet Nam to learn the language and culture and that they will one day love Viet Nam and make it their home. Vietnamese once again and imbued with familial piety, he dreams that his children will invite him to live with them. The repetition of the phrase "they will know" suggests that culture lies beyond the realm of language and that refugee status is lived as an aberration, outside the continuum of a desired and romanticized identity that is located in the past, fixed and stable.

Whereas the protagonist of *South Wind Changing* is paralyzed by grief and nostalgia upon emigration, *Where the Ashes Are* describes an individual who, almost twenty years after his forced departure from Viet Nam, derives both pain and pleasure from the very state of nostalgia. He shows signs of the "restlessness" of those in exile described by Edward Said, which stems from the suspicion that one can neither fully return to the homeland of the past nor be fully at home in the country of resettlement.[23] Such nostalgia is entangled with both the ability to negotiate the desire to return and the awareness of the inevitable process of forgetting. To be too comfortable in the present can thus be perceived as threat.[24] Nostalgia and the idea of being "happy with the idea of unhappiness" can be cultivated. This state of contented "unhappiness" is in *Where the Ashes Are* further heightened by a French nineteenth-century romanticism to which the narrator was exposed to in his French school in Viet Nam.[25] Without a clear sense of home, the narrator articulates home in cultural terms, in relation to the dead. "Where the ashes are, one should make that home," he says, as he brings the ashes of his dead sister from Viet Nam to San Francisco.[26] This phrase, echoed in the book's title, suggests a rejection of the autonomous individual and a move toward a traditional Vietnamese definition of self across generations.[27] But as in *South Wind Changing,* rupture from Viet Nam is associated with death.

Although the narrators of *South Wind Changing* and *Where the Ashes Are* come from different class backgrounds and arrive in America at different times and under different circumstances, both wish to die in Viet Nam, or at least want to be buried there so that their spirits can finally find peace. For these narrators, the boundaries between Viet Nam and America are not blurred, but a clear and constant source of pain that binds and crystallizes their identity.

Collaborations

In an effort to reach a wider audience and remedy the lack of language proficiency and access to the publishing industry, in the 1980s Vietnamese American writers started collaborating with non-Vietnamese writers. Most were white, and many had some connection to Viet Nam during the war. Collaboration came at a cost. For example, in *Shallow Graves: Two Women in Vietnam,* Tran Thi Nga's story may have served as a vehicle for Wendy Wilder Larsen's own voice and story to emerge.[28] Monique Truong argues that "Larsen is the active, narrative-generating bow while Tran is the passive instrument used for the narrative's creation and production."[29] In these early collaborative works, the invisible power differential between the benefactor and the refugee, who lacked access to the publishing industry, helps to solidify a version of history wherein America went to Viet Nam to free its people from evil.[30]

In the mid-1980s, Vietnamese American writers also began

translating into English texts written by Vietnamese writers in
Viet Nam.[31] The translators were younger and primarily concerned with finding new stories. They were also disappointed
by the lack of criticism of communism in Europe toward the
end of the cold war. They turned to stories by dissident writers in Viet Nam that criticized the social consequences of war,
written after the communist government instigated a new policy
of "renovation," known as Doi Moi, in 1986, which brought an
increased tolerance toward different viewpoints. Again, in order to increase their chances of being published, they worked in
tandem with non-Vietnamese American writers who had fought
as soldiers or were invested in other ways in the Viet Nam War.
Nguyen Qui Duc, author of *Where the Ashes Are*, coedited and
translated with John Balaban stories by Ho Anh Thai, Pham Thi
Hoai, Nguyen Quang Than, and Le Minh Khue, among others.
He also translated poems by Huu Thinh with George Evans in
The Time Tree (2003). Nguyen writes in the introduction: "My
work on Huu Thinh's poetry followed a time when I rediscov-
ered poetry, in both Vietnamese and English. And it coincided
with a desire among Vietnamese American writers to portray
Viet Nam not only as a war, but a culture and a people full of
passion and flaws and conflict, and love. Viet Nam is a country,
with many, many tales."[32]

Nguyen's translation is imbued with his desire to introduce Viet Nam as a country and not a war, and to share with
a wide American audience the richness of Vietnamese culture.
On the other hand, his cotranslator was driven by the need to
understand and be forgiven by his former enemies, the North
Vietnamese. Reflecting upon his first meeting with Huu Thinh
and other North Vietnamese poets, George Evans writes: "The
Vietnamese writers, once enemies, were gentler with us and
more insightful about what happened than I could have imagined. They accepted us [American poets] foremost as writers,
but also as part of a vanquished army still marching around in
its memories."[33] Touched by the beauty of Huu Thinh's poems,
regardless of their politics, Nguyen agreed to translate them but

was harshly criticized by Vietnamese Americans who interpreted his attempt to humanize the Vietnamese, which included a
North Vietnamese, as a form of betrayal.[34] George Evans's acts
of redemption through art did not result in criticism and rejection by his own community.

Works of collaboration between Vietnamese Americans and
Vietnamese writers also took place. After the U.S. economic
embargo of Viet Nam was lifted in 1994, Vietnamese American
writers and translators from the younger generation were able
to travel to Viet Nam more easily. Disappointed with American culture, the high cost of living, racism, and the lack of human connections in American society, a few went to Viet Nam
and developed friendships with Vietnamese writers and artists.
They found personal fulfillment and pleasure in these relationships. The discovery that many Vietnamese writers were disillusioned with their own government created common ground
and diminished political tensions that may have existed between
them. As more and more traveled to Viet Nam, pressure from
the Vietnamese American community against having anything to do with Viet Nam also lessened.[35] In 1995, *The Other
Side of Heaven: Post-War Fiction by Vietnamese and American
Writers*, edited by novelist Wayne Karlin in collaboration with
Vietnamese writer Le Minh Khue and Vietnamese American
writer Truong Vu, was published. The volume combines literary
works by writers in Viet Nam and the Vietnamese diaspora, and
by former American GIs. The writers, translators, and editors
saw the project as a vehicle for reconciliation. According to the
editors, the anthology focuses on "the need of literature to tell
uncompromisingly painful truths" about common pain, and the
purpose of the collection was to foster empathy and collective
healing.[36]

A few more translations were published after this in collaboration with other Americans. In 1996, Linh Dinh edited a collection of contemporary Vietnamese short stories entitled *Night,
Again*. Dinh, who translated half of the stories, asserts that his
criteria for selecting the stories was not political: "I wanted to

feature the best, most exciting writers I could find," he says.[37]
As an editor and translator, Dinh's goal, like Nguyen Qui Duc's,
was to bring some of the best work by Vietnamese writers to a
larger American audience, out of cultural and national pride. In
2008, poet, journalist, and translator Nguyen Do worked with
poet Paul Hoover and translated post-1956 Vietnamese poetry
in *Black Dog, Black Night*. The same year, Andrew Pham translated, with the assistance of his father, the famous diary of Dr.
Dang Thuy Tram, which brought the perspective of a young and
idealistic surgeon for the North Vietnamese army in *Last Night
I Dreamed of Peace*.

Anthologies

Vietnamese American narratives found in anthologies and
journals that also include non-Vietnamese American writing
have been selected at times because of their value as commentary
on the war or the refugee experience. Examples can be found in
*The Other Side of Heaven: Post-War Fiction by Vietnamese and
American Writers* (1995), *Tilting the Continent: Southeast Asian
American Writing* (2000), and special issues of the *Manoa Journal*
(2002) and the *Michigan Quarterly Review* (2004).[38] In at least one
instance, editors of a publication generally open to alternative representations of Viet Nam and Vietnamese Americans rejected a
creative piece because they said it was not "Vietnamese enough."[39]

Once upon a Dream, published in 1995, is the first Vietnamese American anthology edited by Vietnamese Americans of
the 1.5 generation—those Vietnamese who immigrated before
or during their early teens. Their goal was to educate the American mainstream about Vietnamese Americans. "I did lots of
translation and was hoping that non-Vietnamese [would] read
the stories so that they could better understand the Vietnamese
plight," explains editor Andrew Lam.[40] The anthology includes
texts from both the older and younger generations. The wish to
represent the community is apparent in sections titles: "Exodus," "Elegies," "VietnAmerican," and "Homecoming." Such

titles suggest that editors selected the works not only for their literary value but also for their social commentary and in reaction to the invisibility and misrepresentations of Vietnamese Americans in general. "The stories, poems, and artwork in this anthology reflect [Vietnamese Americans'] extraordinary will [to survive]," insist the editors in the introduction. The editors say they "selected the stories . . . specifically because they are about Vietnamese-American life in the last twenty years," and dedicate the anthology, perhaps as eulogy, to "all Vietnamese moms and dads [and the] men and women who fought the war in Vietnam."[41] They speak to an identity centered on sacrifice for the nation (or motherland) and filial piety. This early effort to articulate what it means to be Vietnamese American on Vietnamese American terms parallels that of early Asian American cultural nationalists whose primary concern was to increase the visibility of Asian American literature and experiences. Their goal was to help recognize and validate the past, to foster ethnic pride and self-identification that would lead to action for social justice in the United States. For the editors of *Once upon a Dream* however, past experiences are retrieved to denounce past and present injustices in Viet Nam, and if action is to take place, it is mostly there, where parts of their hearts are.

A second anthology of prose and poetry by Vietnamese Americans, *Watermark*, was published two years later, in 1997, and differed markedly in the ways the works were selected, organized, and marketed.[42] On the back cover, readers are told that the stories and poems represent "some of the best writing from a new generation of Vietnamese writers in America," especially as it "goes beyond war."[43] Emphasizing literary value over ethnographic reportage and the pressure to write about the war, the collection gathered stories in a variety of genres, but mostly from those of the 1.5 generation and without any clear organizing principles. The main thread linking the stories is the evocation of water. "The word for 'water' and the word for 'a homeland, a country, a nation' are spelled the same way in the Romanized Vietnamese script and are pronounced the same way: nuoc," explains Huynh Sanh Thong in the preface.[44] The editors chose to evoke "water," Huynh explains, because it holds multiple and emotionally powerful meanings in Vietnamese. He writes: "Water is what makes rice grow, provides life, [it is] the complexion of skin, a way to play cards, people, the nation," and adds: "To say in English that a man has 'lost his country' is not the same as to say in Vietnamese that he has 'lost the nuoc' (mat nuoc). If the English phrase sounds almost abstract, the Vietnamese expression evokes an ordeal by thirst, the despair of a fish out of water."[45] This framing reflects an attempt to free Vietnamese American literature from the weight of representationalism but also holds onto the idea of a collective bound by shared history and culture. The image of water conveys an emotionally charged link to the loss of country that only Vietnamese Americans who experienced forced immigration, even decades ago, can fully understand. Here, identity is not framed in relation to war and ethnic markers but in tandem with the recognized inability and refusal to forget the past.

New Notions of Home

Representations of Vietnamese Americans in contemporary Vietnamese American literature in English differ distinctly from those of the English-language mainstream. The texts are devoid of fantastic colonial tales of adventure and exotic fantasies.[46] Vietnamese people are not represented as childlike, immature, and physically inferior.[47] Contemporary writers show no fascination with the image of a sweet prostitute ready to sacrifice her life for her American lover. Vietnamese American men are not portrayed as lacking masculinity or courage. They are neither perfect math students nor heartless gang members.[48] Vietnamese Americans are not described as desperate and grateful refugees, deprived of agency.

Vietnamese American literature rests at the juncture of various axes of power that contradict, coincide, silence, or enhance the possibilities and direction of its expression. For the writers, writing fulfills a creative impulse. At times, recalling the past through storytelling can contribute to individual and collective healing by making sense of an emotionally incomprehensible past. But for the non-Vietnamese American audience, the texts can serve an individual and collective desire for resolution of the Viet Nam War. One reason for America's current fascination with stories by young Vietnamese Americans who offer chronicles of return to Viet Nam might be the idea that if Vietnamese Americans can go back to Viet Nam, so could they.[49]

Vietnamese American literature has benefited from normalizing relations between Viet Nam and the United States and from the increased importance of ethnic studies in college and universities.[50] The most popular Vietnamese American literary texts today were written by members of the 1.5 generation who combine memories of Viet Nam with discussions of racial and ethnic identity. At the twenty-fifth anniversary of the end of the Viet Nam War, newspapers commissioned tales of return such as Phuong Le's "A Daughter's Journey" and Andrew Lam's "A Child of Two Worlds."[51] PBS featured Andrew Lam in a documentary called *My Journey Home*, and hired Nguyen Qui Duc to narrate another entitled *Vietnam: Looking for Home*.[52] Poet Truong Tran received a grant to travel to Viet Nam and write about his "people" in *dust and conscience*. Andrew X. Pham's travel memoir to Viet Nam, *Catfish and Mandala: A Two-Wheeled Voyage through the Landscape and Memory of Vietnam*, found a prestigious publisher and received national attention.

More emotionally and politically detached from Viet Nam than those of the first generation, these narratives articulate a new concept of home. Identity is depicted to a different degree in terms of movement, one that goes back and forth between North America and Viet Nam, either by actual travel there or by acts of memory, imagined or recollected.[53] Similar concerns pervade, for instance, Cao Lan's *Monkey Bridge* (1997), le thi diem thuy's *The Gangster We Are All Looking For* (2003), Dao Strom's *Grass Roof, Tin Roof* (2003), Aimee Phan's *We Should Never Meet* (2004), Samantha Le's *Little Sister Left Behind* (2007), Lac Su's *I*

Love Yous Are For White People (2009), and to a certain extent, Andrew Lam's collection of essays, *Perfume Dreams: Reflections on the Vietnamese Diaspora* (2005), Lily Hoang's *Parabola* (2008), and Bich Minh Nguyen's *Stealing Buddha's Dinner* (2008) and *Short Girls* (2009). Poetic works such as Mong-Lan's *Song of the Cicadas* (2001) and Kin-An Lieberman's *Breaking the Map* (2008) linger about Viet Nam, although not exclusively.[54] Narratives such as *Monkey Bridge* or *The Gangster We Are All Looking For* take place in the United States, but refer to Viet Nam as a place where life was more complete and made more sense. Memories of Viet Nam play a significant role in these works. The past is assiduously scrutinized, assessed, and evaluated, and if not, evoked as a frame of reference. It is often described as haunting the lives of the narrators like ghosts, at times scary and at others comforting, driving both emotions and actions. The simultaneous engagement with two nations, moving forward in the United States while looking back toward Viet Nam, creates new notions of citizenship.[55]

History

Not all texts published after 1994 are preoccupied with identity, however. Less visible, many are engaged principally with history, tracing and imagining what had happened in Viet Nam before immigration. Those include Huynh Quang Nhung's *The Land I Lost: Adventures of a Boy in Vietnam* (1982), Tran Van Dinh's *Blue Dragon, White Tiger: A Tet Story* (1983), Duong Van Mai Elliott's *The Sacred Willow* (1999), Nancy Tran Cantrell's *Seeds of Hope* (1999), Kien Nguyen's *The Unwanted* (2001) and *The Tapestries* (2002), Jackie Bong-Wright's *Autumn Cloud: From Vietnamese War Widow to American Activist* (2002), Anh Vu Sawyer's *Song of Saigon* (2003), Trinh Do's *Saigon to San Diego: Memoir of a Boy Who Escaped from Communist Vietnam* (2004), and Andrew Pham's *The Eaves of Heaven: A Life in Three Wars* (2008). *The Unwanted* by Kien Nguyen is perhaps the best-known of this group. Nguyen ends his memoir with the following remarks:

> My reason for writing this book at first was purely per-
> sonal. I just wanted to heal myself. But, as the story pro-
> gressed, I thought more and more about the other Amera-
> sians I had encountered. . . . As dark as my memoir may be,
> it is not unique by any means. It's estimated that fifty thou-
> sand Amerasian children shared my fate, or worse. . . . I
> kept writing in hopes that these innocent victims' lost
> childhoods might finally be mourned, and their buried se-
> crets at last revealed.[56]

The narrator's investigation of the past and exploration of Vietnamese culture in the postwar context differs from efforts by
earlier Asian American writers who were preoccupied with
claiming America and striving for acceptance. Kien Nguyen's
main motivation is to denounce human rights violations against
Amerasians and to call upon America to take more responsibility for its foreign policy.[57]

Not all texts concerned with history center on condemning North Vietnamese communism. Duong Van Mai Elliott's
The Sacred Willow follows the journey of her family over four
generations.[58] Her hope is to contrast the life of her educated,
urban middle-class family and the ideological and ethical conflicts they faced during colonization and war with stereotypical
depictions of Vietnamese in Hollywood movies, which she sees
as confined to "Vietnamese villagers in combat" and "Saigonese
soldiers and bar girls."[59] Elliott's story traces the excruciating
choices her family was forced to make in a country at war. It
offers a vivid critique of French colonialism, Japanese occupation, and the American war in Viet Nam, showing how they are
all connected. Spanning over two hundred years, *Sacred Willow*
accuses foreign powers of having torn her family apart and of
having fueled the rise of a certain kind of communism.[60]

The Book of Salt

Monique Truong's *The Book of Salt* (2003) received the most
national and international recognition of any book written by

a Vietnamese American author. It was reviewed by the *New York Times*, and has been translated into ten languages so far.[61] It breaks from previous Vietnamese American works in genre, style, and content. The *Book of Salt* follows the complex thought processes of its narrator Binh, a Vietnamese cook for Gertrude Stein and her partner Alice B. Toklas in 1930s Paris. A delicate, highly sophisticated stream-of-consciousness narrative, the book underscores what it means to function outside the realm of nationalism, to be a man without a nation. He is not a patriot like the man, later known as Ho Chi Minh, he meets on a bridge in Paris one evening. The attraction of the story does not lie in the action but in the language and flow of Binh's thoughts and insights, themselves shaped by colonization, exile, poverty, and the homosexuality that his father never accepted. More precisely, it is about access to language. Situated in a locus of dislocation and displacement and in a state of alienation and servitude, Binh is invisible as a human being. When he is seen, the color of his skin triggers exotic fantasies of Asia in the minds of the people he serves.

And never is he heard. His place in the household is below than that of the dogs. A servant only kept on for his cooking skills, who is not supposed to express feelings, his voice seems unreliable and appears to drift *above* emotions. Insignificant to his employers and others, Binh takes on the role of observer. The tone of his voice, at once monotonous and passionate, detached and alert, reflects elision, detachment, alienation, and freedom. When he left Viet Nam, Binh says he had "no intention of reaching shore."[62] He sees no point of arrival, no resolution, and no possibility of wholeness. Yet no one owns him and no one can know him, readers included. The repetitiveness, sameness, and intensity of Binh's language, prickled with moments of cool clairvoyance, keep readers at bay. The sophisticated prose of *The Book of Salt* invites readers to reflect upon their own privilege and the exclusionary practices engendered by labels of race, sexuality, or history. In Monique Truong words, she "alienates readers without them knowing it."[63]

Second Generation

In 2006, the Vietnamese Artists Collective, based in San Francisco and composed mostly of second-generation Vietnamese American artists, published an anthology entitled *As Is*. In their call for submissions, the collective wrote that they were "open to everything and anything from traditional forms to the risky and experimental."[64] In the introduction to the anthology, editor and contributor Danny Thanh Nguyen writes:

> I, like many, sometimes forget why people make art: a drive to educate, a means of survival, a need to build camaraderie, a cheaper form of therapy, etc. And in losing sight of the reasons behind intention, we become not unlike those who simplify us into labels: as immigrants, as Vietnamese, as other, as working-class feminist hemophiliacs. But in spite of these obstacles we continue to seek an audience that will accept us without the need for justification.[65]

These emerging artists started the collective because they wanted to come together as friends who share common interests, such as writing, and experiences as Vietnamese Americans. For most of them, sons and daughters of refugees, struggles are not exclusively bound to memories of the Viet Nam War. They want to be heard but do not wish to justify or explain themselves. *As Is* speaks of Mexican Americans, French colonization, generational conflicts, imagined memories of war, love, death, grandmothers, working at a nail salon, and of daily life unmarked by ethnicity or race. The contributors write about sex openly and with humor.[66] These young writers are emotionally further from the refugee experience and have more access to certain resources than those who came before them.[67] "What we want," Nguyen says, "is to find a home in a broad Asian Pacific Islander community." Refusing to represent Vietnamese Americans as a whole, he says the characters he creates "simply happen to be Vietnamese Americans but do not necessarily talk about ethnic culture, roots, or history."[68] These young artists use the refugee and ethnic platform to their benefit or when they need to, while rejecting bluntly and without fear the limitations of these categories.

Performance and spoken word artist Bao Phi may be the established artist of most appeal to the second generation. Some of his poems revisit Viet Nam's history and reflect upon ethnic identity, while others are free from ethnic markers. His strong, in-your-face poetics denounce as much as they inspire, with their intonation and rhythm adding to content. They address anger and rage but also offer solace and the exploration of daily life. Bao Phi performed at the Oakland Museum as part of the "What's Going On" exhibit discussed in the previous chapter. His presence came about as a result of the Southeast Asian delegation's demands for Vietnamese American inclusion. Phi read a poem called "No Offense" about "frat boys" to an audience of young Vietnamese Americans and older white liberal supporters of the antiwar movement. Phi said he wrote the poem in response to so-called Mekong Delta parties held by a fraternity at the University of Florida, at which men were asked to dress up as GIs and women as Vietnamese prostitutes. The party drew protests from Vietnamese Americans from the first year it was held. Fraternity members defended themselves by saying they did not mean to offend anyone. The next year, they did it again. In the large Oakland Museum amphitheater, Bao Phi's voice resonated loud and clear:

> You wanted a Mekong Delta party
> So party on
> as your frat house is bombarded
> the roof is on fire
> the roof is on fire
> you will dodge bullets on the dance floor
> your parents will be chained to sewing machines
> to make your uniforms and costumes
> your brothers will turn against you
> your sisters will become prostitutes

you will starve
you will get malaria
you will not get a job
tanks will roll into your neighborhood
your children will play with shell casings
in crater filled suburbs
there will be nothing left
there will be nothing left
after we come for you
there will be nothing left
no offense.[69]

Bao Phi's role reversal highlights the racism of the American war in Viet Nam and its persistence today. He accuses the young fraternity men of blindness, privileged arrogance, ignorance, racism, sexism, and blind patriotism. In this unapologetic reversal of history, Bao Phi highlights the latent violence that pervades the Mekong Delta party, under the pretense of "having fun." The repetition of the pronoun "you" is a provocative reminder of the power inequality between America and Viet Nam. The anger that emanates from the poem underscores the revulsion at having to point out that Vietnamese women are actual human beings from a third world country that was torn apart by civil war and cold war dynamics, not cartoon characters playing at war, nor is their mission in life to please young white American men. Bao Phi's poem and tone shook the comfort level of the exhibit organizers and others in the audience who had come to see an exhibit on the impact of the Viet Nam War in California. Vietnamese American voices had been included as an afterthought and under political pressure. After the reading, an older white woman stood up and said she was offended and called Phi a racist. Her fear of his words denotes a naïve liberal belief in the moral standing of America in domestic and world affairs, a luxury.

How one interprets and reads Vietnamese American literature, or any literature, is political in nature. Because of the monumental amalgam of images and predetermined notions attached to the word "Vietnam," it is crucial to understand the social context from which that literature emerged and then transformed itself. Who are the Vietnamese Americans, we need to ask, and why are there so many of them? Why do they write what they write? How are their stories received? Because most Vietnamese Americans who initially emigrated to the United States had not planned nor desired to do so but were instead forced to by their circumstances, the theme of history and a redefinition of home is prominent in their writing and that of their children.

Recommended Readings

Michelle Janette, "Vietnamese American Literature in English, 1963–1994." *Amerasia Journal* 29.1 (2003): 267–286.

Russell C. Leong, Brandy Liên Worrall, Yen Lê Espiritu, and Nguyen-Vo Thu-Huong eds., "'30 Years AfterWARd': Vietnamese Americans and U.S. Empire." *Amerasia Journal* 31.2. (2005).

Monique Truong, "The Emergence of Voices: Vietnamese American Literature 1975–1900." *Amerasia Journal* 19.3 (1993): 27–50.

3 /   Hybridity

> For the recently arrived (such as Vietnamese
> Americans) . . . their cultural specificities and historical
> relationships with U.S. imperialism may be much more complex
> than has been recognized in an identity politics derived largely
> from East Asian American experience.
>
> SAU-LING WONG, "DENATIONALIZATION RECONSIDERED"

> The aim of judgment in historical or literary-critical
> discourse . . . is not that of determining guilt or innocence.
> It is to change history to memory: to make a case for what
> should be remembered, and how it should be remembered. This
> Responsibility converts every judgment into a judgment on the
> person who makes it.
>
> GEOFFREY HARTMAN, "JUDGING PAUL DE MAN,"
> IN MINOR PROPHECIES

Asian American Studies

I committed to the field of Asian American studies instead of
anthropology because of its emphasis on race, class, and gender,
and because I believed fighting for social change needed to start
here, in my new American home. In France, critical discussion
of race was nonexistent in high school. Asian American studies
classes resonated with me. I could relate, for example, to Maxine Hong Kingston, who grew up in Stockton, California, in the
1950s, and her struggles with the act of speaking. Like her, I was
almost mute as a child. I read Vietnamese American literature in
part to better understand my mother, myself, and the diasporic
Vietnamese culture I grew up in. But what I found during my
years of study was that the field of Asian American studies addressed primarily immigrant experiences within the boundaries
of the nation-state. Asian American literary studies, in particular,
minimally covered Vietnamese American literature.[1] The goal of
This Is All I Choose to Tell is to contribute to filling this gap.

But why does such a gap exist in a field so concerned with race and class? The relative absence of Vietnamese American scholarship in Asian American studies is commonly attributed to the ideological premises associated with the creation of the field.[2] Tied to the civil rights and antiwar movements, early Asian Americanist activists indeed often empathized with America's enemies, the North Vietnamese, who were referred by the military and in Hollywood movies as "gooks."[3] Very few of the early activists at the birth of Asian American studies expressed solidarity with the South Vietnamese who fought alongside Americans. Sucheng Chan explains that early Asian Americanists eventually

> had to find ways to come to terms with [Vietnamese American students'] vehemently anti-Communist political perspectives and their proclivity to adopt the most conservative currents in American political ideology. This fact created a dilemma for Asian American Studies faculty members, many of whom espoused antiestablishment and anticapitalist beliefs in those early years of the field's development.[4]

Some students who had come from South Viet Nam did not agree with the leftist politics of the field, and did not subscribe, at least initially, to the notion of panethnicity. That is, they did not identify as Asian American but as Vietnamese. They did not necessarily welcome ties with Chinese Americans, in light of the history between Viet Nam and China. China had occupied Viet Nam for a thousand years, and Vietnamese culture is rife with tales of legendary figures fighting Chinese occupation. During the French occupation of Viet Nam, colonialists used ethnic Chinese as middlemen, supporting them with mercantile enterprise. And during the Viet Nam War, China gave financial and military aid to the North Vietnamese. Vietnamese Americans did not easily trust Japanese Americans, either. During World War II, as Germany occupied France, the Japanese military occupied Viet Nam. In 1945, Allied bombing, drought, and Japanese appropriation of coal, minerals, and rice resulted in famine in northern Viet Nam, killing over one million Vietnamese.[5] And although they were often referred to as Southeast Asian Americans, Vietnamese American students did not necessarily feel a sense of solidarity with Cambodians or Laotian American students. Viet Nam has had a long history of border disputes with Cambodia; and some Vietnamese had long-held prejudices against people whose skin color is darker than their own, especially tribal peoples without clear national borders, like the Hmong.

Many of the first Vietnamese American students who took classes in ethnic studies were the children of those who had wanted America to continue the fight against communist North Viet Nam. Most of those who left Viet Nam as adults felt deeply betrayed and abandoned when American troops left. For them, the end of the war meant the loss of their country and the beginning of life in exile. For the majority of those who came in 1975, immigration also represented a loss of economic and social status. Unlike the antiwar protesters, including those who started the field of ethnic studies, most Vietnamese Americans who attended Asian American studies classes were adamantly anticommunist. These students were critical of proponents of the antiwar movement, which included many of their teachers. Early Vietnamese American supporters of Asian American studies were students like Chuong Chung, who immigrated prior to the end of the war, or like Yen Le Espiritu and Hien Do, who were trained in other disciplines.

But early Vietnamese Americans' support of the continuation of the war and anticommunist sentiments do not entirely explain the lack of Vietnamese American scholarship in Asian American studies.[6] Inherent in the formation of the field lies the notion of self-determination and the assumption that researchers whose ethnic background matches that of their subjects can better understand the experiences and complexities of the people they study. These assumptions have influenced the rate at which Vietnamese American scholarship is produced in

Asian American studies. Vietnamese Americans began to arrive in large numbers in 1975, but it took time before a new generation of Vietnamese Americans was able to acquire a secondary education, and years before any became interested in Asian American studies.[7] This slow incorporation was compounded by refugee parents' influence; they pressured their children to go into what they considered to be practical and safe fields such as accounting, computer sciences, nursing, or engineering. They discouraged their sons and daughters from engaging in the social sciences or the humanities.

At a theoretical level, early focus on East Asian immigrants did not provide a fertile ground for the development of Vietnamese American scholarship. Elaine Kim, the first literary critic to integrate Asian American literary voices in a book-length study in 1982, defined Asian American literature as "published creative writings in English by Americans of Chinese, Japanese, Korean, and Filipino descent," a definition that does not include the writing of Vietnamese Americans.[8] Her framework was adopted by literary critics Sau-ling Cynthia Wong, King-Kok Cheung, and David Leiwei Li, whose works largely focus on East Asian American literature.[9] Most of the stories they analyze are situated largely in the United States and bring to light racial and gender discrimination.

The privileging of East Asian experiences was not challenged until the early 1990s, when Filipino American and South Asian scholars argued that Asian American studies did not sufficiently take into account the experience of people marked by histories of colonialism and U.S. imperialism.[10] Reading Filipino American literature as a "literature of exile and emergence" instead of as a "literature of immigration and settlement, whereby life in the U.S. serves as the space for displacement, suspension, and perspective," Oscar Campomanes challenged the claims of established Asian Americanists.[11] A change in Asian American demographics, combined with subsequent questioning of the East Asian paradigm, opened doors to the study of Vietnamese American literature.[12]

Asian American literary critics started examining Vietnamese American literature in the 1990s. In 1993, Monique T. D. Truong published the first comprehensive essay on Vietnamese American literature from 1975 to 1990 in *Amerasia Journal*.[13] In 1996, Lisa Lowe devoted a few pages of her book, *Immigrant Acts: On Asian American Cultural Politics*, to Monique T. D. Truong's "Kelly," a short story about a young Vietnamese American woman who recalls her life in the South in a letter to her old friend, once an outcast like her.[14] Soon after, editor King-Kok Cheung and critic David Palumbo-Liu each dedicated a chapter to Vietnamese Americans and their literary productions in their respective works.[15] In 2006, Asian Americanist historian Sucheng Chan published the first book in the field about Vietnamese Americans, in which she provided historical context to her Vietnamese American students' papers about their refugee experiences.[16] With the second war in Iraq, renewed discussion of the Viet Nam syndrome ironically created openings for Vietnamese American studies scholarship.[17] In 2003 and 2005, two issues of *Amerasia Journal* were dedicated to Vietnamese Americans.[18] In the 2005 issue, scholars emphasized the consolidation of the American empire. Leading scholar Yen Le Espiritu writes: "Vietnam appears to be well on its way to become yet another 'satellite regime' of the ever-expanding American empire. In this 'New World Order,' Vietnamese refugees, and their insistent demand for 'history,' are cast aside, yet again."[19]

Hybridity

> *When does death begin? How to count the dead? Whose death*
> *matters? Who owns the dead? What about the living dead,*
> *who live as a shadow, already a ghost, never allowed to be fully*
> *present? And what about those who are kept alive but always "in*
> *a permanent condition of 'being in pain'"?*
>
> YEN LE ESPIRITU, "THIRTY YEARS AFTERWARD:
> THE ENDINGS THAT ARE NOT OVER"

> *The national project of "remembering" the Vietnam War—who*
> *its heroes were, who must be forgotten, who may mourn—is a*
> *crucial site in which the terms of "membership" in the national*
> *"body" are contested, policed, and ultimately redefined.*
>
> LISA LOWE, *IMMIGRANT ACTS*

Lisa Lowe's use of the concept of "hybridity" provides a strong departing analytical framework to approach Vietnamese American identities. Hybridity, for her, refers to "the uneven process through which immigrant communities encounter the violence of the U.S. state, and the capital imperatives served by the United States and by the Asian states from which they come, and the process through which they survive those violences by living, inventing, and reproducing different cultural alternatives."[20] Many Vietnamese American experiences are products of the violence between competing empires and of resettlement marked initially by downward mobility and racial tensions. I use the term "hybridity" here to refer more specifically to those experiences and identities shaped by colonialism, war, immigration, and racism. By addressing the uneven process through which Vietnamese Americans encounter the violence of the U.S. state and the Viet Nam state within the context of colonialism and the cold war, I wish to draw a complex discussion of what it might mean to be and to represent Vietnamese Americans. It provides me the possibility of examining tactics of survival through modes of simultaneous resistance and accommodation, without ready-made judgments that would exclude one or the other. It permits for an exploration of gray areas like the shutting of the heart, the cost of women's sacrifices, the enormous resilience of the human spirit, the emotions, and what people do in order to craft an existence without a place in history. This framework does not blame the victims or make people heroes in order to serve a political agenda, but rather makes visible the complexities and contradictions that occur when the abandoned enter the nation that has abandoned them but emphasizes having rescued them. It helps tackle the contradictions that ought to take place when one is invisible and afraid, without giving into fears of this inquiry to be appropriated by racist and imperialist perspectives.

The concept of hybridity is useful because it incorporates *all* Asian American identities, regardless of politics, and takes in account power relations between nations and between the state and its citizens. Hybridity is not to be confused with the notion of a bridge between cultures, for this concept presupposes an equal footing in two cultural locations, which is never exactly the case. Donald Ranard writes, for instance, that Vietnamese Americans of the 1.5 generation—those who belong neither to the first generation of adult immigrants nor to the second generation of U.S.–born children—are "a bridge between two cultures," living "in two worlds with two sets of languages, rules, and customs."[21] This common understanding, when taken literally, runs the risk of reinforcing Orientalist conceptions of first and third worlds. It can overshadow the reality that subjectivity is for the most part more rooted in one location than the other and, more important, that there are major power differentials between the United States and Viet Nam, a superpower and a third world country.

Hybridity is not positive or negative in itself. The readiness to embrace those located at the margins as potential bearers of positive change capable of repudiating domination, or to treat in-betweenness as a gift, an enigmatic access to language that may possibly reveal an opening in ourselves and the world we inhabit, can mask the immense difficulty, stress, pain, and contradictions that arise to various degrees when the people involved are located on the margin at the intersection of cultures.

It hides the existence of foreign policies that dictate who can become American and who cannot, who belongs and who does not. The concept of hybridity, for instance, provides a framework to the story of Viet Dinh, who from 2001 to 2003 was assistant attorney general of the United States. Dinh said that he was drawn to the Republican Party because of his hatred of communism. As a seven-year-old boy, he saw communists take his father away to reeducation camp.[22] At the age of thirty-six, his job was to enforce the Patriot Act, which effectively expanded the authority of the American government to conduct searches of its citizens.[23] The Patriot Act allows federal agents to conduct surveillance, investigate libraries and mosques, and detain people without charge as material witnesses.[24] In short, it takes away the liberties and basic rights of democracy. In a context in which the majority of Vietnamese Americans vote Republican because it is perceived as more anti-communist than the Democratic party, the concept of hybridity shifts the focus from political differences to that of questions of survival and empire.[25] It invites discussions that draw connections between domestic race relations, geopolitics, and U.S. global power.

Because they were American allies and because the Viet Nam War was lost, Vietnamese Americans have been pushed out of American and Viet Nam history. It is no coincidence that the recollection and processing of the past in Viet Nam plays an important role in Vietnamese American literature. Because of the involuntary nature of departure from that country, texts written by Vietnamese Americans cannot be read as *any* text, as certain postmodern thinkers suggest, nor always in isolation of an author's intent and experience.[26] For some, the act of writing itself is intimately linked with the wish to rectify social history, to serve as witness to the past, and to foster individual and collective healing and self-definition. Vietnamese American memories do not coincide with American normative social history of the Viet Nam War. The repetition of normative representations over time perpetuates the production of distorted images of Viet Nam and the United States, which in turn displace Vietnamese

American perspectives. The word "normative" points here to the marginal location of Vietnamese American representations in society.[27]

What are normative images of Viet Nam? I often begin my Vietnamese American literature class by asking students to say what first comes to mind when they hear the words "Viet Nam." The same responses surface: "war," "helicopters," "jungle." . . . The list is quickly exhausted and the room falls silent fast. Because of the Viet Nam War, Vietnamese American authors are writing in a context of representation where South and North Vietnamese have been infantilized, exoticized, and the men feminized. The war has been recreated and rewritten in Hollywood studios, fictionally won by brave and white American soldiers and their machine guns while the Vietnamese merely serve as backdrop.[28] When depicted at all, they are the cold-blooded communist soldier, the corrupt South Vietnamese official, the prostitute, or the Dragon Lady. The shadowy image of the Vietnamese in America's imagination made room for the images of lonesome young white men losing their innocence but regaining masculinity despite strides in feminism, through the exotic.[29] In Hollywood's version of the Viet Nam War, American soldiers are seldom shown torturing or killing Vietnamese prisoners or cutting the ears and teeth of enemy soldiers as trophies, acts performed on Asian enemies but considered unimaginable against European enemies.[30] Absent from Hollywood narratives are the one million Vietnamese civilians killed in a war in which more bombs were dropped on a country two-thirds the size of California than in all of World War II.[31]

While the distinction between South and North Vietnamese tends to be blurred in the American imagination, specific images in the media came from the South: a monk engulfed in flames,[32] a naked little girl crying and running away from a napalm attack,[33] a North Vietnamese man killed point-blank by a South Vietnamese general,[34] a stream of Vietnamese desperately trying to climb into a helicopter perilously poised atop the American embassy,[35] and boat people weakened after days at sea without food or water. In all of those, Vietnamese, allies and enemies alike, are imprinted as either victims or bad subjects. The images have forged one-dimensional representations of the Vietnamese, which in turn impact how Vietnamese Americans are seen, understood, and perceived, and by extension, may influence how they choose to represent themselves.

Discussions of hybridity are not always welcome. There has been and still is strong resistance in Asian American studies to incorporate dimensions that lie beyond the national border. In 1995, Sau-Ling Wong argued forcefully against the denationalization of Asian American cultural criticism. Changes in Asian American demographics and an embracing of poststructural theories have complicated identity politics and lead to an increased interest in the field of subjects and topics that reach beyond national borders. The move toward what she calls a "diasporic perspective," threatens she says, a "domestic perspective that stresses the status of Asian Americans as an ethnic/racial minority within the national boundaries of the United States."[36] Wong warns that diaspora studies, and the over-deconstruction of identity that ensue (that is, "an ever-evolving, never-resolved subjectivity characterized by instability, endless movements, boundary transgression, and multiple reference points"), creates an invisible hierarchy among Asian American studies scholars. While they are becoming more popular, Wong contends that diasporic approaches contribute to the depoliticization of the field and to an overall forgetting of history. They have also damaged coalitions that originated with the pan-Asian American movement of the 1960s. The denationalization of the field, Wong fears, could ultimately result in the "reabsorbtion" of Asian American studies into what she calls the "master narratives."[37] It elides domestic race relations and obscures issues of class, she says, as not everyone can afford to travel and forge nomadic cultures. It can also lead, she adds, to the privileging of recent immigrant experiences over those of the American-born. Wong insists that it is crucial for Asian Americanists to come together as people of color and to continue claiming America and establish an "Asian

American presence in the context of the United States' national cultural legacy and contemporary cultural production," something she says is pushed aside by denationalization. "Coalition of Asian American and other racial/ethnic minorities within the U.S. should take precedence over those formed with Asian peoples in the diaspora," she concludes.[38]

Wong's vision of racial equality and justice in America is important. Yet a domestic perspective alone limits full understanding of Vietnamese American perspectives. It does not address, for example, the story and identity of an older Vietnamese American man who speaks French, knows a few Chinese words, had contact with American culture prior to immigration, and expresses his identity in relation to virulent anti-communist views while professing pride in his people for defeating the French, even though the French were largely defeated by communist forces. Such a man may live in the United States, but his mind constantly travels in time and space away from this nation. Nor does a domestic perspective help analyze the story of the younger narrator of *Catfish and Mandala*, who reflects on his life in Viet Nam and in the United States. It does not explain the anxieties of a student like Mai in *Monkey Bridge*, who has no tragic war memories of Viet Nam herself but who appears to carry her mother's fears as if she had suffered the same trauma at the end of the war. And neither does it facilitate the understanding of a text like *dust and conscience*, shaped by the very notion of nationlessness. Perhaps even more important, a domestic perspective does not take into account Vietnamese Americans' insistent demand for "history."[39] It does not adequately explain identities and experiences of a people who came to this country relatively recently. For some, issues of life and death, loss of nation, or of domestic violence both in Viet Nam and in the United States, come *before* or *with* the desire and need to claim America. What happened prior to immigration and what caused immigration are crucial to a great many Vietnamese Americans. If these concerns are real, as suggested by the Oakland Museum controversy, and if they are found in their literary texts, then they cannot be ignored by political choice.

One argument that encouraged the formulation of *This Is All I Choose to Tell* is again that of Lisa Lowe in *Immigrant Acts* (1996). Lowe argues that Asian Americanists were strong enough institutionally to afford rethinking "the notion of racialized ethnic identity in terms of differences of national origin, class, gender, and sexuality rather than presuming similarities and making the erasure of particularity the basis of unity."[40] This rethinking of Asian American identity as more than a shared history of facing de jure and de facto racism in the United States is crucial to the development of Vietnamese American scholarship in Asian American studies. This argument has been strengthened in the early 2000s by Kandice Chuh in *Imagine Otherwise: On Asian Americanist Critique* (2003) and by Viet Nguyen in *Race and Resistance: Literature and Politics in Asian America* (2002). Chuh suggests that Asian Americanists examine the impact of transnationalism and globalization, put forward a more direct criticism of U.S. practices of empire, embrace postcolonial studies, and engage more systematically in interdisciplinary work. Citing Michel Foucault, Chuh argues that if we cannot "ignore identity politics, . . . neither can we rely upon it to effect radical social change." We must continually ask, she adds, how what is believed to be the truth came to be so.[41] Viewing produced knowledge as discourse, Chuh considers scholarship formed in Asian American studies as another form of discourse, and as such, one that needs to be more reflective of its own ideological premises.

Viet Nguyen makes a similar argument in *Race and Resistance* as he examines the consequences of a lack of political introspection. Nguyen argues that ideological rigidity and lack of self-reflexivity have led Asian Americanist literary critics to misread Asian American texts only as sites of either resistance or accommodation. In the process, says Nguyen, Asian Americanists have transformed race and racial identity into commodities, and have missed other important aspects of narrators' experiences and, therefore, part of their humanity.[42] Neither Lowe, Chuh, nor Nguyen dismisses Asian Americanists' success in making visible the relevance of race in understanding America and their active role in promoting social justice. What they insist on, however, is that how one defines and treats identity *does* matter. A narrow view of identity, they agree, can be problematic and potentially reproduce racist and nationalist tendencies.

This Is All I Choose to Tell uses and applies the notion of hybridity in ways that appreciates the analyses and recommendations of Lisa Lowe, Kandice Chuh, and Viet Nguyen while remaining mindful of Wong's cautionary remarks on the danger of a certain kind of dehistorization and depoliticization. When asked what they mean when they talk of "American culture," my students say they are reminded of white Anglo-Saxon heterosexual middle-class values. This cultural association is reinforced in academia and echoed by the media and politicians. Viet Nguyen's emphasis on ethnic studies' ideological premise and the role it plays in limiting the reading of Asian American texts is not to mask the fact that other academic fields are also imbued with ideology. Ethnic studies and race theories by intellectuals of color were formed in reaction to established fields for a reason. Academia has historically omitted the history and perspectives of people of color to guide and determine the cultural, ideological, and political fabric of the nation.[43]

Ethnic studies has played a critical role in altering ideology invested in the maintenance of white hegemony. The initial mission of ethnic studies was to create a space in academia that would redress historical alterations and forgetting, and in the process, formulate new theories and articulations of what it means to be American. Early founder Sucheng Chan writes that ethnic studies scholars "exist to challenge and remedy the neglect of our history and the issues confronting our communities in the university curriculum."[44] In the 1920s and 1950s, assimilation theories were central, for example, to the development of sociology. One of the founders of the field, Robert Park, argued in the 1920s that assimilation, after various phases of contact, competition, and accommodation, was natural and irreversible, and was the best way to fight racism.[45] Thirty years later, sociologist Milton Gordon elaborated on Park's theory and argued that a modern capitalist society should be based first and foremost on meritocracy and not along ethnic lines.[46] In order to speed up the assimilation process and reduce racism, he said, people of color ought to have more close contact with white Americans. Various versions of this color-blind argument have since been put forward to counter affirmative action policies.[47] An extension of this claim is found in today's assertions of postracial America.[48]

Ethnic studies scholars have fought hard and continue to do so against arguments that view culture as static and assimilation to Anglo-Saxon middle-class values as synonymous with progress. Those who can assimilate are not superior, however, to those who do not fit into this ascribed model, and not everyone can assimilate everywhere, due to the color of their skin. American society is not as open, fair, and free as many claim to be. This belief ignores relations of power and obscures America's history of conquest, exclusion, and exploitation of minorities of color. Chinese immigration, we need to remember, was prohibited by law from 1882 to 1943 strictly on the basis of race, and racial segregation in schools did not become unconstitutional until 1954.[49] The racial limit on naturalization rights was lifted for all only in 1952.[50] And not all Americans became Americans of their own free will, such as Native Americans, black slaves, Mexicans in Texas, and Asian wage laborers in the nineteenth century. The experiences of Vietnamese American refugees go against assimilation assumptions as well, as these refugees do not immigrate to North America by choice but by force.

Reading Is Political

How one reads and interprets a text matters. It is a political act that holds political ramifications. Vietnamese American literature cannot be understood solely within the same framework as other Asian American immigrant texts because not all authors and narrators are immigrants, but rather refugees. To read them this way would ignore a large portion of what is being said and the unique circumstances of departure that impact their lives or the narration itself. But Vietnamese American texts cannot be read strictly as refugee stories, either. To do so would obscure the humanity of Vietnamese Americans, similarly deny their full history, and potentially limit them to the role of passive victims, paralyzed by grief.

Vietnamese American literature works with, against, or aside from normative narratives of the Viet Nam War and its aftermath. When Vietnamese literary critics Hoanh Ngoc Hien and Nguyen Hue Chi visited the United States in 2000 and 2001, they were dumbfounded to find that, like them, Vietnamese American writers felt pressure to conform to the expectations and tastes of mainstream public and publishers.[51] Because of the highly visible and emotional space occupied by the Viet Nam War in American society and culture, and of America's need for its citizens to heal and forget the Viet Nam syndrome as it consolidates and continues to expand its empire, a unique dialectical relationship between Vietnamese American cultural production and the mainstream audience has formed. The word "mainstream" is not meant here to fix identity or create new stereotypes, as the diversity of readership and the importance of a Vietnamese American audience must be recognized. I use the term "Vietnamese American" and the word "mainstream" instead strategically to delineate the imbalance of discursive power between majority and minority.[52]

Vietnamese American literature is born and produced on U.S. soil, in a nation that lost international respect and moral authority with its defeat in the Viet Nam War. The continued American culture with images of that war and the associate pressure to write "the" refugee experience, with a special fascination for stories of "boat people," has pushed young Vietnamese American writers and scholars to articulate Vietnamese American identities in reaction to this enormous weight, and to affirm that they have nothing to do with the war. "We refuse to perpetuate telling war stories," writes Danny Nguyen in the first collection of creative writing by the second generation, *As Is: A Collection of Visual and Literary Works by Vietnamese American Artists*.[53] Nguyen is frustrated by what he sees as preconceptions about Vietnamese Americans and the Viet Nam War on the part of publishers, reviewers, and readers, limiting the possibilities for his generation to be understood or even considered.[54] Reading Vietnamese American literary texts only in relation to the Viet Nam War and the refugee experience can indeed reinforce stereotypes of Vietnamese Americans as paralyzed by grief, and as passive and pathetic subjects ultimately in need of professional care, and deprived of agency.[55] To survive violence and losses does not in itself produce a pathological condition. And as Danny Nguyen reminds us, the second generation has no memory of the war. To view Vietnamese American texts only as refugee narratives restricts the full recognition of Vietnamese American experiences and identities.

But to view Vietnamese American literature outside the framework of war, in reaction to dominant representations and expectations, is also limiting. Poet Barbara Tran wrote in 2004: "It is not the right time to 'move on' from the war, for there are still too many who cannot do so because the past has gouged too deep a hole in their lives. They keep falling back in."[56] Yen Le Espiritu adds that the "decoupling of Vietnamese Americans from the Vietnam War risks assimilating Vietnamese into the apolitical and ahistorical category of 'cultural diversity.'"[57] As the United States is currently at war in Iraq, it is necessary to remind politicians and others that wars do not end with the signing of documents and treaties. War and its consequences continue to affect the lives of the survivors and their descendents. The war against the "Axes of Evil" had been suppressing discussion of American imperialism. It is difficult in this context to discuss the Viet Nam War and Vietnamese immigration to the United States as not an aberration in American history but rather a phenomenon situated along a historical continuum based on an infernal logic of foreign interventions, invasions, and conquests. In a climate of patriotism and nationalism, recognizing and addressing the legacy of the Viet Nam War while raising issues pertaining to resettlement is political. In accordance with Yen Le Espiritu, "rather than doing away with the term 'refugee,'" I wish to imbue it in *This Is All I Choose to Tell* with social and political critiques that "critically call into question the relationship between war, race, and violence, then and now."[58]

For these reasons, much attention was given in this first section to the social and historical contexts, as well as debates surrounding the interpretation of Vietnamese American literature. Viewing Vietnamese American literature in relation to the notion of hybridity, despite my own political desire to uphold Vietnamese American texts as modes of resistance, facilitates paying close attention in the second part to issues and themes raised within the texts themselves, regardless of the positive or negative images they may convey. I will then take notice when a narrator vacillates between power differentials in relation to the first and third worlds or racial hierarchies; or grapples simultaneously with memories of Viet Nam, trauma, resettlement in the United States, and citizenship. I will also look at what happens when a narration lets go of the attempt to represent identity in what has become expected refugee discourse. Behind these readings stands a concern for the significant dialectical relationships between history, society, and cultural production, as well as limitations of identity politics, while at the same time embracing its necessity in certain times and locations.

Recommended Readings

Sucheng Chan, *Asian Americans: An Interpretative History*. Boston: Twayne, 1991.

Renny Christopher, *The Vietnam War, the American War: Images and Representations in Euro-American and Vietnamese Exile Narratives*. Amherst: University of Massachusetts Press, 1995.

Lisa Lowe, *Immigrant Acts: On Asian American Cultural Politics*. Durham: Duke University Press, 1996.

PART TWO

INTERPRETATION

4 / Survival

In this life is reincarnated
Myself a migratory bird
Traversing the immense ocean
The way back unmapped
THANH NHUNG, "LOSS"

Memory forms the fabric of human life, affecting everything
from the ability to perform simple, everyday tasks to the
recognition of the self. Memory establishes life's continuity; it
gives meaning to the present, as each moment is constituted
by the past. As the means by which we remember who we are,
memory provides the very core of identity.
MARITA STURKEN, *TANGLED MEMORIES*

Vietnamese American communities originated with war. As in
the Philippines (1898–1910) and in Korea (1950–1953), American intervention in Viet Nam (1959–1975) was a manifestation
of empire building.[1] In contrast to those conflicts however, the
Viet Nam War was highly visible, both domestically and inter-
nationally. The Vietnamese allies of the Americans were forcibly
displaced, deprived of their nation, and their clans and families were broken up. Depending on the conditions and time of
departure, and their length of stay in refugee or reeducation
camps, some from the first and 1.5 generations faced death repeatedly, inevitably shaping their common identities and those
of their children.[2] Those who were not able to leave until 1978
or later continued to face extremely difficult, if not traumatic,
experiences well after the events of 1975. Trauma subsequently
surfaces in literature as social and cultural discourse in response
to "the demands of grappling with the psychic consequences of
historical events."[3] Everyone who experiences and copes with
trauma develops survival strategies differently. In Jade Ngoc
Quang Huynh's *South Wind Changing*, for instance, religion

plays a significant role in helping the narrator find meaning and accept his fate in reeducation camp. In Nguyen Qui Duc's *Where the Ashes Are*, the narrator's strong family ties and connections enable his articulation of identity. But what of those who do not have the support of religion, family, or community?

Society slowly includes those on the margins into the normative narrative of the nation, partly through stories that recollect or evoke the past.[4] This inclusion occurs through struggles and insistence from those who are on the margin. The concept of historical trauma, or the cumulative emotional and psychological injury over a lifespan or across generations, is found in Native American, African American, Jewish Holocaust, and Japanese American studies. Genocide, enslavement, organized terror, and population displacement, as well as battery and assault, represent known sources of extreme human suffering that cause trauma.[5] Although these experiences occur in different degrees of magnitude, they have generated stories that reflect common themes and emotions such as anger, sadness, guilt, and shame.[6] These stories are terrains of mourning, but also of contestation, depending on who reads and interprets them. As they are produced, along come new formulations of self and emotion, and by extension of perception and identification, potentially promoting healing from trauma, as well as strategies to make sense of the past and the present and pave the way toward a more peaceful future.[7]

Memories or altered memories about Viet Nam, literally recollected in memoirs or through fiction, play an undeniably crucial role in the identity formation of the narrators presented in this chapter. By identity, I refer to the relation between the self, discovered through the articulation of remembered emotional disturbances, and the group. The concept of historical trauma is, I suggest, relevant to some Vietnamese American narrators because, like many others, they were forced out of their country and associate departure with death. Writing to evoke the past is not always about creativity, nor is it always a matter of choice. The act of returning to fragmented memories reflects what Derrida calls "learning to live with ghosts," a condition that disrupts normative fixed binaries and oppositions such as the "other" versus the assimilated, individualism versus collectivism, and cultural nationalism versus transnationalism.[8] Trauma and the lack of support from family, community, and nation as well as downward mobility produce, I suggest, a deep sense of vulnerability that leads to survival strategies heavy with contradictions that manifest themselves differently along gender and ethnic lines and are heightened by lack of financial resources. The emotions that drive the narrators' actions and gazes in Andrew Pham's *Catfish and Mandala* and Lan Cao's *Monkey Bridge* create, I show, alternative visions that illustrate the concept of hybridity discussed earlier, in ways that do not necessarily imply resistance *or* accommodation alone. In these texts, fear can be passed down from one generation to the next, or is intertwined with memory, history, and invisibility. Investment in gender and ethnic identities serve sometimes as a mask to shield the vulnerable self from emotions not yet digested and perceived as unbearable.

Catfish and Mandala: Bicycle Cowboy

> We rarely admit even to ourselves the circumstances and the cost of our being here.
>
> PHAM, CATFISH AND MANDALA, 238

In *Catfish and Mandala*, a work of "creative nonfiction," fear is tied to domestic violence and the impact of the war and its aftermath. An, the book's narrator, grew up in an unstable environment. An's family escaped Viet Nam by boat in 1977 and came to America when he was eleven years old. An's father, who once led a thousand men into battle, now works as a janitor. An's mother, an active businesswoman in Saigon, becomes a housewife who does not speak English, lost in American society. The book opens with An's reflection on his own death. An believes his life is intimately linked to that of his sister Chi, a transsexual who commits suicide at the age of thirty-two. An's and Chi's destinies were foreseen by a Buddhist monk when they were born. Shortly after Chi's suicide, An's grandmother asks him whether he wants to know his own future. Fearing the power of an irremediable destiny spoken aloud, he declines her offer, quits his job, and undertakes a cycling odyssey. Evaluating his life in relation to his sister's foreseen death, An cycles across the northern California coast, Mexico, Japan, and finally Viet Nam.

FEARS

Along his journey, An remembers something his mother once told him: "Your father is unstable in the head, An. His father made him kneel all day in the summer sun. The sunstroke changed him. Made him violent."[9] A violent man, An's father was abused by his own opium-addicted father, a vice encouraged under French colonization.[10] An's father in turn beat him and his siblings, his oldest sister Chi in particular, with uncontrollable rage.

An tells us his father beat his sister mercilessly when she was a child: "Like striking vipers, the canes blurred through the air, swishing, biting into Chi, one after another. Thwack! Thwack! Thwack! She howled. I cringed, covering my ears, knowing well the taste of bamboo, the way it licks out at flesh, first a jolt like electricity, then sharp like a fang, then hot like a burn. The canes broke over her back" (170). Although it is culturally acceptable to hit children to discipline them in Viet Nam, it is not acceptable to use such excessive force that it threatens a child's life or mental health. "The neighborhood women ... muttered that Dad's cruelty was a curse upon our house," An recalls (56). His father breaks the cane over Chi's back. He has no control over his own behavior. His blows, An tells us, are like "striking vipers," unpredictable, fast and potentially deadly. Although Chi survives the beating, she takes refuge in their grandmother's house and develops "an eerie knack for sensing [their father's presence] around corners" (57). Afterward, An recalls, Chi "never wholly came back into [their] lives again" (57). She lost her trust in her father and perhaps in others as well.

In the United States, An's father continues to "whip" his children (195). As the first son, An is expected to discipline and hit his own siblings: as the eldest son of the family, An carries the weight of his parents' sacrifices and high expectations.[11] Asian American immigrant writings often speak of intergenerational conflicts.[12] But in this particular story, the line between generational conflicts and domestic violence is blurred. Violence is not only physical. It is also emotional. The narrator describes a scene where the family is seated for its first Thanksgiving dinner. An's mother, not knowing how long to cook it, serves the turkey before it's done. An describes the turkey as "a frightful thing that resembled a boiled hen dipped in honey" (167). Disgusted by the meal, An and his siblings refuse to eat it. An's father lashes out in anger, whacks the table with a yardstick and snarls: "EAT!" He proceeds to lecture them about the war, the poor people in Viet Nam, and the famine he had to endure as a boy. "I'm too lenient with you," he says. "Your grandfather was strict. He would have whipped you and let you starve." The violence and dysfunction in this family does little to uphold the model minority myth, which attributes the success of Asian American children to traditional Asian culture.[13] The father's own experience of violence as a child turns An and his siblings into wasteful slaughterers. His anger cannot inspire compassion for his pain and sacrifices on their part. Instead, An and his siblings are consumed by fear of their father and his violent temper.

An's continued experience of domestic violence is compounded by the sense of abandonment he felt during the war when his parents were away, as An's mother left him alone for days while trying to secure his father's release from prison. His mother left him with a "magic pot" of catfish. An recalls:

> She locked me inside our three-story building and said, "By the time you finish this pot, I'll be home."
> So I ate it fast. It was all gone in two days. There was nothing left in the clay pot except sauce, bones, and the big catfish head. . . . For the next meal, I would add a lit-

tle water, maybe a dash of pepper, and boil it again. When there was no more meat, the pot magically kept on yielding plenty of peppery, fishy, sweet, salty, buttery sauce, tasty enough to be poured on plain white rice for a meal. And sure enough, Mom came home before the clay-pot catfish ran out of magic. (97)

The magic of the catfish is a fantasy that An embraced as a child to allay the anxiety of separation from his mother, his fear of losing his father, and the reality of being left alone in a big house. His only link to the world is his mother's promise that she will return before the pot of fish is empty. The magic lies in the ability of the catfish to continue yielding sustenance and in his mother's capacity to keep her word. This magic allows him to postpone and temper his anxiety, and for the magic to work, the object of desire—his mother's return—has to be delayed. The power of the catfish masks a profound sense of abandonment, which An, the child, painfully tries to evade and control by measuring his consumption.

An also appears traumatized by his escape by boat, or what he calls his family's "last gamble" (61). The boat they are meant to board is late. When the boat finally arrives the family has to make a run for it. An falls and is terrified of being left behind, but Chi stops and helps him. As they then swim toward the boat, he struggles in the waves and panics (89). The boat's captain jumps into the water and rescues him. Once aboard, the situation only intensifies. Not only are they afraid of getting lost at sea and of being caught, they also face engine failures, the indifference of a passing French boat, lack of food and water, sharks, and violence among the crew (91). On the third day aboard the leaky boat, which does not have enough fuel to reach another shore, An says, "our end was written all over a sky as impenetrable as stone" (119). Lost at sea, the passengers and crew are ready to die. They are rescued by an Indonesian ship just as their boat is sinking. While climbing the rescue ship's ladder, An stumbles again:

I couldn't hold on much longer. Somehow, I knew I

wouldn't make it onto the ship. I felt my arms surrender-
ing, my legs going limp around his waist.... I was falling.
Tai screamed over the howling wind, reaching back to grab
me. The rope ladder twisted. I fell. A shoulder-wrenching
jerk. I was hanging by one arm. (120)

Exhausted and terrified, An thinks he's going to die and be
swallowed up by the ocean. A crewmember leans over the rail
and grabs his wrist just before he falls. The sound of the "howling wind" in the above passage connotes danger and An's total
loss of control in the face of nature's terrible power. The child
comes close to death repeatedly, all in a short span of time: on
the shore, in the water, on board, and during the rescue. Though
the experience is traumatic, An does not have words to name it.
Instead, his memories are made of images that continue to haunt
him until he is finally able to put the experience into words.[14]

After these life-and-death experiences, racial tensions in the
United States seem less significant, but race still heightens his
sense of vulnerability. An recalls: "I grew up fighting blacks,
whites, and Chicanos. The whites beat up the blacks. The blacks
beat up the Chicanos. And everybody beat up the Chinaman
whether or not he was really an ethnic Chinese" (328). Down-
wardly mobile, An's family lives, at least initially, in poor neighborhoods regimented by racial dynamics. Regarded as Chinese,
he is immediately relegated to the bottom of a system he describes as a sort of food chain. If this is not experienced as a
matter of life and death, it becomes, he said, a matter of "shame"
(328). Poor race relations compound the trauma of escape and
family violence. Vulnerable, An wishes he could pass as white.
Sharing his thoughts, he said: "I don't mind forgetting who I
am.... I don't mind being looked at or treated just like another
American, a white American. No, I don't mind at all. I want it.
I like it" (327). Passing, for him, means creating a fantasy world
where he would not be marked by difference and would not
represent anyone or anything. This desire for erasure of ethnic
and racial identity is a response to fears, for he knows he can be

struck at any moment with insults, physical violence, rejections, criticisms, and "racist love."[15] The accumulation of fears made him "quick and deft," for he said "there is no greater fear than the fear of being caught wanting to belong" (339).

Anger and Guilt

During his yearlong journey, An struggles with his inability to control his life. His mystical association at birth with his transsexual sibling Chi frightens him, but it also gives him inspiration and strength. His constant memories of Chi suggest that she lives on in him. Chi was a refugee who never fit into American society or in her own family. An outcast, she died alone committing suicide, and is not talked about in the family. She is a casualty of immigration and a transgender in a normative, conservative society. Walking "out the door to destinations unknown, spending the sum of [his] breaths in one extravagant gesture" is An's "last ticket," his "last hand to gamble" (33). More than a process of authentication, An's travel to Viet Nam is a desperate attempt to confront his destiny and conquer his fears. In order to control his future and escape these fears, An must face his past. Embarking on a reckless journey, he exposes himself to dangerous situations and possibly new encounters with death to make sense in part of why he survived. But reflecting upon his past, what he uncovers are anger and guilt.

As an adult, An's accumulated fears turn into anger.

> "'I am violent, Mom."
>   "A curse in my father's line."
>   The rage was passed on to another generation. A monster in me, for I am violent. A few years down the road, I cane Hien [brother] with a spark of Father's fury. And Hien, barely ten, comes back at me with a knife. (170)

The narrator acknowledges the violence he inherited from his father as he himself is asked to hit his sibling, which he does to excess. The cycle of physical violence ruptures connections between parent and child, between siblings, and between child and others. An realizes: "I've left everyone I loved. I've failed people I loved" (134). He has difficulty communicating his anger and is unable to trust others. Anger drives his action and pushes him to run away from complex situations that he cannot control.

Anger causes him to deride his father, mimicking him in a derisive tone:

> "You do job best you can. You get promotion. You get new job. You say, 'Thank you very much, sir' and you go. Think about future. You are Asian man in America. All your bosses will be white. Learn to work."
> Yes, father. Okay, father. I will, father. I can't be his Vietnamese American. (25)

An is angered by his father's passive capitulation to racial hierarchy and mocks his words in Pidgin English. He views his father as a weak and submissive man, someone who would have him sacrifice his manhood for the sake of career advancement and security. He sees first-generation Vietnamese Americans' pragmatic acceptance of stereotypes as complicit in white America's racism. Rejecting his father's disregard for his individuality, An crafts an identity in opposition to his father's.

By extension, An condemns Vietnamese Americans who, in his view, act polite and submissive toward their white bosses: "I hate their slitty-measuring eyes. The quick gesture of humor, bobbing of heads, forever congenial, eager to please," he says (25). He does not want to be bound by necessity, but rather wants to be a man with physical strength, courage, independence, and pride. Unlike his father, An sees Vietnamese Americans' pragmatism and resilience in the face of injustice as an infirmity.[16] Like Frank Chin's relationship to older Chinese Americans, An's relationship to first-generation Vietnamese American men is partly and initially one of contempt for their sacrifice and their willingness to swallow their pride for economic survival.[17] "Vietnamese. Honor. Obligations. Respect. I hated it all," he says (107).

If some of An's actions represent resistance to racism, they also underscore a potential for self-destruction. An chooses not to hold onto his stable job because of conflicts with his racist boss. As the first son and main beneficiary of family privilege, An is pressured by his father to succeed financially. He graduates from UCLA with a degree in aerospace engineering and enters the workforce. There he encounters the model minority myth: "I like you people. Orientals are good workers. Good students, too. Great in math, the engineering stuff . . . I think you'll do just fine here. We won't have any trouble at all," An's boss tells him on his first day at work (25). But the young engineer refuses to become a so-called "meek" Asian American. Frustrated, An eventually quits his job in an extravagant gesture:

> When I finally resigned, I was no longer a "good Oriental."
> I even left behind in my desk three files titled "Stuff Paul
> Rejected Because He Doesn't Know Any Better," "Stuff
> Paul Rejected Because He Didn't Want to Jeopardize His
> Promotion," and "Stuff Paul Rejected Because They Didn't
> Originate from Engineers but from Mechanics Who Have
> More Practical Experience on the Subject" (25)

An blatantly denounces the incompetence of his boss, who had prevented him from being promoted under false pretenses and thought he could get away with it because he assumed Asians were passive and easily exploited. The incident suggests the existence of a glass ceiling that still hinders the advancement of Asian Americans like An into top managerial positions. By resigning, An challenges accepted notions of equal opportunity, regardless of skin color, as well as common notions of meritocracy. An also challenges stereotypes, for he is neither agreeable nor confrontational. He does not behave like an "entitled" and "confrontational" white American man who fights for his rights, but he also refuses to be a "powerless" Asian American man who accepts his lot without complaining. The manner in which he quits his job and the incriminating files that he leaves behind also reveal anger. Though the files are intended to redress past injustices, they are also designed to destroy his boss's career. After An resigns, his "supervisor-bossman Paul was moved 'laterally' into a cubicle labeled 'independent contributor' on the third floor, where," An tells us, "they put troublemakers out to pasture"(25). While his gesture represents an act of resistance to racist assumptions, it also suggests hidden anger and desire for both justice and revenge.

Anger is expressed more openly when An recounts an event that occurred while he was biking along the northern California coast. A man in a truck calls him "Jap" and throws water at him. The man's friend makes fun of him, laughs, make "Chinese eyes" at him, and yelps triumphantly: "Yeah! Right on the head!" (39). An eventually catches up with the men when he recognizes their truck parked outside a bar. He says:

> Part of me wants to go inside and confront the truckers. Part of me wants to slash their tires. I want to feel my fists smacking into their fleshy red faces. Giving them the full force of my righteous fury. Realizing how badly I want to hurt them, I am glad I don't have the gun my brother Huy and his boyfriend had offered to loan me. (38)

An is rightfully angered by the racist incident. His desire to confront his tormentors shows his resistance to social injustices. Yet after a moment's hesitation he also comes to realize that his anger is excessive. At the height of his anger, it is not only justice or an apology that he seeks, but the opportunity to hurt or even kill.

An seems to be more comfortable expressing guilt, an emotion that gnaws at him and similarly impacts all of his actions.

Guilt is an emotion that An shares with his father. Reflecting on the way he raised his children, An's father eventually admits: "'My father was violent, I was an abused child,' Father said. 'He was abusive. And . . . I was abusive.' . . . With this conception of his having been an 'abused child' . . . he could not survive, for all his guilt, real and imagined, came crashing down on his age-brittle shoulders" (321). His father eventually realizes he was abusive to his children and expresses deep regrets and guilt, all of which are linked to fears. Fear does not originate in one single event. Rather it is something that is reinforced over time through generations, each new experience reaffirming An's sense of not deserving to live.

During his travels, An opens himself up to the past and future. He realizes then that his guilt poisons all of his memories and is manifest in almost all his relationships. When his father beats his older sister, An is frightened. But he also remembers that he blamed himself for the violence. Feeling "full of first-son righteousness," An told his father that Chi disobeyed him, prompting their father to beat her with rage (56). Rather than being angry with his father, An the child feels there is something wrong with him and blames himself for the violence he witnesses.[18] He cries, "cowering in the hallway terrified," and tells himself that it was he who "brought these blows on her." Because of what he later sees as his "first-son righteousness," An loses a sister whose strength and independence he admires (56).

An blames himself for situations that are out of his control. Without Chi, An has to carry the responsibilities of a first son, bringing an end to his life as a carefree child. An's family left Viet Nam because his father, a former lieutenant and director of propaganda for South Viet Nam's government, feared for his life after Saigon fell to the communists. An explains that the communists hated most those in charge of propaganda. After 1975, his father is sent to a reeducation camp. He survives thanks to the resourcefulness of his wife, who bribes guards with the money she makes through her running a shady massage business. The revenue from this business helps An's extended family pay for their departure from Viet Nam, but later becomes a source of shame and tension within the family (254).[19] After being released from the prison camp, An's father decides to take the family out of Viet Nam (59). Since fleeing is illegal, their plan to leave has to remain secret. If they were discovered, the entire family could be jailed and An's father executed. But An, then a child, reveals his family's secret plans to escape to a friend.

Haunted by feelings of guilt for what he did, An feels responsible for his family's survival (61).[20]

His sister's death uncovers the overwhelming sense of guilt that has permeated his life since the day she suffered from the blows inflicted upon her by their father.

An also endures survivor's guilt. Survivor's guilt usually refers to the guilt of those who survived war. Chi is not directly a victim of war, however, but a victim of unsuccessful resettlement due to the end of the war and domestic violence. In the United States, Chi initially lives with their family, but violence continues inside the home. While An's father beats him to mold him into a "responsible" son, he hits Chi to make her become a "good" daughter. When a counselor notices a bruise on Chi's body and sends the police to arrest their father, Chi runs away in panic. "I can't come back here. Dad will kill me." "She really believed that," An says (214). She also wanted to prevent their father from going to jail "because of her," and through her sacrifice allows the family to stay together.

After Chi leaves, talking about her becomes taboo in the family (254). But the silence around her departure only magnifies her absence (315). A boyish-looking refugee teenager who doesn't speak much English, Chi wanders the streets of 1980s San Francisco and ends up as a garment worker. In contrast to his sister, An, the eldest son of what is now a middle-class family, pursues an aerospace engineering degree at UCLA and embarks on a professional career. Chi is a casualty of immigration and resettlement while An is the beneficiary, which weighs heavily upon him.

First Vietnamese-American Hero

A survivor does not have the luxury of counting his blessings.
PHAM, *CATFISH AND MANDALA*

With a sense of not belonging to any nation and unable to accept support from his family because of domestic violence, An seeks a way to protect himself from his fears. To do this, he surrounds himself with a shield of masculinity to help him manage and hide the anger and guilt that derive from his fears.[21] "All my life I have held pain in check, kept grief at a distance," he says (108). To feel these painful emotions is a luxury he cannot afford. An frames the process of crafting an identity in terms of cultural markers, such as the Vietnamese belief in destiny, karma, or mandala, which contrasts sharply with the American belief in free will. His purported goal is to attain real freedom so he can control his destiny. In the process of moving forward in space while looking backward in time, he experiences new emotions, allowing a new identity to emerge.

Masculinity, Gail Bederman writes, is displayed when "men claim certain kinds of authority based upon their particular type of bodies."[22] In this particular instance, An does not resist the status quo but rather upholds its normative definitions. An despises white racism. He resents being called a "Jap!" (37, 38, 39) and being viewed as a model minority. Yet he is attracted to what he regards as the masculinity of white men. The identity he claims for himself reflects romanticized Hollywood images of lone, rugged, adventurous men. An recalls "riding out [his] front door on a bicycle for the defining event of [his] life" as "so American, pioneering, courageous, romantic, self-indulgent" (29). His decision to go to Viet Nam is motivated by his encounter with Tyle, a U.S. Army veteran he meets in the Mexican desert, who projects exactly these qualities. An describes Tyle as a "charismatic" man who moves with "an idle power" that he says he envies. He compares Tyle to a "giant," a rugged man with "carved leathery lines crafted into his legend-hewn face of fjords and right angles," a man he says who speaks in a "dry, earthen voice" (5). An associates masculinity, located primarily in the body, with the ability to survive on his own and to conquer an abrasive environment. For him, controlling a harsh environment is tantamount to the power to conceal anger and guilt, and ultimately maybe also his fear of death and physical and emotional violence.

Masculinity also helps him navigate or evade contradictions

generated by hybridity or the process through which he survived the violence of the United States and Viet Nam by "living,
inventing, and reproducing different cultural alternatives."[23] Indeed, he lives with many contradictions. French schools taught
him that he was superior to other Vietnamese, while American
movies showed him that he was inferior to white Americans.
Normative American history has trained him to think that he
was a loser of war, while Vietnamese in Viet Nam inform him
that as an American, he is a winner. American multiculturalism tells him that a certain kind of difference is desirable, while
Vietnamese tell him he can never be physically equal to a white
Westerner. As the eldest son in his family, An is supposed to be
strong and provide for his family, but his sister Chi is stronger
than he is, and it is she who keeps the family together through
her sacrifice. Vietnamese culture teaches An to prioritize the
interest of the family over individuality, but mainstream American culture insists on validating individual dreams. His physically trained body assures him that he is capable and strong, but
emasculating stereotypes of Asian American men tell him that
he is not a real man.

Investment in masculinity helps An navigate contradictions
of hybridity. For instance, An tells us that in Viet Nam his parents "put aside a small fortune to enroll [him] in the best school
in the country, a private French institution for boys" (97). Although An felt out of place there because the other children were
"rich," "smart," and "had private tutors," he develops enough of
an association with privilege and colonial culture that he looks
down on other Vietnamese and distances himself from them,
something that is further reinforced by his "adoption" by American society. According to Albert Memmi, in the process of ac-
quiring the education and language of the colonizer, "the colonized's mother tongue, that which is sustained by his feelings,
emotions and dreams, that in which his tenderness and wonder
are expressed, thus that which holds the greatest emotional impact, is precisely the one which is the least valued."[24] Imbued
with colonial education and subsequently disempowered by

America's emasculation of Asian men, An's self-loathing mixed with anger is projected onto first-generation Vietnamese Americans like his father and Vietnamese in Viet Nam. Throughout the book, he describes Vietnamese as "knifish," "snakes, and "rats," "disposable [like] little spiders ready to be plucked by a breeze," and expresses harsh criticism of Vietnamese Americans in general (127). He sacrifices the people near him in order to build his manhood.

In Viet Nam, as in America, An finds that his physical abilities as a man are questioned because of his race. A Vietnamese tour operator named Binh gives him the following advice when An tells him of his plan to cross Viet Nam from south to north on bicycle: "You won't make it. Trust me, I've been around a long time. Vietnamese just don't have that sort of physical endurance and mental stamina. We are weak. Only Westerners can do it. They are stronger and better than us"(77). Faced with Vietnamese interiorization of colonial ideology and American television stereotypes, which historically depict Asian American men as inferior subjects in both mind and body, An wants to show the Vietnamese that an Asian man can be the equal of a white man. He experiences the same anger and urge to prove others wrong as when his American boss made derogatory comments about Asians and his father told him to know his place and obey. It is not An's love for cycling, an activity he did not care for before his trip, that pushes him to bike across the challenging terrain, but rather a desire, similar to that of early Asian American cultural nationalists, to show that Vietnamese American men are not "lacking daring, originality, aggressiveness, assertiveness, [and] vitality."[25] An wants to prove that he is not, as some Vietnamese seem to believe, his father's Vietnamese American or, as some Vietnamese seem to believe, a Viet Kieu who has become soft and weak "like a woman" in the United States. "Don't be such a wimp, drink up," orders his cousin, offering An the beating heart of a snake in a "shot glass half filled with rice wine" (84). Viet Nam becomes a testing ground that enables the narrator to emerge as the first Vietnamese American hero. In the 1970s,

Frank Chin called himself "Chinatown Cowboy" to counter the perceived loss of Chinese American manhood. In the late 1990s, this young Vietnamese American man portrays himself as a "Bicycle Cowboy" riding into a "Hanoi sunset" after drinking the beating heart of a snake (219).[26] It is a persona and gender identification primarily modeled on the iconic white American man, one that asserts his sexuality as a straight man and his ability to conquer Vietnamese women.[27]

Navigating the Absurd

A survivor of the violence of the United States and Vietnam, An is seen as someone he is not everywhere he goes. He crafts an identity by building shields around himself and by "living, inventing, and reproducing different cultural alternatives."[28] Sharing food and drink one evening with the American GI Tyle, who is wandering through the Mexican desert, An is struck by the man's request: "Forgive me. Forgive me for what I have done to your people" (8). An resists this request and remains silent, a preferred strategy when people want something from him he cannot give.[29] He reflects instead on the meaning of the term "his people."

> No. No, Tyle. How can I forgive you? What have you done to my people? But who are my people? I don't know them. Are you my people? How can you be my people? All my life, I've looked at you sideways, wondering if you were wondering if my brothers had killed your brothers in the war that made no sense except for the one act of sowing me here—my gain—in your bed, this strange rich-poor, generous-cruel land. . . . I am the rootless one, yet still the beneficiary of all of your and all of their sufferings. Then why, of us two, am I the savior, and you the sinner? (9)

For An, the location he inhabits is absurd. He is too removed from Viet Nam to identify with Vietnamese with whom he has had no contact since he left as a child, but too closely associated with the Viet Nam War and those perceived as racially "other" to be accepted into mainstream America. Yet he recognizes that he has benefited from the sacrifices of Americans and first-generation Vietnamese Americans. The repetition of "my people" reflects a state of exile and removal from land and nation and challenges any simple notion of people. The phrase betrays the ruptures and violence of civil war and the losses derived from immigration. Without a sense of belonging to a clearly defined people, An uses creativity and memory, which are shaped by how he is treated by others and the contradictory values and beliefs he has learned at home and in society. Because of how he looks, many Americans may see him as an other that needs to "go home," and by virtue of his American citizenship, the Vietnamese, with whom he shares a common language and culture, view him at times as traitor.

The contradictions and difficulties of having no easily identified position in the accepted context of representation recur, regardless of time and space. After An has spent more than two months traveling in Viet Nam, an old man, "a stranger-once-enemy," invites him into his home. The old man speaks of his close relationship to the land and his views of American GIs. "No, I do not hate the American soldiers. Who are they? They were boys, as I was. They were themselves, but also part of a greater creature—the government. As was I. I can no more blame them than a fish I eat can be blamed for what I do," the old man says (267).[30] From the old man's perspective, the young man standing in front of him is like a benevolent ghost. Those whom he speaks of, the ones who matter in the old man's eyes, are the Vietnamese in Viet Nam and the American GIs, not the Vietnamese Americans. In the old man's hut, An does not find the connection he is looking for but only an answer for Tyle, the American GI who evoked his desire to visit the country of his birth. "When you go to Vietnam . . . tell them about me. Tell them about my life, the way I'm living. Tell them about the family I've lost. Tell them I'm sorry," Tyle says (9). To which the old man in the hut replies months later: "Tell your friend Tyle. There is nothing to forgive. There is no hate in this land" (267). The old man does not talk to An but *through* him. Despite the remoteness of the site and the poverty of his host, An is relegated to the role of messenger. Both the American GI and the Vietnamese Northerner view him as a bridge, a kind of mediator who triggers their memories, as though he were a convenient ghost from their past. They do not *see* him. He exists only as a signifier of the war, a narrative from which he is totally absent.

Hybridity in itself does not always make him a reliable narrator.

> I am a mover of between. I slip among classifications like water in cupped palms, leaving bits of myself behind. I am quick and deft, for there is no greater fear than the fear of being caught wanting to belong. I am a chameleon. And the best chameleon has no center, no truer sense of self than what he is in the instant.
>
> No guilt . . . the perfection of our intention is enough. (338–339)

An describes himself as a "mover of between," a fluid man free from classification, a "chameleon" able to change color, form, and shape according to circumstances. He says he melts into backgrounds and finds freedom in passing. An's idea of selfhood without center, without adherence to any specific attributes, qualities, or behavior, all of which he says change depending on the person he is in contact with and the circumstances he is in, is questionable. If he functions outside certain established discursive spaces, can hold multiple visions,[31] and contest master narratives, his investment in masculinity represents a central part of his identity. Like the tea he drinks without sweetened condensed milk, An takes refuge in a fixed and reassuring view of what it means for him to be a man. It is a position of privilege he assumes to the fullest, one he describes as good, bitter, but also wholesome like a "desert shore" (336). On this shore, An is utterly alone. His sole companion, his sister Chi, is a ghost. Like other postcolonial subjects, An in America is "incapable of integrating himself, incapable of being invisible . . . [and goes] on conversing with the dead."[32] Although he might be, like a catfish, someone who needs very little nutrient to live and is free to roam the environment as he pleases, the narration suggests that the act of freeing oneself from historical and personal trauma is not a matter of choice or of sheer will. And it cannot be muscled through.

Healing

To be free from many of his fears, An has to feel his anger and guilt and accept them as part of who he is. These emotions slowly subside after an incident occurs in Viet Nam when he is open and unguarded. There he sees a girl begging for money in a market. Her face suddenly reminds him of his old girlfriend. And in that instant, he tells us, anger and guilt came rushing toward him, as if crushing him. He recalls:

> A grayness swept through me, but I wanted to feel the pain. Deserve it. All my life I have held pain in check, kept grief at a distance. . . . I couldn't stop and I didn't trust—didn't know—the wetness welling up behind my eyes. . . . Blue exhaust teared my eyes, seared my nostrils. In the circling, my mood spiraled downward, inward, powerless. There was nothing I could tear down. Nothing to smash my fists into. Roaring. A monster eating my heart. (108)

The incident is cathartic. Unexpectedly awash in memories of a time when he was in love, he is struck in this crowd of anonymous faces by the pain he had kept at bay with physical exertion and emotional detachment. Safe amid strangers, his anger finally culminates in a burning rage he experiences as a "monster eating [his] heart." An feels the pain and holds on to it. Overwhelmed by guilt, he interprets this pain as a form of punishment for all he has done, for having survived. He feels he deserves it. It is as if he is facing death itself. This scene makes visible the violences he encountered in Viet Nam and the United States, and perhaps more important, his vast capacity for resilience. How did he survive with all of this anger and guilt inside of him without destroying others and himself? After he feels these emotions, tears and sorrow come and finally begin to release him from what had become an encaged world. The memory of his sister allows him to go through the release. "I was weeping for myself because I was not there in the month before [Chi's] death" (109).

After the incident in the marketplace, An puts himself in less dangerous situations and eventually travels more like a tourist, and even hangs out with some. He shifts his attention away from his father, war, and resettlement to a rationale that allows him to live without guilt and excessive anger. He remembers Crazy Ronnie, a woman he met on the road before leaving for Viet Nam. She had told him: "The perfection of intention, in the end, it is all that matters" (338). This resonates with him and helps to further alleviate some of the guilt he feels over his sister's death and her troubled life. Like a catfish that feeds on waste to sustain life, Chi has throughout her life asked for nothing. She sacrificed her life for the well-being of their family. Drawing on his memories of his sister, An tries to emulate her, but no matter how hard he tries, he tell us, he never had her courage, strength, or innocence (33). "She will always pee further than me," An says (185). And no matter how hard he struggles, his pain will never equal hers. Unlike Chi, An will not and cannot take his own life. He is straight, well educated, and the eldest son in a traditional family. He benefits from greater acceptance in his family, in America and in Viet Nam. But An does not want to believe that Chi lived a short and painful life so he could be free. He no longer blames her for his guilt. He is able to accept that it is not his fault his sister died.

At the end of his journey to Viet Nam, An seeks resolution. He reflects: "I know my love for her now, refelt my love for her then and all the love I felt for her in the between years. It isn't forgiveness I seek. All my sins, my sorrows but a drop of ink in this blue vastness" (185). An acknowledges for the first time the connection with his sister and the love he has for her. And he forgives. Perhaps the most courageous deed he accomplishes during his travels is not the conquest of the environment and his ability to control physical pain, but this brief moment of openness and vulnerability at the market.

Going to Viet Nam, a poor country devastated by wars, is not like going to modern Japan and being easily empowered, like David Mura in *Turning Japanese*. Retrieving his roots does not lead to "recovery of wholeness."[33] "The sight of my roots repulses me," he says (193). Rather, Viet Nam becomes a vehicle that facilitates a return to memories and allows painful emotions to be released and possibly digested. To drop "ink in this blue vastness" is, for him, an integral part of this process.

Having begun to heal, An deals with contradictions of hybridity differently. He looks upon the world more kindly. At the end of the book he describes an encounter with an old woman at the beach, near the end of his journey through Viet Nam. After sipping some Vietnamese coffee, which he describes as "good, bitter, but wholesome like this desert shore,"[97] he recounts:

> She says something in English, but I can't understand her, so I keep smiling and nodding. She laughs, I laugh with her. She tries a phrase in French. I shake my head. Never thinking I could understand her, she prattles in Vietnamese, It is beautiful, no? Very beautiful, very peaceful here, isn't it?
>
> I smile.
>
> I smile at her from my anonymity, refusing to answer in our common tongue. I don't want to disappoint her with my commonality, to remind her of our shared history. So, I let her interpret my half-truths. At this I am good. (338–339)

By not responding verbally to the old woman, An the traveler creates a space in which he is not known and therefore cannot be judged, rejected, or disempowered because of ethnicity and origin through language. By remaining silent, he prevents the old woman from making a connection that would mark him as a bridge, a national traitor, or a benefactor. He eventually chooses anonymity and silence. It is no longer the negotiation of difference that concerns him, but the management of commonalities. What matters is the joy shared in the present moment without being reminded of the past. The ability to feel safe in the present holds the promise of a new identity.

For An, who emigrated to America from Viet Nam by boat in the 1980s, to be a man "of between" does not signify being a bridge between cultures. Instead, it is a constant struggle that forces him to confront and even embrace painful contradictions that cannot be easily resolved by a balanced sense of self, or a total, pure, idealized, and subversive stance. His search for roots eventually turns into a search for home, which is primarily articulated as a search for safety from others and from himself. Before he left, he had interiorized his father's warning: "Don't ever think America is yours. It isn't" (191). Upon returning to America after spending a year in Viet Nam, where he finally feels emotions born of compounded trauma stored in his body, he begins to accept his host country. He tells an older Vietnamese man sitting next to him on the plane: "Welcome home" (342). And he tells himself that "nowhere else are we safer than in America" (183). An becomes Andrew. For him, home is where safety is most present. This voluntary and new embrace of America mirrors a transformation from refugee to immigrant, an experience that is no longer defined by fears, but by trust in one's ability to control the present and the future.

Monkey Bridge: Fear in a Handful of Dust

> *There is always order to tend to, chaos to push swiftly away.*
>
> LAN CAO, *MONKEY BRIDGE*

> *Forms of individual and collective narratives are not merely representations disconnected from "real" political life; nor are these expressions "transparent" records of histories of struggle. Rather, these forms—life stories, oral histories, histories of community, literature—are crucial media that connect subjects to social relations.*
>
> LISA LOWE, *IMMIGRANT ACTS*

Fear and the need to take control of one's life and surroundings are even more visible and clearly articulated in *Monkey Bridge*. The opening page of the novel warns readers that they will find something "different" from their "shadow." The book begins with a quote from T. S. Eliot's *The Waste Land*:

> (Come in under the shadow of this red rock),
> And I will show you something different from either
> Your shadow at morning striding behind you
> Or your shadow at evening rising to meet you;
> I will show you fear in a handful of dust.[34]

Readers are told at the outset that in this book they will not find a mirror of their expectations, but instead "fear in a handful of dust." But unlike An, Mai, the book's narrator, has little knowledge of her mother's past and cannot make sense of her behavior. In order to protect her daughter from her "destiny," or bad karma, and avoid transmitting her "wound" to her child, Mai's mother lied about her past. Without any reliable memory of her own, the narrator grows up in the void of the unspeakable. Yet, fear of death is passed down from mother to daughter and generates a deep sense of vulnerability that also complicates the reading of the text. Mai's actions and gaze are dictated by her need to be protected from perceived dangers and from her deep desire to belong. Mai's vulnerability creates anger and sadness. Her identity becomes marked by a back-and-forth movement between self-defense and attack. Her shield is her mind.

Mai is not an emblematic victim, nor does she embody the plight of the Vietnamese people.[35] Mai remembers the French villa where she lived with her family in Viet Nam as a nurturing sanctuary that she misses deeply, and not as a terrain of war or misery. For her, Viet Nam evokes "sweet memories" (128). Unlike the narrator of *Catfish and Mandala*, Mai did not have to undertake a hazardous journey by boat to leave Viet Nam. She boarded a plane. Mai comes from a privileged background. Her father was a professor of French philosophy and her mother a well-educated woman who did not have to work outside the home. Her father passed away in his sleep in Viet Nam before she immigrated to the United States. In America she lives alone with her mother, who subsists on welfare. For Mai, immigration does not represent progress or safety, but an unimaginable downfall and rupture with what was once a very good life.

Although she did not have to face death in the way that An did during his harrowing journey by boat, Mai nonetheless experienced her departure from Viet Nam as traumatic. She associates the act of leaving with violence and death. She says: "The fear of separation I suddenly understood that day to be a fear as primordial as the fear of death. Once felt, it stays forever trapped, like a child's muffled cry, inside one's chest" (97). That Mai recognizes her fear is lodged inside her body, despite the relatively safe circumstances of her departure, suggests that trauma does not affect people equally, but is experienced differently according to one's level of resilience and sense of vulnerability at that particular moment. For Mai, a child who had recently lost her father and was forced to leave behind the world she knew and board a plane without her mother, the experience is similar to facing death. When Mai's mother finally joins her in the United States a few months later, after the fall of Saigon, Mai no longer trusts her mother's ability to protect her and no longer sees her as a source of "comfort and sanctuary" (137). In the United States, Mai's mother loses her "motherly authority" to the point where she becomes increasingly "alien" to her (137–138). Growing up, Mai, like An, is attracted to an American culture that promotes individualism, rationality, and straight-forward communication. As a teenager, Mai, feeling alienated from her mother, is frustrated by what she perceives to be her mother's lack of control over her environment and the extreme anxieties that seem to consume her. Mai describes her mother as absent, gnawed by the guilt of having left her own father behind in Viet Nam in the midst of her chaotic departure in 1975. Mai views her mother as someone who lives with a sense of "impend-ing doom" (24). Because she left her father behind, Mai's mother says she believes she has brought bad karma upon herself and will have to suffer the consequences.

Fears Passed on from One Generation to the Next

> *To articulate the past historically . . . means to seize hold of a*
> *memory as it flashes up at a moment of danger.*
>   WALTER BENJAMIN, *ILLUMINATIONS*

In Viet Nam, Mai had enjoyed her status as a member of the elite upper class. She resents the fact that people in America can only see her as a poor refugee. Mai has no memory of having confronted death directly, aside from the journey by plane that brought her to America. And yet, she is plagued by fears. Where do these fears come from?

The narrative suggests that they are passed down from Mai's mother through the body.[36] According to Mai, her mother sees "danger everywhere, danger screaming out of the earth and the sky and even the birds" (24). Mai says: "My mother could be a fugitive even in her own home. She had an instinctive distrust for everyone" (46). Her mother's paranoia disturbs her. But Mai discovers that she, too, is prey to irrational fears. In a scene where she travels to Canada with her best friend Bobbie to con-tact her grandfather (during the U.S. economic embargo against Viet Nam, relations between the two countries was prohibited, so Mai had to travel outside of the United States to contact her grandfather), she is struck by what it means to be a refugee upon reaching the border. She hears her mother's voice: "[Americans] jump at the chance to send us all back. Nomads, that's what we've all become" (15). Her mother's distrust of Americans stems from what she has heard. "The Americans, rumors had it, could forbid us to return if we stuck so much as half a foot outside the perimeters of their country," she says (14). "Besides," Mai adds, "I knew from my own reading that refugees were a burden to the economy" (15). Faced with the prospect of repatriation, Mai panics. She says:

> Any movement, however slight, could crack the Chevy wide open like an uncooked eggshell. I was miles away from the possibility of victory tonight. The Canadian frontier, prodigious and uncrossable, looked flat and wide, a horizontal plateau so utterly open there couldn't possibly be a spot anywhere in that land for a person to hide. . . . I was, after all, without the protection of American citizenship. (29)

At the border, Mai sees her car as her only protection. It becomes for her a fragile "uncooked eggshell" that could crack wide open at any instant. Any slight movement on her part and everything could be destroyed. "One wrong move, and the entire mess can just disarrange itself and collapse like a hundred pieces of flying metal for the whole world to see," she recalls (257). Like the wide open and barren Canadian landscape spread out before her, Mai feels naked and unprotected. She is unable to control her fears. She realizes she has absolutely no safe place she can call home (29). Crossing the border to contact a lost family member represents a possible crime. National borders are real, significant. They signal the possibility of deportation, which for Mai is comparable to death. Her fears of deportation are heightened by her mother's fears: "I could have warned Bobbie about my mother's paranoia, but, then, it had never occurred to me that her terrible sense of the world could circulate inside my skin" (17). Mai says, "My mother was my karma, her eye my inheritance," suggesting that fears are passed from one generation to the next, independently of memory (20).

Sharpened Vision

> *History operates more efficiently when its agents are dead.*
>
> MARITA STURKEN, *TANGLED MEMORIES*

Like An, Mai sees herself as a chameleon. She moves between various cultural spheres without fully fitting into any. This ability creates what Edward Said calls a "sharpened vision," one that is acutely aware of the constructiveness of cultural regimes of truth, which Mai only partially inhabits and navigates haphazardly.[37]

Mai rejects outright normative American humanitarian rhetoric that posits the United States as the savior of the "free world" (151, 203). Commenting on America's glorified image of itself, Mai makes the following observations about the movie *The Deer Hunter*:

> In one hallucinatory scene after another, against a disturbing background of incomprehensible grunts which supposedly constituted spoken Vietnamese, the roulette-like spin of a gun as arbitrary and senseless as Vietnam would dictate the life and death of American innocence. Vietnam was becoming a huge allegorical hold into which all things primeval could be sucked. (100–101)

Mai sees white American characters in *The Deer Hunter* as righteous, in denial, and ignorant of Vietnamese culture and history. The word "supposedly" implies that the actors improvise their own version of Vietnamese, which they degrade to "incomprehensible grunts." Her descriptions of "hallucinatory" scenes contest dominant representations of American soldiers as innocent prey to wild, exotic, and evil spells commonly associated with Asia. Mai discards the notion that Americans are simply victims of their circumstances, an idea that the majority of Viet Nam War movies promote. The terms "American innocence" and "allegorical hold" denounce American revisionist views that use Viet Nam as mere background for the psychological development of its young white men. Missing from this self-serving portrait, Mai suggests, are the Vietnamese people, their fears, their sense of desperation, and their humanity. And perhaps more important, absent from these portraitures is the deep sense of abandonment and betrayal that South Vietnamese felt following the sudden departure of American forces from Viet Nam.

Mai's attitude of utter rejection toward Hollywood, the media, and the U.S. government's representations of the Vietnamese comes to the surface in a daydream she has after watching televised reports of the fall of Saigon in April 1975. She says:

> Then, suddenly, in a voice of mingled sorrow and surprise, a network newscaster announced, "It all began with the best of intentions." Behind him, on top of the U.S. Embassy, American marines pointed their bayonets and rifles like sharks' teeth against their astonished old allies, in fear, the newscaster explained, of an American massacre by a frightened local population desperate enough to try anything, anything at all, to keep the Americans from leaving, from abandoning. (99–100)

In this dream sequence, Mai dares to give a different version of what happened in Viet Nam at the end of the war. To Mai, Americans are neither victims nor heroes, but traitors. Seen from her perspective, Americans are responsible for her state of exile, losses, and a life lived in fear. In the dream sequence, Americans are compared to "sharks," a word that denotes power, heartlessness, and greed. As "sharks," Americans are described as monsters chomping on panicking South Vietnamese bodies, Vietnamese who made the mistake of believing in America's false promises and its protective power as leader of the free world. In Mai's dream, the victims are the South Vietnamese who have been used, betrayed, and left as live bait to be eaten by another dreadful shark (98).[38]

Mai does not trust normative history. Her memories do not match textbook versions of the war and its aftermath. Her denouncing of an America-centric view of the Viet Nam War is bound by the erasure of the South Vietnamese from it, one that is entangled with the subsequent distorted representations of Vietnamese Americans. In Mai's view, American representation of the South Vietnamese served as a means to justify American intervention in Viet Nam. America's "fictional tales of victory" rewritten in Hollywood movies and its renewed interest in Vietnamese American voices and memories are motivated, she says, by a collective desire to "re-fight the war and produce a new ending" (153). The United States, she concludes, is a "country in love with itself" (31). It is concerned with either forgetting the war or rewriting it so as to fit its own image as the good fighter of the free world (153). The majority of Vietnamese in Viet Nam, she suggests, have moved on and do not want to talk about what they call the "American War." The removal of America from the center of the narrative provides an alternate and impassioned view of history as a social construct governed by power. For Mai, history is not an abstraction or postmodern construction. It is real—something she has lived through and that has impacted her life and caused enormous losses and voids that cannot be filled. Her voice effectively makes visible the "bundle of silences" that buries Vietnamese Americans' experiences and identities.[39] Because her memories are not validated by the history she was taught in school or sees on television, they enter the realm of the sacred and become central to her identity.

Mai's vision also contests models of assimilation as well as paradigms that assume that all Asian immigrants come from a pure and untouched Asian culture. Speaking of her mother's friends' decision to open a French ice cream store in Little Saigon in Virginia, she says:

> Mr. and Mrs. Hai, who used to work in the ice-cream business in Saigon, had decided that nostalgia could be exploited—with sensitivity, of course. Their ice-cream parlor would specialize in replicating with unwavering precision the decor, arrangement, atmosphere, and taste of the old Givrard and Brodard ice-cream parlors in downtown Sai-

gon, where coconut, pineapple, orange, and other fruit-
based ice cream would be served in their natural fruit
shells. (143)

Mr. and Mrs. Hai capitalize on Vietnamese Americans' nostalgia for the past and their love-hate relationship with the French
to further their business interests. They reappropriate symbols
of French colonialism as a vehicle to attain *their* American
Dream. The exploitation of Vietnamese Americans' colonial
past complicates notions of progress, nationalism, and immigration. The couple's nostalgic gaze is transfixed on an idealized
and revisionist past that glosses over the realities of colonization
by ranking intruders according to the lesser of their worst qualities. As such, French colonialism, as compared with Chinese
rule or the Japanese occupation, for example, was not perceived
to be so terrible by certain members of the Vietnamese elite, as a
number among this group in the South also benefited economically from access to French education and the infrastructures it
established.[40] Symbols of French colonialism, like this ice cream
parlor, are prominent markers of Vietnamese Americans' nostalgia for the past. The couple is moving forward in America by
looking back to a past changed by foreign conquests.

Americans, she emphasizes, are not the only ones to rewrite
the past. Some Vietnamese Americans did so as well. Far from
romanticizing her community, Mai recounts some of the aber-
rations of resettlement. She says:

Like all of us who made up the refugee community, Little
Saigon too was preoccupied with the possibility of astro-
logical and historical revisions. . . . There was an odd ele-
ment of righteousness in this transformation. Out of the
ruins came a clatter of new personalities. A bar girl who
once worked at Saigon's Queen Bee, a nightclub frequented
by American soldiers, acquired a past as a virtuous Confucian teacher from a small village in a distant province.
Here, in the vehemently anti-Vietcong refugee community, draft dodgers and ordinary foot soldiers could become

decorated veterans of battlefields as famous as Kontum and Pleiku and Xuan Loc. It was the Vietnamese version of the American Dream; a new spin, the Vietnam spin, to the old immigrant faith in the future. (40)

Some Vietnamese Americans, enticed by the notion of the American Dream, believe that anything is possible in America, including the reconstruction of the past. If America can erase and make up the past, so can they. This version of the American Dream possesses mythic qualities beyond notions of America as the Gold Mountain.[41] America is seen as a place inhabited by childlike, innocent, and blindly trusting people who believe everything they are told by their government, the movies, the media, and those around them. The blind trust and naïveté of those who live in a superpower can be exploited to their benefit. The same blind innocence that accepts uncritical erasure of America's South Vietnamese allies from history can now be used to lay the ground for a terrain where rebirth is possible, as phantasmagoric as it may be. In this version of the American Dream, destinies can be salvaged, redeemed, and controlled.

"Control, Everything Is Order and Control."

Mai is preoccupied with controlling her environment through the power of her mind and intellect. Her sense of vulnerability makes it very difficult for her to live without the security offered by a recognized identity. Her fears stored in her body produce anger and also sadness that at times harden her sharp vision to a point of detachment so that she can no longer see the humanity of those standing in front of her. For Mai, freedom in America is tied to her ability to control her destiny and her future, which means breaking with the past while simultaneously holding onto a nostalgic evocation of Viet Nam that offers comfort in times of perceived danger. "Control, everything is order and control," Mai says (257). She believes that if she fails to control her environment everything will collapse. Without control, the monkey bridge made of bamboo reeds on which she metaphorically walks alone over a precipice would break, and she would fall and die. Mai's perception prompts her state of alertness and restlessness. Mai's hyperconsciousness holds the potential for destruction and self-destruction. Like An, Mai is both the rejected and the one who rejects.

Mai is also excessively critical of Vietnamese Americans of the first generation, whom she describes as being trapped by "brute anticommunism" and ignorance. She says:

> Detached, I could see this community as a riot of adolescents, obstreperous, awkward, out of sync with the subscribed norms of American life, and beyond the reach of my authority. I could feel for them, their sad shuffles and anachronistic modes of behavior, the peculiar and timid way they held their bodies and occupied the physical space, the unfailing well-manneredness with which they conducted themselves in public—their foreigners' ragged edges. (146)

Mai's vision is harsher than that of a gawking tourist visiting a Vietnamese American enclave. She compares older first-generation Vietnamese Americans to childlike creatures who, unfortunately, cannot fit into American society. The succession of words: "riot of adolescents," "obstreperous," "awkward," and "out of sync" denotes a gaze colored by a strong concern that white Americans might associate "them" with her, and thus prevent her from being fully accepted into American society no matter how Americanized she becomes. Like An, Mai identifies herself in relation to the gaze of what she regards to be the dominant society, or what An called the "cream-colored giants who make [first-generation Vietnamese Americans] and [those of the 1.5 generation] look tribal, diminutive, dark, wanting."[41] Like him, Mai fears rejection by whites and being misunderstood as one of "them"—or those she views as awkward first-generation Vietnamese Americans. Mai is frustrated not only by stereotypes but also by the fact that she cannot control the behavior of older Vietnamese Americans, whom she says escape "the reach of [her] authority."

Mai manages her lack of control by imagining another kind of community, one that does not counter stereotypes but conforms to them. If there must be differences between Vietnamese Americans and whites, in Mai's view, then Vietnamese Americans should acquire differences that are desired by the mainstream. She imagines turning the first generation into "more palatable possibilities—sultans and genies flying out of bottles and lamps, flamboyant turbans of paisley and silk" (147). If they cannot assimilate into the mainstream, Mai reasons, Vietnamese Americans could at least contribute to the multicultural spectacle. If only their appearance and behavior coincided more with Orientalist and Vietnamese iconographic images, she says with a touch of sarcasm, they would find a place in America, and so would she. "If you have to be different, you have to be acceptably different," she affirms (147), concluding sadly that "Americans had rendered us invisible and at the same time awfully conspicuous" (42).

On the margin of the margin, and without a recognizable history valorized by institutions to which she can anchor her identity, Mai feels alone and unsafe. As critic Nguyen-Vo Thu-Huong explains, "one does not become recognizably human until one acts in one's history. And for that, one needs to have history."[42] Immigration to America has not given Mai the sense of security or entitlement she needs. She does not have a sense of place. Alienated, Mai uses misconceptions and stereotypes to her own advantage. She also strategically appropriates and transforms Vietnamese legends and historical events to manage her fears. During a college interview, Mai is afraid she will not be accepted to the college of her choice. To maintain her composure, she puts on an imaginary mask, positing herself as the legendary Vietnamese woman warrior Trung Trac, who is lauded by Vietnamese for winning battles against Chinese invaders. Mai's appropriation of Trung Trac represents an abrupt return to an imagined Viet Nam from which she can retrieve heroism and pride. Mai recalls her father's words: "We had driven back five Chinese invasions, three Mongol, and two French" (118).

The evocation of national victory overshadows for an instant the painful memory of losing the country and the reality of what she calls her "blemished" life (118). Her use of the word "we" during times of stress and perceived danger helps Mai reduce her fears and alleviate the discrepancy in power between her and the college interviewer. National pride momentarily becomes her shield and strategy of survival, regardless of the fact that a segment of the Vietnamese population who fought the French consisted, for the most part, of communists who later became her enemies.

Mai consciously uses stereotypes as a defense mechanism. During the college interview, Mai sees herself as a woman warrior in close combat with a tiger. The interviewer, Ms. Layton, is the tiger. Threatened by the woman's power to deny her entry to the college of her choice and throw her off balance, Mai feels vulnerable and suddenly regards the interviewer as an enemy. When Ms. Layton asks her in a casual and "unreadable voice" if she was "there the whole time the war was going on" Mai tempers her impulse to ask "Which war?" (126–127). Shielded by the armor of the Trung warrior, she is tempted to attack the interviewer's American centrism, her ignorance of Viet Nam's long history of wars, and the diversity among Vietnamese Americans. But Mai is conflicted because she does not want to reveal the complexity of Viet Nam's history for fear that she might lose the special attention that she is currently being given as a stereotypical refugee. If she unveils her elite background she fears she will no longer receive the compassion she may benefit from. Like a "warrior" faced with a stronger opponent, she then plays the role of the recognizable and vulnerable "refugee." Mai deflects the question and provides a vague and unsatisfactory answer without being overtly offensive: "In Saigon, right in the downtown section," she says (127). When the interviewer asks, "What was it like over there?" Imagining what a woman warrior like Trung Trac would do with a tiger (120), Mai steps carefully to one side, and uses her own momentum to throw the interviewer off balance: "It was . . . different," she replies. "It's very hot there and humid. . . . I thought seventy degrees was cold when we first arrived. My mother put up the heat" (129). Mai employs here "a drunken monkey style" used by the woman warrior, the "most bewitching," she says, "of all styles . . . [a] riot of freewheeling movements that seemingly contained no pattern and no discernible rhythm, best designed to confound an opponent" (120). Mai manages to circumvent the discussion without having to lie or confront Layton's preconceived notions (129).

Mai calls her response "the poor person's weapon," which Michel De Certeau defines as a "tactic" of the weak, a "clever trick," a "maneuver," a "polymorphic simulation" that uses "joyful discoveries, poetic as well as warlike."[44] Like a Vietnamese woman warrior's guerrilla tactic, Mai successfully manages and controls Americans' national guilt over the Viet Nam War without compromising herself and showing her anger.[45] Ms. Layton responds, "Uh-huh . . . Good thing you didn't start out right away in New England." In a final punch, Mai throws the interviewer off guard and steers the discussion away from war stories and toward more benign discussions about the weather. Mai successfully evades Ms. Layton's assumptions and maintains intact the interviewer's preconceptions about the refugee experience, because at this very moment it serves her. Mai has "turned the tables," in De Certeau's words, "on the powerful by the way in which [she] makes use of the opportunities offered by the particular situation," making her "weaker position seem the stronger."[46] Hence Mai effectively controls the situation by turning stereotypes to her own advantage.

Yet strategies of survival do not always serve Mai and her mother well. By lying to her daughter, Mai's mother created a rift between the two. Mai's mother's trauma is revealed at the end of the novel, when both the reader and Mai learn that her mother had witnessed her adoptive father (Mai's grandfather), who became a "Viet Cong," kill her biological father just before she left Viet Nam to be reunited with Mai. Mai's biological grandfather, a rich landlord and beneficiary of the French colonial system, forced her grandmother to have sex with him in exchange for letting her keep the land.[47] At the end of the war, Mai's adoptive grandfather kills the man who took away his pride and manhood and hurt his family so deeply. Keeping this terrible secret had tormented Mai's mother for years.

Throughout the novel Mai compares her position to that of a girl walking alone on a bridge made of bamboo reeds suspended over a steep precipice, always on the verge of falling. Like An, Mai has "no emotional attachments that carried the length and depth of space" (226). While she was alive, her mother hid the horror of her adoptive father killing her biological father to protect Mai from a history of "bad karma," a system that believes present lives are affected by deeds committed during past lives. In America, destiny can be changed and altered. Past lives may even be dissociated from present ones, perhaps because the spirits of the past remain in Viet Nam. To be a safe place, America has to be freed from ghosts. When Mai is accepted into college, her mother commits suicide. She sacrifices herself both to free her daughter from filial responsibilities and so that she can finally find peace from her torment. It is only then that Mai is free. She can once again feel and accept her connection to her mother and to Viet Nam. The novel ends with this sentence: "Outside, a faint sliver of what only two weeks ago had been a full moon dangled like a sea horse from the sky" (260). The present is entangled with the past. Viet Nam, a country shaped like a sea horse will, from this moment, remain with her. Like An, Mai can only trust and receive support from the dead.

Catfish and Mandala and *Monkey Bridge* are multifaceted texts written from the perspective of the 1.5 generation. They are neither refugee nor immigrant texts alone, and that what happened prior to, during, and after the time of immigration is central to understand the formations of the narrators in search for a recognizable and livable "I." Both offer a critical gaze of the ways in which American society looks at Viet Nam and Vietnamese Americans and how this, in turn, impacts their identity. Yet both direct anger and frustration toward Vietnamese Americans of the first generation or the Vietnamese in Viet Nam and white

Americans. They fear that the behavior of Vietnamese elders tarnishes the way white Americans look at and judge them. This anger and frustration points to a marginality entangled with postcolonial conditions, the high cost of war, domestic violence, and downward mobility associated with immigration, as well as with the fear of death passed on from parents to their children.

For the protagonists of *Catfish and Mandala* and *Monkey Bridge*, hybridity means that living without fear is a luxury they do not have. They cannot let go of their fears through sheer will alone. Living without resorting to tactics to hide these fears and manage their anger, sadness, or guilt is not something they can afford. They do the best they can by trying to control their environment through body and mind, utterly alone and without support or models to emulate or guide them. Acutely protective of themselves, they hold their breath, trusting no one but the dead. At times, they gain control by internalizing or mimicking what they perceive to be genuine power, especially along ethnic and gender lines.[48] Both are located at the intersection of the world of their parents, who remain in part emotionally in South Viet Nam, and an America that is more concerned with making amends with North Viet Nam than with its South Vietnamese allies. These difficulties are compounded by the fact that other communities, both white and nonwhite, in the United States and in Viet Nam do not seem to acknowledge or understand the refugees' collective grief over losing a nation. An and Mai live life as though they are walking on a thin bamboo bridge that may collapse at any moment. On each side of the bridge is an amalgam of memories of loss and violence. They react to these forces in ways that cannot be qualified as resistance or accommodation alone.[49] But what cannot be denied from these stories is the high degree of resilience and creativity generated in face of intense contradictions and violence generated by empires.

Recommended Readings

Michel De Certeau, *The Practice of Everyday Life*, translated by Steven Rendall. Berkeley: University of California Press, 1984.

Allen Douglas and Ngo Vinh Long, eds., *Coming to Terms: Indochina, the United States, and the War.* Boulder: Westview, 1991.

Stuart Hall, "Cultural Identity and Diaspora." In *Identity: Community, Cultural, Difference,* edited by Jonathan Rutherford, 223–237. London: Lawrence and Wishart, 1990.

Marita Sturken, *Tangled Memories: The Vietnam War, the AIDS Epidemic and the Politics of Remembering.* Berkeley: University of California Press, 1997.

5 /   Hope and Despair

that the only true audience is the one not listening to know that
i write despite of you the more i write the less you know to know
that you i define as the reader this is all you need to know this is
all i choose to tell.

TRUONG TRAN, DUST AND CONSCIENCE

We live and act as though "life" is real and "art" derivative; art
at its best makes the opposite feel true.

NAM LE, INTERVIEW WITH KY-PHONG TRAN

Mikhail Bakhtin has argued that literature does not fully reflect the real but rather "a social struggle for unity."[1] Although Vietnamese American texts can be used carefully and strategically to draw commentary about the experience of the group, they are creative works that respond to what Bakhtin describes as "the quotidian pressures and opportunities in life."[2] Vietnamese American authors, like all authors, are creating within and in relation to the context in which they are being read. Those who write in English respond in particular to a majority culture in which their country of origin represents a thorn in the psyche of the nation in search of resolution of the Viet Nam War. The following chapter examines what happens when authors let go of the weight of representationality and normative refugee discourse. Complex questions of powers between first and third worlds as well as issues of violence, and ethnic and gender identity constructions continue to be raised.

dust and conscience: A Narrative of Hope

Truong Tran emigrated to the United States when he was five years old in 1975, by plane. He has hardly any memories of Viet Nam or of his departure, and no interest in telling *the* Vietnamese American refugee story. The narrator of his book of prose poems, *dust and conscience*, published in 2002, is concerned rather with the possibility of letting go of the weight of representationality. The author works against societal pressures to represent Vietnamese Americans and "his" people through both content and form.

In *dust and conscience*, Truong Tran wove a story of self within poetic fragments.[3] The book opens in the conditional: "if only i were a dissident poet i could claim my poems were once written in a cell scraps of paper brought to me by a rat on a string."[4] The speaker is referring to Nguyen Chi Thien, a poet and prisoner of war known for his collection of poems, Flowers *from* Hell, which he wrote after 1975 while imprisoned in a reeducation camp. Nguyen had then brought the manuscript to the British Embassy, which cost him another twelve years in prison. The book, however, was translated into seven languages and many of the poems were made into songs. In 1985, Nguyen Chi Thien received the International Poetry Prize in Rotterdam. While many loved his poems, others questioned the poetic value of his work and claimed that it garnered acclaim partly because of the political circumstances under which it was written.

Tran's book directly addresses the relationship between identity politics and art. What is art and what is political appropriation? At what point and to what extent do the two intersect? When will Vietnamese American literary texts be appreciated for their literary quality and not only for their origin. When and how can Vietnamese American writers be freer from external pressures and from their own past to tell their stories and those of others? How could Tran possibly write about his experience and that of the Vietnamese people without his work being consumed by an audience hungry for authenticity and resolution of the Viet Nam War?[5]

In 2000, Truong Tran was commissioned to travel to Viet Nam to write about his experience and encounters with "his" people. The grant was awarded to coincide with the twenty-fifth anniversary of the end of the Viet Nam War, which saturated American media for several weeks. Tran pondered how to tell his story and the stories of those he was commissioned to write about without giving in to what he regards to be an exotic National Geographic-type narrative, which he opposes.[6] Like Andrew Pham and Lan Cao, Tran is acutely aware, to use Lisa Lowe's words, that "there is always a politics of identity, a politics of position, which has no absolute guarantee in an unproblematic, transcendental 'law of origin,'"[7] especially when this origin is Viet Nam. Ambivalent, but also welcoming of the opportunity to be paid to travel to Viet Nam, something that would be difficult for a poet to refuse, Tran accepted the grant, went to Viet Nam, and produced *dust and conscience*. He met the terms of his contract with his funder without making compromises. He does not bare his soul to an audience, nor does he engage in an anesthetized multicultural rhetoric. This ethical position is articulated at the cost of linearity and clarity, for imbedded in language itself, he suggests, are the very associations he seeks to deconstruct.

HOME

By privileging form over content, Vietnamese American identity emerges within the fissures of fragments, memories, and inventions as something that, like all identities, is incomplete, in the making, and impacted in excess by the continuous and enormous impact of the Viet Nam War, the mixing of American and Vietnamese culture and the vast power inequalities between first and third worlds. Without developmental narratives as carriers of formal constructs and free from the categories "Vietnamese Americans" and "Vietnam," Tran's speaker begins: "the line which connects the perceptions to the perceived is crossed with the line of the needs and necessities and there at the crossing are the casualties fragments to stories some still struggling to find the beginnings" (12). The speaker introduces himself by considering many possible beginnings. Without a clear idea of

what home is and without a clear origin to locate himself, he ut-
ters multiple articulations of the concept of home. Home brings
to mind various stories and memories, all of which resonate
with what home could be, without ever arriving at a clear definition that coincides with the real. Instead of proposing an answer,
the narrator fully lets go of the security of a fixed identity and
begins by exploring what home means to others.

What does home mean, he inquires for instance, to a Vietnamese man visiting indefinitely his children in the United
States? Tran writes: "to preserve the bitterness he scattered his
children in four directions sat back in his chair and proceeded
to grow old he waited until the time was right he paid them a
visit when they went to kiss their father he licked their skin he
found the bitterness still clinging to his tongue he tells his children i want to go home" (11). This older Vietnamese man, like
other Vietnamese at the end of the war, sent his children overseas. When he joins them years later, the connections have loos-
ened. The children have grown up in America and are busy with
their lives. The man concludes that he cannot live with them, no
matter how prosperous they may be. He ultimately decides to return to Viet Nam, a poor country with fewer human rights. For
him, the notion of home is clear, yet because it means separation
from his children, the connection and emotional attachment to
home is also a source of pain. Without a clear identity linked to
a national origin, the narrator crafts a subjectivity in relation
to what he is not. His identity is unlike that of the Vietnamese
man who cannot live in the United States because he misses Viet
Nam too much.

Home does not mean the same thing as it does for the speaker's mother, either. He recalls his mother sitting "in her new car
she listens to the cd she is reminded of home she is overwhelmed
with sadness she is parked in her garage she is reminded of
home" (17). Regardless of her material satisfaction in the United
States, his mother, who has lived there for over twenty-five years,
misses Viet Nam deeply, a place that she still calls home without
hesitation, in spite of her American citizenship. The speaker of

dust and conscience is not, like his mother, living in a state of exile. His memories of the country he emigrated from are too faint or nonexistent for him to mourn. He cannot miss a place that he has hardly any memories of. But like his mother, he is not fully at home in the country of resettlement.

During his trip to Viet Nam, the narrator realizes that although he does not feel American, he is not Vietnamese, either. It becomes clear that he has no place he can call home. Home is neither here nor there.[8] Without a home, without a recognizable identity, or a clear "I" to point to, how then would a poem from a Vietnamese American perspective begin? The speaker hesitates. Although the theme of nation or nationlessness is central to the text, not once does it mention the name of a country, a common marker of identity. The first sentence of "the book of beginnings" opens with the line: "inception incipience debut dawn," words that evoke beginnings without reference to a location with national borders, or an actual time.

The absence of nation suggests that such a connection to a home is not available to the narrator. What the narrator mourns is not the loss of home but the absence of home. In Viet Nam, he imagines writing a note to his friends in the States: "it is not that I am forgetful or lazy I have written letters to each and every one of you but I choose not to send them for such an act means that the existence of home would then be confined to one or the other" (21). While the achievements of an exile, according to Edward Said, are permanently undermined by the loss of something left behind forever, such achievements are here undermined by the inability to mourn a home, a point of reference that would anchor him.[9] In *dust and conscience*, the authorial subjectivity is located *before* the attempt of inscription of wholeness. "Where would i begin if not at home," he asks. Since the term "home," he reflects, does not have clear meaning or associations, it can therefore *only* exist as a question. Home exists only in the search itself. All the narrator can do is debate the question of home and wonder about the land of Viet Nam and America. This question serves as a guide, an arrow that points him to a direction. It provides a degree of strength and support, and as small as it may appear, still allows the narrator to move forward with his utterance. This articulation of self contrasts sharply with modernist binaries, like home/not home, homeland/adopted land, in which "home" is clearly linked to a nation and holds the potential to heal the wounds caused by uprootedness.

The absence of a home coexists with the absence of identity. How, the narrator also asks, can the "I" be told ethically and without compromise when the "I" does not have a place in society and when the "I" has not fully come to terms with the contradictions inherent in the crossing of cultures, war, immigration, and absence from history? And more specifically, how does one begin to speak of what it means to be on the margin, to be a gay man and a second-generation Catholic Vietnamese American from a poor refugee family who writes poetry?[10] *Dust and conscience* traces a journey of becoming without a predetermined and charted path.

The speaker insists he is not a victim. If sadness can be detected from the tone and rhythm of the poems, there is also something freeing about being in that location. Whereas an exile like his mother is inconsolable about her past, bitter about the present and the future, the narrator is detached from loss and without nostalgia and bitterness. Deprived of an origin to which he wishes to return, the beginning for him is not a matter of geography but more a matter of time. Beginning, or the formulation of a recognizable "I" belongs to the realm of the future. One day, he hopes, he will arrive and have access to a language in which the "I" will not require reverting to a mask, its representation will not resort to tactics of survival, and his texts will no longer be read only within the framework of war. Such a task, he suggests, is not yet possible.

The "book of endings" speaks of the narrator's search for an evolving voice. Out of the fragmented memories and reflections of his life, the narrator crafts what Pierre Bourdieu calls a new habitus, a social, political, familial, linguistic structure that may not be home, but instead *represents* the possibility of home, located in the future.[11] Unlike exile narratives of the first generation that seek timelessness, boundlessness, predictability, reliability, stability, and universality, the narrator accepts and opens himself to the unknown.[12] He writes:

> every word of every image is a step towards the end this urgency dictates that the sentence as we know it no longer an option grammar is obsolete stories once told in detailed chapters have been reduced to a noun a verb the father dies the lover leaves in search of his own ending perhaps now the writing can finally begin. (74)

The speaker does not return to a specific time or a specific location. Instead, he faces the multiple ruptures that mark his life, the rupture with a place, a lover, and the living. From the composites of these breaks, the assimilation and acceptance of these ruptures will eventually, he hopes, begin to take place. Only then will he be able to come into language and begin a text with "I am."

In the meantime, the narrator of *dust and conscience* speaks about himself and others through "a *suspension* of language," where truth is understood as belonging to the realm of perception and from a standpoint of being emotionally detached from the past. The narrator wishes for a freeing of language from social constrictions and unitary meaning prescribed by categorization. Without the support of a preexisting "I" in society, the speaker retrieves serendipitous moments, fleeting memories punctuated by silences, observations, imagined interventions, and unanswered questions that come before and during the formulation of identity. The result is a series of poetic fragments seemingly detached from one another. None of the marks that commonly break conventional sentence structure, and hence the conventional ordering of thoughts into linear and causal expressions, are present. The speaker describes his narration as one that is "mangled but cohesive weighted [and serves] the purpose of anchoring" (27). The possibilities are endless. The fragments are like blocks that he and readers can pick up at anytime, anywhere. Piled on top of each other without any prescribed order, they indicate the *preparation* of home.

SELF-REFLEXIVITY

Vietnamese American identity, the text suggests, is elusive. It calls for a rethinking of languages and of the act of representing, especially the people of Viet Nam. The narrator, to borrow from Trinh T. Minh-ha, tries to "maintain a self-reflexively critical relation toward the material, a relationship that defines both the subject written and writing subject, undoing the I while asking 'what do I want wanting to *know* you or me?'" (76). For example, in the "book of ruptures" Vietnamese characters enter the narration and talk back at the narrator.[13] One character says: "pardon the interruption but there is a scorpion a woman a frog and a ghost all wanting to come in they insist on entering into the book" (63). The Vietnamese characters appear to break from the narrator's control and authority. They enter a narration designed to protect them from an exotic and exploitative gaze.

But the objects of representation, now suddenly subjects, say they are not satisfied with his approach. In one passage in which the narrator describes sitting on the beach watching a child sell soft drinks and cigarettes to tourists, a sand crab suddenly enters the narrative. He reads the text and says he does not like it: "enter the sand crab from a previous poem he looks around examines his surroundings the page is a bit off it feels nothing like a poem" (65). The sand crab hides the representation of a destitute Vietnamese child who survives by selling soft drinks and cigarettes to tourists on the beach. But the sand crab says he does not like what he sees and does not approve of the narrator's framing of him—this "feels nothing like a poem." The unstructured poetic fragments do not correspond to the cultural markers of what he considers to be a "good" poem. He does not particularly like to be called a sand crab, either. It is not beautiful, he explains.

In an earlier scene in the "book of beginnings," the narrator had said:

> i met a sand crab in a deserted beach and we sat there
> among the dunes discussing the crab's fortitude i asked
> what is it about you that allows you to survive this scorch-
> ing heat and unrelenting environment to which the crab
> answered my skin and my legs for it pays to have thick skin
> if you can even call it that and you know what else when
> running sideways i surprise the likes of people like you.
> (33)

The narrator uses the metaphor of a sand crab to resist subject-ing the native to a voyeuristic gaze that looks at natives like ani-mals at a zoo, and only so as to find resolution for a lost war. But again the "sand crab" does not understand, stating in the "book of ruptures" that "he's not used to being stared at with such disdain" (65). The native Vietnamese feels betrayed. Instead of being compared to a sand crab, he would prefer maybe to be cel-ebrated and romanticized, his existence and ancestry glorified and transformed into a symbol of national pride, as proponents of Negritude have done in the past. The sand crab's intervention suggests the unbreachable ruptures caused by colonialism, wars, culture, immigration, and differentials of power between first and third worlds. Ethical and nationalist representations do not go hand in hand.

In *dust and conscience,* the narrator does not join, make sense, unify, and represent what it means to be Vietnamese American or Vietnamese. The book escapes categorization within fixed notions of maturity, progress, and assimilation. Situated on the margin of the margin, the narrator challenges first and foremost his readers: "if i wrote about the blue skies would you look up point to god in a pillow of clouds if i wrote about the blinding sun would you stare with faith see for the first time i mean truly see" (7). Like the dissident poet Nguyen Chi Thien, the narrator of *dust and conscience* suspects, because of the author's national origin, that he will neither be appreciated nor criticized for only the reasons he intends. While he refuses claims to authenticity and representationality, he insists on speaking in spite of the knowledge that he cannot truly speak. He says what is not yet formed and free to be formed from both the outside and the inside. To do this, words are placed carefully and hesitantly on the page at the expense of clear meaning and readership. Each poetic fragment stands like a brick with shades of blue and gray that both soothe and subvert common desires for revelations and resolutions.[14] The lack of clarity in turn asks for readers' active participation and self-reflection about what they expect to uncover from a Vietnamese American text.[15] Working outside the more popular genre of Asian American autobiography, Truong Tran, like Theresa Hak Kyung Cha in *Dictee,* writes against interpellative narratives of assimilation and shakes the parameters of prescribed notions of what it means to be Vietnamese American.[16] In this narrative, freedom of Vietnamese American cultural expression is foreseen to be possible one day. It holds hope.

Fake House: Narrative of Despair

Fake House is a collection of short stories. Like *dust and conscience,* it does not tell the Vietnamese American refugee and Vietnamese experience in a way that corresponds to mainstream expectations. The first half of the book is set in the United States and the second in Viet Nam.[17] Dedicated "to the unchosen," *Fake House* intertwines multiple narratives about social outcasts, the forgotten, the social misfits, and in Linh Dinh's words, the "fuck ups and losers, people rejected and humiliated by a winner-takes-all glamour culture."[18] The short stories highlight problems of alienation, communication, and the attainment of subjecthood by recent Vietnamese immigrants to the United States, indigenous Vietnamese villagers, and marginal white characters. Dinh captures sites of survival and the contradictions exacerbated by class, race, and gender polarizations, and shows the brutal effects of marginality across geographical lines.

Unconcerned with offending readers, Dinh denounces the hypocrisy of Vietnamese, Vietnamese Americans, and American patriarchy. At the same time, Dinh comments upon the crises of masculinity that mark postwar Vietnamese and Vietnamese American identities.[19] The short stories systematically traverse and displace static and fixed antinomies, punctuate how such crises perpetuate dysfunctionalities and exacerbate the subjugation of women. In this world of the disenfranchised, women bear a high cost of demasculinization caused by war and globalization. Upheld as symbols of nationalism to counter "masculinized humiliation" vis-à-vis colonial and imperial conquests,[20] low-income Vietnamese American and Vietnamese women are, *Fake House* suggests, situated somewhere toward the bottom of an infernal transnational food chain. For them and other outcasts and forgotten, there is absolutely no hope.

In the story "555," Thanh is a recent Vietnamese immigrant to the United States who visits prostitutes for sexual relief and human contact, which gives him temporary release from a life destroyed by war and incarceration in reeducation camps. Thanh describes the appeal of prostitutes in terms of necessity. Seeing a young "not bad looking" white American man waiting to visit a prostitute, he asks himself: "Why would a kid like this go to a whorehouse and pay almost a hundred bucks to get laid? Can't he find a girlfriend?" (106). Thanh's front teeth have been "punched out" by "V.C." He does not speak English and feels he does not belong in America. As one of the "girls" soaps his back, he recalls that "someone had thrown an egg at him from a passing car" the night before (107). In the United States, Thanh is the target of racism and classism. Like the protagonist Old Pete in Jeffery Paul Chan's "Jackrabbit" story, Thanh seeks the company of a Korean or Chinese prostitute to soften the life of de facto forced bachelorhood, the lot of other recent immigrants like him.[21] But unlike Old Pete, Thanh does not go to Asian prostitutes to be in tune with his ethnic identity.[22] On the contrary, Thanh chooses a brothel in Chinatown that has mostly Korean prostitutes because in racially stratified America, they are cheaper and different enough to be objectified.[23] When he realizes the prostitute he chooses is a Vietnamese woman, his "prick . . . suddenly" goes "limp" (108). Discovering their common origin, the prostitute asks Thanh in Vietnamese, "What's your name, Brother?" Thanh immediately interrupts any possibility of connection and intimacy and says, "What are you doing in a place like this?" Thanh does not see the parallels between their debased lives. To escape his own displacement reflected and embodied by this young woman, Thanh takes refuge in patriarchy. He pays the prostitute generously for her time but does not have sex with her. In exchange, he asks her to conjugate the verb "to be" in French. For a short time, Thanh lives the illusion that he still functions in a system where patriarchy takes precedence over racial and immigrant status. The recital of "Je suis. Tu es. Il est. Elle est . . ." conveys the message that "to be" a recently arrived poor Vietnamese immigrant in the United States is not a choice, but a condition situated on the continuum of colonization (109). For Thanh, the conjugation of French words with a Vietnamese accent has a sweet and familiar ring. A man once incarcerated in a communist reeducation camp after 1975, Thanh may have been a former officer of the South Vietnamese Army and attended French language school as a child. The French words allow him to break the intimacy of a common culture and at the same time bring him back to a time of peace when a French education was the key to upward mobility into the elite upper-middle class. Language triggers the memories of old privileges. "555" suggests that unlike colonial times, today resistance against a common enemy is nearly impossible. This situation offers absolutely no glimpse of hope.

Like "555," the story "Hope and Standard" proposes that politics, culture, and economics are inextricably intertwined, creating a dynamic filled with hopelessness. In "Hope and Standard," Dinh shows how forced marriages of Vietnamese women to Viet Kieu—Vietnamese men from overseas who are considered foreigners—has become a strategy for Vietnamese to escape poverty.[24] In this dynamic, attractive Vietnamese women from poor families are trapped by both American white male fantasies and Vietnamese patriarchy. In the story, a Vietnamese father marries his daughter off to a white American. The father plans to retire and "build a little brick house" with the money from the transaction (145). He says:

> My daughter did not marry a Taiwanese! We have much higher standards than that! She didn't even marry a Viet Kieu but an American. A real American! She will sacrifice her youth to suck this guy dry! Within five years we'll get a divorce. Then she'll get her American citizenship. Then she'll bring me to America. I'm not that stupid! (146)

The father subscribes to a worldview that assumes racial, national, and gender superiority and dominance. For the Vietnamese father, white American men are situated at the top and Vietnamese men at the bottom of globalization's hierarchy. At the very bottom is the Vietnamese daughter forced to fulfill her filial obligations for the benefit of her father by marrying a man she does not love. The victim is also the American man, naive enough to believe in myths about submissive Asian women. By sacrificing herself to facilitate her father's dream of coming to the United States, the Vietnamese bride embodies the figure of Kieu in Viet Nam's national epic poem *The Tale of Kieu*. Kieu, who was forced into prostitution, is upheld as a paragon of chastity in Viet Nam because she sacrificed her body to save her father. In "Hope and Standard," the father's matter-of-fact tone and the commonality of the situation dissipate all trace of *The Tale of Kieu's* romanticism, heroism, and glorification of Kieu's sacrifice. All that is left under neocolonial capitalism is the act of sacrifice detached from morality and ethics. Unlike *The Tale of Kieu*, the selling of one's body is not presented in *Fake House* as an expression of love for one's family, but rather a harsh act imposed by patriarchal violence. According to the narrator, the father had "beaten" his daughter "into making this decision" (146). The story shows that globalization is not always linked to progress. Compared to the title character Kieu, the young

Vietnamese woman in Dinh's story is deprived of agency and freedom. Sacrifice is not portrayed as a romanticized choice but a debased condition.

The violation of women is shown to be intimately linked in "Hope and Standard" to the emasculation and disenfranchisement of Vietnamese men. Unlike Thanh in "555," Vietnamese men's sense of masculinity is determined not solely in relation to class and gender but also to nationality. Unlike Vietnamese women, Vietnamese men do not have the option to be "bought out" by prospective spouses in more privileged nations. Even a broken man like poor and toothless Thanh may be viewed as more attractive in Viet Nam than a healthy Vietnamese man because of his American citizenship. For the male narrator of "Hope and Standard," Vietnamese women are all "waiting to be hooked up with a Viet Kieu" (144). "No Viet Kieu or foreign women have ever come to our village to claim any one of us," he adds with a sigh. From his perspective, poor young Vietnamese men, southerner and northerner alike, are the losers. Young destitute Vietnamese men are disempowered by their inability to compete with foreign men and privileged Viet Kieu, and by their undesirability, which prevents them from being sold like their female counterparts as exotic commodities to foreign partners. This emasculation, the story implies, worsens the treatment of women. Once symbols of nationalism in white *ao dai* (Vietnamese dress), they are now resented and seen as unattainable objects of desire to be forcibly sacrificed to patriarchy, their exotic appeal exploited.

Fake House names the ugliness that emanates from corners of the world that many who have access to publishing are uncomfortable writing about or see as too risky because it will not find readers. The juxtaposition of multiple voices from many locations underscores how individuals on the margin can be trapped in cycles of violence. The narrators of *Fake House* are in various states of disempowerment and disenfranchisement. They are driven by the desire to survive and conquer in spite of, but also through, society's discursive rules. All potential for connections between human beings, men and women, is violently interrupted and truncated. The characters stand at odds with the modern institutions of the state. The abused becomes the abuser. Dinh's characters are the "debris," the victims and enemies of a transnational system. In *The Politics of Culture in the Shadow of Capital*, Lisa Lowe and David Lloyd write that our "moment is not one of fatalistic despair; faces turned toward the past." The goal, they say, is not "to make whole what has been smashed, but to move athwart the storm into a future in which the debris is more than just a residue."[25] *Fake House* examines spaces saturated by ruthless displays of power. If hope is to be found and fatalistic despair refuted, the process to "move athwart the storm" does not reside in the present, the future, or in the stories themselves, but rather in the very process of telling. By placing a mirror in front of the ugly, however distorted that mirror may be, *Fake House* asserts without apology, the ugly will remain.

Dust and conscience and *Fake House* are books that do not seek to represent *the* Vietnamese American refugee and Vietnamese experience. In *dust and conscience,* the possibility to speak and to articulate identity freely is located in the future. This, the author emphasizes, can only be achieved through a rearticulation of language, inventions, and letting go of the desire to arrive at a center and represent Viet Nam. Like *dust and conscience*, *Fake House* rejects conventional representationality. The characters in *Fake House*, regardless of race and ethnicity, are driven by their struggle to survive and by their ruthless quest for power and existence, which often come at a cost to others. It makes visible what Michel Foucault calls heterotopia, or the institutional and social practices that code certain spaces as public and others as private, some legal and others illegal, and exhibits spaces of crisis marked by illiteracy, deviance, or subversion whereby Vietnamese and Vietnamese American women hold a space among others that have been used and forgotten.[26] For *Fake House* and *dust and conscience*, the cost of speaking differently about Vietnamese American and Vietnamese identities and experiences has been, to a certain extent, their reception by the public. Tran's work is at times ignored because of issues of accessibility, and Dinh's work because of its use of crude language. Both texts ask and provoke readers to reflect upon their own gazes and assumptions through a reappropriation of language.

Recommended Readings

Cynthia Enloe, *Bananas, Beaches and Bases: Making Feminist Sense of International Politics*. Berkeley: University of California Press, 1990.

Trinh T. Minh-ha, *Woman Native Other: Writing Postcoloniality and Feminism*. Bloomington: Indiana University Press: 1989.

Ghayatri Chakravorty Spivak, "Can the Subaltern Speak?" *Wedge*, 120–130. 1985: 7–8.

6 / Reception

Vietnamese American writers are peddler[s] of fiction, not Viet Nam experts.

MONIQUE TRUONG

It is taken as an unspoken truth that to realize its counterhegemonic potential, minority discourse must access hegemonic apparatuses.

DAVID PALUMBO-LIU, *ASIAN/AMERICAN*

In a recently published, highly acclaimed book of short stories entitled *The Boat,* author Nam Le explores issues of authenticity.[1] Speaking to a journalist about the first story in his collection, "Love and Honor and Pity and Pride and Compassion and Sacrifice," Le talks about pressures of containment that writers of color often face. "One of the chief ambitions of the story," says Le, "was to play with that idea of what we consider to be authentic, how much autobiography is implied or assumed, how we read something differently if we think it's been drawn from the author's life."[2] In the story, the narrator Nam is a young writer who attends the Iowa Writers' Workshop. Nam suffers from writer's block and is stressed over an approaching deadline. He struggles with the idea of writing a story about his father's experience during the war, what he calls his "ethnic story," or whether to deliver a "universal" story that is not based on his *"background or life experience."*[3] Because of the popularity and commoditization of literature by writers of color, writing about his family and personal experience has become stigmatized. Commenting on the commercial value of autobiographies by minorities, a writing instructor at Iowa encourages Nam to tell his "ethnic story." "Ethnic literature's hot. And important too," says the instructor (9). "You could totally exploit the Vietnamese thing," a friend tells him (10). Contemplating the idea of giving in to the demand for unchallenging multiculturalism, Nam imagines himself "standing in a rice paddy, wearing a straw conical hat" (10). Like Nam, Vietnamese American writers receive the message from reviewers and publishers that they are better off telling "their" refugee stories with an ethnic identity angle in order for their work to be published and made accessible to a mainstream American audience.

David Palumbo-Liu defines minority discourse as texts that offer "resolutions to a generalized 'problem' of racial, ethnic, and gender identities."[4] According to him, "such perceptions deeply inform the contracting, marketing, and distribution of Asian American literature, which in turn influences the (re) production of representation of the successful formation of a particularly constructed Asian American subjectivity, as well as the institutionalization of these texts within academic and popular culture."[5] Vietnamese American literature, like all discourses, occurs in dialogue with prior discourses and is in correspondence with a socially constructed reader. For Vietnamese American literature, the national crisis triggered by the unfavorable outcome of the Viet Nam War makes this dialectic even stronger. Expectations of certain kind of minority discourse are compounded by a certain type of refugee discourse dominated by departure of Viet Nam by boat and memories of Viet Nam before the end of the war.

Vietnamese American writers have addressed the delicate dialectic that both restricts their freedom of expression and provides them with a forum from which to speak directly within the texts themselves. In *Monkey Bridge*, Mai's mother writes in her journal:

> No one in my new family was cruel to me. No one pulled my hair or slapped my face or insulted me. Perhaps, if Mai were to read this, she would ask: Is that all? My daughter, like the American accustomed to hearing about the

savagery of foreign lands, might expect much more dra-
ma from a life in a country back there. Where's the cruel
mother-in-law, where's the rape, the floggings, the bandits
and the cannibals, the savage dismemberments? she would
ask. What she wants to see is a good exciting movie of adventure set in a foreign land where people are as capable of
inflicting brutalities—of the kind no one here could be ac-
cused of inflicting—as they are of enduring them.[6]

Mai's mother challenges her daughter to reflect upon her search
for roots and history. She questions her daughter's use of stereotypes to negotiate her present life and craft a place for herself
in American society as a victim. She suspects that her daughter desires to possess a good and painful "refugee story" so that
she can offer it to her American counterparts in order to better fit in. She points to her daughter's apparent interiorization
of Orientalist and nationalistic views, saying that she, "like the
Americans," searches for signs of "savagery" and Asiatic "adventures," allowing her voice to be used as a vehicle for "Americans"
to shed responsibility for the conflict. Mai's mother accuses her
daughter of self-hate, not because she denies her cultural background, but because she repackages Vietnamese culture and history in accordance with predetermined images to facilitate her
incorporation and acceptance into America. Through this lens,
Mai's appropriation of the legendary Vietnamese woman warrior Trung Trac can be seen as mimicking Maxine Hong Kingston's use of the legendary Chinese woman warrior Fa Mu Lan
in *Woman Warrior* (1975), a tactic used to make the narrative
recognizably Asian American.[7] Like Jade Snow Wong in *Fifth
Chinese Daughter,* which was published 1950, Mai also takes on
the role of a cultural guide in order to be better included and accepted by mainstream America. For example, she intermittently
interrupts the flow of narration with ethnographic explanations
about mundane aspects of Vietnamese American culture:

In Vietnam, we said "come here" to humans differently,
with our palm up and all four fingers waved in unison—

the way people over here wave goodbye. A typical Vietnamese signal beckoning someone to "come here" would
prompt, in the United States, a "goodbye," a response com-
pletely opposite from the one desired.[8]

She uses "our," "we," and "typical" to assert her authority in
representing Vietnamese American and Vietnamese culture.
As Elaine Kim noted over two decades ago about early Asian
American writers, Mai readily assumes the role of an anthropo-
logical informant and takes readers on a guided tour of aspects
of a community and culture that might appeal to and do not dis-
turb non-Vietnamese American readers.[9] Drawing broad generalizations, Mai takes on the task, as her mother anticipated, of
representing Vietnamese Americans based on their "palatable"
differences. These tactics and strategies show Mai's vulnerability
as a member of a relatively new community and demonstrate
the relevance of contemporary issues of authenticity and au-
thorship. It is noteworthy that with the publication of *Monkey
Bridge*, Lan Cao became the first Vietnamese American writer
to be compared by reviewers to other renowned Asian American
writers Bharati Mukherjee and Maxine Hong Kingston.[10] Only
a few years before *Monkey Bridge,* Vietnamese American texts
were mostly reviewed as political or foreign texts.[11]

Reviewers

A brief look at some of the reviews of this literature sheds
more light on the particular gaze through which these texts tend
to be read, interpreted, and included in American culture.

Shortly after the publication of *Catfish and Mandala* in 1999,
The Metro, a local Northern California newspaper, featured the
book on its front page with the following endorsement: "Former
Silicon Valley engineer Andrew Pham left Vietnam as a child in
a leaking boat and returned 20 years later as a grown man on bicycle. The published account of his odyssey reveals the secrets of
his family's past, the heart of humanity and the deepest wounds
of war."[12]

The reviewer privileges the author's memory of Viet Nam over that of his experience as an immigrant. The use of the word "reveal" assumes an audience curiosity for Vietnamese family secrets, as if they might provide an answer to why America lost. Andrew Pham is reluctant, however, to carry the burden and assumption of representation. He calls *Catfish and Mandala* a work of creative nonfiction to highlight the selective and creative processes inherent in recollecting the past.[13] He does not wish to represent the Vietnamese people. The protagonist makes a point of introducing himself without Vietnamese ethnic and refugee markers before he begins the process of telling his story. He describes himself as someone who likes to go to the movies, eat Italian food, and play sports, a man who does not wear "yellow, red, orange, or anything bright" because these colors "complicate the laundry process." He says he likes "buying cookbooks more than cooking" and knows little of the Viet Nam War.[14] An's introduction of himself as an ordinary middle-class man in America without specific ethnic and war markers responds directly to expectations to represent the refugee experience before he engages in this very task. "And in my fraudulence," he reflects, "I know I have embarked on something greater than myself," he says after giving "the absolution that is not [his] to give" to Tyle the American GI.[15] In a similar fashion, the story, by virtue of the author's name, cannot escape a politics of representation of race and war. This ambivalence is evident in a scene near the end of the book. The narrator describes the excitement of a Vietnamese chef who explains to two customers how he cooks a fish without killing it. The chef promises they will be able to eat the fish "alive and gaping."[16] An, who is sitting with a tourist, serves as translator. Like the tourist, he is appalled by what he sees. And yet in his role as translator, and given his specific history, he finds himself in a situation that makes him a bridge between cultures. At this juncture, he identifies with the fish. If the story of his life must be consumed, An, with eyes wide open like a gaping fish, stares back at his reader. This ambivalence of serving *the* refugee story to appease national guilt and facilitate

America's return to Viet Nam is made even more bluntly at the end of the book, when he catches "a glimpse" of himself in the Vietnamese tour guide Calvin, who tells him: "It's very hard being a tour guide. Sometimes I feel like a pimp."[17]

Reviews of *Catfish and Mandala* are similar to other predictable and sometimes disparaging reviews of Vietnamese American texts. In 1994, Jade Ngoc Quang Huynh's memoir *South Wind Changing* was reviewed by Lowell Weiss, who wrote:

> The end of Huynh's story, not recounted in his memoir, is disappointing. Huynh, close to finishing his second book, is back in Bennington, but he is bedridden with ulcers and supporting himself on food stamps. In the past months, several college-level teaching positions have fallen through. Huynh has survived objectively worse predicaments, but struggling as an almost literally starving artist in a land of opportunity has become a challenge more painful than Huynh could have imagined. Once again, without warning, the South Wind has changed.[18]

Weiss takes the liberty of publicly finishing the author's life story for him and judges it as "disappointing." This comment demonstrates the reviewer's abidance by the model minority myth whereby Asian Americans are perceived as succeeding easily because of their alleged innate family values and hard work. Absolved from this judgment is the American government's responsibility toward those who have been traumatized in reeducation camps.[19] In his arbitrary and mundane disavowal of the historical and social contexts of Huynh's book, Weiss resorts to indirectly blaming the marginalized author, whose functional life ends with the removal of American troops from Viet Nam, for his inability to succeed in America. In so doing, the reviewer maintains intact the normative narrative that posits the United States as a place of freedom and opportunity. Huynh's narrative does not talk much about his life in America because it is not the story he wants and chooses to tell. In the United States the narrator says his soul dies and what happens in the United States is not as important to him as what happened when he was struggling to survive oppression in Viet Nam. His primary concern is to denounce human rights violations in Viet Nam after 1975, after the Americans left.

Adair Lara, who reviewed le thuy diem thuy's *The Gangster We Are All Looking For* also reads the text as autobiography, regardless of the fact that the author insists her own story differs from that of her narrator's. "It's not me. It's a work of fiction because many things happen in this book that never ever happened to me or to my parents," said Le in an interview with *Nhà Magazine*.[20] Yet Adair Lara writes:

> We want to follow the girl when she flees—find out where she went, how she managed. She is interested in the father, but we are interested in her. But perhaps this book tells us all we need to know about who she turned out to be, which is a writer of great promise. She just needs to learn to trust us. Or forgive us.[21]

Adair's motherly advice to the author to trust and forgive her readers indicates a lack of understanding of the high cost of war and immigration, wherein secrecy and hiding are not a choice but a mode of survival. Adair's wish for more revelations misses the narrator's described state of voicelessness and her attempt to explain what it means to grow up in an environment where absolutely no one can be trusted. "There is not a trace of blood anywhere except here, in my throat, where I am telling you all this," says the narrator.[22] Violence permeates the story and trust is a luxury the narrator does not have. What matters to her, as implied by the poetic and detached form of the text, is not the ability to tell, but the ability to hide. In constant fear of losing ground, the narrator focuses on the small things that allowed her to evolve as a child, in spite of the lack of support and safety in her life. She takes recourse in her imagination, and out-of-body experiences, and engages in reckless behavior as a teenager. Adair's disappointment in the narrator and author is reminiscent of gazes historically placed on the lives and stories of so-called inscrutable Asians.[23] And had the author, like Amy Tan, elaborated on the difficult relationship between the narrator and her mother, the narrative might have been more praised for its acute sensitivity and poetic beauty.[24]

Reviewers tend to blur the distinction between Vietnamese Americans and Vietnamese. Reviewing *The Gangster We Are All Looking For*, David Mehegan writes: "Le intends her novel to reveal the Vietnamese spirit and culture through the specifics of one child and her parents."[25] But Le's story does not take place in Viet Nam and does not reveal the Vietnamese spirit and culture. The story is about resettlement, memory, and the processes of becoming Vietnamese American in the context of poverty and uprootedness from one's culture. It is about cultural dislocation. Viet Nam exists only in the novel in terms of fragments and reference points from which the child negotiates her American life. For her, Viet Nam does not represent an anchor but an incomprehensible rupture and loss.

Publishers sometimes do not take into consideration the political differences among Vietnamese Americans. For example, Oxford University Press markets Duong Van Mai Elliot's *The Sacred Willow* as "the first book" about "what Vietnamese history has meant to the Vietnamese themselves."[26] This claim of representationality is at odds with the perspectives of first-generation Vietnamese Americans who left Viet Nam after 1975. Like her narrator, Mai Elliot left Viet Nam in 1973, sided with the anti-war movement, and denounces in her book the corruption of the Southern government. She is an immigrant who did not experience postwar Viet Nam. She does not represent all the Vietnamese whose perspectives on history differ, depending on which side they were on, nor does she represent Vietnamese Americans' voices.

Publishers at times make decisions based on their perceptions about the racist assumptions of the public. Although *The Book of Salt* garnered wide success, it initially encountered resistance from publishers. The first publisher that acquired the manuscript asked Truong to simplify the language because they said a Vietnamese cook could not possibly have such sophisticated thoughts and the language was too poetic for an uneducated Asian character.[27] "I cannot imagine a white writer being told that," laments Monique Truong.[28] Once published, this novel was loved for reasons the text itself seeks to counter. In his review of *The Book of Salt* in the *New York Times*, Christopher Benfey says he is tempted to borrow Toklas's prose to describe the book as "insecure, unstable, unreliable but thoroughly enjoyable." Benfey writes that the narrator "tells his story with a lush and exoticizing expansiveness, more sweet than savory." "Cooking, for Binh," he adds, "is a 'way of remembering the world.' [Binh] concocts both Vietnamese delicacies of Proust's madeleine and [adds] an exotic spice for poignancy." If Benfey points to the two women's racism and the postcolonial nature of the text in his essay, he concludes that Truong has, "against the odds . . . made unsettling art from precisely such exotic cuttings and transplantings."[29] Like reviews of Maxine Hong Kingston's *The Woman Warrior* thirty years before, Benfey measures the book to a certain degree against the stereotype of the exotic, and by extension inscrutable, and mysterious Oriental.[30] His use of the adjectives "insecure," "unstable," and "unreliable" is reminiscent of Orientalist attitudes aimed at defining Europeans as "rational, peaceful, liberal, logical, and capable of holding real values without natural suspicion."[31]

Christopher Benfey is not the sole reviewer who finds *The Book of Salt* an exotic culinary delight. Joy Press writes:

> In her debut novel, *The Book of Salt*, Monique Truong imbues food with all . . . danger and darkness. . . . Truong weaves a sumptuous tale of gastronomy, language, cravings, and cruelty around a pseudo-historical figure: the mysterious Vietnamese cook who worked for Gertrude Stein and Alice B. Toklas. His name is Binh (or ThinBin, as Stein calls him), and he recounts his life story in deliciously acid tones.[32]

Press lures readers with evocations of French food cooked by a

Vietnamese man she associates with "danger," "darkness," and "cruelty," the combination of which the reviewer finds "mysterious." Press's words evoke once more old stereotypes of Asian men as sinister and dangerous creatures.[33] But unlike past writings, these alleged dark, mysterious, and dangerous qualities are presented as alluring and spicy, like the food Binh cooks. Through the prism of food, the postcolonial space is reduced and controlled, and Truong's novel is turned into a sophisticated pleasure accessible to a trendy elite and well-traveled reader.[34] Distracted by the French Vietnamese mixture, which she finds appealing and delicious, Press fails to see the mirror *The Book of Salt* places in front of the readers' eyes.

A pivotal scene in *The Book of Salt* shows, for instance, that it is not intended to bring exotic pleasure to readers. At the end of the book, Binh's "Mesdames," Stein and Toklas, decide to return to the United States. At the train station where he accompanies the women and carries their luggage, a small group of photographers surrounds them. Their picture appears in the newspaper a few days later. Binh cuts out the picture and reflects: "It captures my Mesdames perfectly. I am over there, the one with my back turned to the camera. I am not bowing at Gertrude Stein's feet. I am sewing the button back onto her right shoe."[35] Binh is in the background, his face unseen. All that is shown of him in the photograph is his back, bent forward at the feet of the famous lesbian writer, an image that elevates the woman, the appearance of his servitude a sign of her prestige. In the safety of a space where the expression of emotions is not his to have, he does not expect to be seen and framed by the camera. But looking at the photo in the newspaper, Binh makes the rational and calm distinction between servitude and work. He does not bow to his master like a monkey, but is sewing a button on her shoe like a man at work. Unlike reviewers' claims, *The Book of Salt* is not a book designed to be consumed for its exoticism and culinary prowess. It is a well-crafted work saturated with the voice of the powerless. *The Book of Salt* is an attempt to move the margin to the center, a state the narrator shows is imbued with loneliness, resilience, and sharp vision.

Dinh's use of raw language in *Fake House* has caused some reviewers to criticize his work as vulgar and sexist.[36] Indeed, why write about prostitutes or sold daughters when stories of Vietnamese prostitutes and "easy Vietnamese women into white American men" pervade representations of the Viet Nam War? Vietnamese Americans and other Asian Americans have for a long time condemned this practice as misrepresenting Vietnamese women and culture. The repetition of these images does indeed perpetuate the analogy between Vietnamese women and the country Viet Nam as passive victims. Yet *Fake House's* representation of women differs from these common portraits. If it depicts women as degraded sexual objects, their portrayal is not synonymous with embracing patriarchy, but rather denounces it. When Thanh in "555" meets the narrator at a bar, he tells him: "I came to town today to fuck a whore."[37] The word "fuck" leaves no doubt about the nature of the transaction. Unlike the Broadway musical *Miss Saigon*, there is no possibility of romance between prostitute and client. The woman Thanh meets that day is "short, small-breasted, with a cheery, innocent face" that pleases him because she helps him take a shower and rubs his back.[38] In "Hope and Standard," the young woman is described as having "an upturned nose and a face like chinaberry."[39] The narrator points out the fact that her teeth are "real." The "only drawback," he says, "was that she had no breasts and had to wear a padded bra."[40] The use of the term "girl" in reference to a young woman implies the male narrator's assumed superiority. The reference to the woman's teeth is reminiscent of a master's attitude toward a subject for sale, one mediated by colonial aesthetics that places value on an "upturned nose" and large breasts.

There is a "complex dialectic of reinforcement" between readers and writers, Edward Said emphasizes.[41] The experiences of readers are determined by what they read and see, which in turn can influence certain writers to take up subjects defined by readers' experiences.[42] But in this dynamic who does the speaking matters. Let us turn for a moment to Robert Olen Butler's 1993 Pulitzer Prize-winning story collection *A Good Scent from a Strange Mountain* and its depiction of Vietnamese American prostitutes and Vietnamese women. Robert Olen Butler, an unknown author prior to winning the Pulitzer, was suddenly grouped with Toni Morrison, Alice Walker, Ernest Hemingway, and John Steinbeck. Butler says he takes particular pride in his development of Vietnamese women characters: "The ultimate maleness is to be able to yield into the woman's voice you are intimate with," he said.[43] In Butler's "Fairy Tale," the female protagonist gives the following description of herself:

> I am twenty-five years old and my titties are small, especially in America, but I am still number-one girl. . . . I give some man love when he is alone and frightened and he wants something soft to be close to him. . . . I am not sexy bitch, wiggle it baby, oh boy oh boy it's hot, it feels good. . . . In the morning I go into the bathroom and he is in the tub and I kneel beside him and take his hands and I have a cuticle file and I clean the grease away. He kisses my hands when he leaves.[44]

The young prostitute is depicted as sweet and childlike, the tone of her voice light and unthreatening. She is eager to please her client. This self-portrait parallels Tony Rivers's caricature of white men's fantasies of Asian women in an article published in *GQ*:

> She has no tits. . . . She is, of course, always young, a lot like a child, an obedient daughter. . . . She cares for you and always forgives, grants you refuge and soothes you with the stillest part of her female psyche. . . . When you get home from another hard day on the planet, she comes into existence, removes your clothes, bathes you and walks naked on your back to relax you. And then there is sex. . . . She's fun you see, and so uncomplicated.[45]

Like the prostitute in *A Good Scent from a Strange Mountain*, Rivers's caricature of the Asian woman revolves around her serving her man as a daughter, a mother, and a sex object. It is noteworthy that reviewers have responded in drastically different ways to Robert Olen Butler's and Linh Dinh's work. The language of Butler's Vietnamese American characters has been described as "rather charmingly broken,"[46] while the language in Dinh's stories has been dismissed for being marked by "tricky dialogue rife with pointedly racist misinformation, linguistic confusion, and dunning vulgarities."[47] In the award-winning *A Good Scent,* Butler uses language that ranges from broken English to the "extreme of sing song lyricism" that gives the impression that people of Vietnamese descent are all overwhelmingly "good."[48]

Unlike Butler's representation of the Vietnamese American prostitute, Dinh's representation is not dominated by sweetness, submissiveness, and childlike innocence. The cost of colonialism, war, immigration, and poverty as well as of certain physical attributes is manifested through the use of language itself. The environment is harsh and the people are harsh, and therefore the language is harsh. In the short story "555," after rubbing Thanh's back, a prostitute named Huong tells her aroused client to wait for her while she takes a five-minute nap. When he ignores her request and removes her panties, "she yanked them back on" and snaps, "My ass is cold!"[49] The ostensibly crude use of the word "ass" removes readers from a world of fantasy. Instead of depicting a doll-like object ready to serve her man of the moment with a fixed red innocent smile, Dinh shows readers a tired, hardened, and aggressive human being. Huong is accustomed to being violated by men. They do not respect her and she does not respect them. Her attitude changes initially when she finds out her client is Vietnamese American. Bound by ethnicity, she reverts to speaking Vietnamese and asks: "What's your name, Brother?" using the proper Vietnamese form of address to an older man.[50] When Thanh speaks to her, he only addresses her by her first name: "How old are you, Huong?" clearly delineating her lower social status.[51] Initially curious and open, Huong quickly realizes that their common national identity is linked to patriarchal judgments that debase her in ways men of other national origins cannot. It makes her more vulnerable. Although she momentarily "cheers up" when he tells her that he no longer wants to "fuck," she tells him in confidence that she is also a student, but becomes indignant when he asks her to conjugate the verb "to be" in French. "You must think I'm stupid," she blurts out defensively.[52] She agrees to recite the verb conjugations, neither to prove her submissiveness to a client nor to show respect toward a man who shares her ethnicity, but under the condition that he never return to see her. Unlike Butler's representation of the Vietnamese prostitute objectified as a woman of pleasure and bound to other Vietnamese Americans by ethnicity and language, Huong does not recite the verbs obediently, lightly, and dutifully, but blurts them out with "vehemence," accenting "each syllable." Readers are left with a sense of having witnessed an act of violence that is subtle, complicated, and suggestive of a harsh reality.

While reviewers have a difficult time with *Fake House*'s use of crude language, they still insist on extracting "the" Vietnamese American experience from it. In *Publishers Weekly*, for instance, the reviewer writes: "The first half of [*Fake House*] focuses on Vietnamese immigrants living in the U.S," although out of the nine stories in the section set on U.S. soil, only two include Vietnamese American characters. The narrators of Dinh's stories are not only Vietnamese or Vietnamese American. Some of the stories are also told from the perspective of white men and white women. Linh Dinh responded vehemently to these readings in a personal interview in 2001:

> From slave narratives to fiction: it's one thing for the slave to reclaim his own story; it's another for him to tell everyone else's secrets. In reading the memoirs and the autobiographical novels, the public can congratulate itself on becoming interested in the colored man, but as soon as the colored man starts to talk from behind it! for it! through it! the public freaks the fuck out!!

Linh Dinh's anger brings to the surface the place of the ethnic author in society. Who does the speaking and from which
location? White authors have always written about and from
the perspective of people of color. Why then is it so difficult
for reviewers to accept it when people of color write from the
perspective of white people? Why is Robert Butler rewarded
a prestigious literary prize for his portrayal of sweet and offbeat Vietnamese American caricatures, and Linh Dinh's work
denigrated and dismissed for addressing the ruthless reality of
life on the margins, which includes caricatures of offbeat white
characters? To those who criticize Linh Dinh for his sexism and
vulgar language, he says: "I'm actually hyperconscious of power
relations of all kinds and never side with agents of power. . . . I
write about the abuse of female domestic servants, ridicule the
culture of prostitution in Vietnam, and Vietnamese machismo
in general."[53] Linh Dinh's transgression of refugee narratives
makes him a "bad subject," to borrow philosopher Louis Althus-
er's term. With its raw language and unflinching examination of
the ugly and the grotesque, *Fake House* gives a raw glimpse of a
world marked by the legacy of colonialism, war, emigration, and
globalization, a language that is rarely heard in the narrative of
the nation.

The association of Vietnamese American literature only with
the Viet Nam War is problematic because it obscures the complexities of hybridity, the subjects' postcolonial, refugee, immigrant of color, and transnational experiences, and therefore
misses a large part of what is being said and presented in the
texts. It also limits the range of cultural expressions available to
Vietnamese American writers. And yet, it also provides a forum
for Vietnamese American writers located on the margin of the
margin to be heard, and to process painful memories. Michel
Foucault has argued that the name of the author should be erad-
icated because of its function as "a means of classification" that
characterizes the mode of existence of a text. A text, he explains,
"points to the existence of certain groups of discourse" and refers to its status within society and culture.[54] Foucault points

out that the practice of naming an author produces meaning that exceeds the limits of their work and therefore should not be used. But he has Marx, Freud, Shakespeare, and Radcliffe in mind. When reading Shakespeare or Radcliffe, reviewers do not address their racial and ethnic background. The aura evoked by these names transcends the scope of their works. Restricting as it might be, the category Vietnamese American, linked to an original loss of national identity as unquestioned fighter of the free world, has created a special forum from which to speak and be heard. An imperfect space is better than no space at all. But because of this specific context of reception, how one locates, reads, and interprets Vietnamese American texts matters a great deal.

Recommended Readings

Elaine Kim, *Asian American Literature: An Introduction to the Writings and their Social Context.* Philadelphia: Temple University Press, 1982.

David Palumbo-Liu, *Asian/American: Historical Crossings of a Racial Frontier.* Stanford: Stanford University Press, 1999.

Monique Truong, "The Reception of Robert Olen Butler's 'A Good Scent from a Strange Mountain': Ventriloquism and the Pulitzer Prize." *Viet Nam Forum* 16 (1997): 75–94.

Conclusion

In writing this volume, I walked a fine line between the desire to represent, primarily for the purpose of social justice, and the desire not to replicate the logic of domination that can take place when abiding by a nonself-reflective and nonstrategic essentialist approach.[1] The main goal of *This Is All I Choose to Tell* is to introduce, despite such challenges, the large scope, diversity, and complexity of Vietnamese American literature, to facilitate teaching and contribute to the inclusion of Vietnamese Americans in Asian American studies and in American society in general. I also engaged with theoretical debates in ways that are accessible to a larger audience. Vietnamese American literary texts vary in terms of the narrators' time of arrival, generation, and degree of trauma. They speak of hope and despair, resistance and accommodation, identity and history, remembering and forgetting, claiming America and maintaining transnational ties. Many of the texts, but not all, work against the national forgetting of Vietnamese Americans' loss of country and craft a new notion of home.[2]

This Is All I Choose to Tell suggests that the category "Vietnamese American," as restricting as it may be, facilitates the exploration and understanding of the experience and identity of

Vietnamese Americans. Vietnamese American authors function and respond to a culture in which Viet Nam represents, as I have explained, a thorn in the psyche of the nation. Those who write in English are well aware that reviewers tend to look for and emphasize connections to the Viet Nam War. These authors both resist and at times use to their benefit this complex "interplay between authorial design, available social space, and accessible cultural resources," a process characterized by negotiation.[3]

Emphasizing the dialectical dynamics between the audience and cultural production does not mean downplaying the importance of memoirs, autobiographies, creative nonfiction and novels linked to Viet Nam. Memories of the Viet Nam War still weigh heavily on many Vietnamese Americans, especially painful ones associated with being forced out of the country. There are still many ghosts and many secrets that continue to gnaw at individuals, families, and communities. As the erased segments of Andrew Pham's letter on a leaf on the cover of this book suggest, silences and self-censorship still protect the living. Secrets are kept to protect children from unresolved karma, or they are shared selectively within families to maintain a collective identity.

In the process of telling, withholding from, and adapting to their audience, Vietnamese American writers are not only articulating new ideas about what it means to be American but also generating new ideas of Viet Nam. "As the country itself is in flux, so too should be our ideas of Viet Nam," says poet Barbara Tran, referring to the war in Iraq.[4] These stories are best understood when they are read in relation to the social and historical contexts that shaped them. Domestic racism and shifting foreign policies in the United States (such as the lifting of the economic embargo) as well as in Viet Nam (for instance the *Doi Moi* policy that focuses on a socialist-oriented market economy, and more recently, the ability of Vietnamese to obtain visas to America) are relevant to Vietnamese American identity. Whether Vietnamese Americans who return to Viet Nam are treated as foes or friends fundamentally impacts their sense of who they are and influences the production of their stories. The same holds true when Vietnamese Americans encounter violence in America, either inside or outside their homes. Identities are shaped by how we are looked at and treated by others. As cultural productions, Vietnamese American stories, whether they abide by, resist, or sidestep the pressures to conform to predetermined images and preferred topics, have the power to affect the ways we think of ourselves and our citizenship in America and how we view and function in the world. Soon, more stories will be published. With time, there will be less holding back, more fictions, and perhaps more exploration, in addition to the "here" and "there," to the "over there" stories of Vietnamese in other parts of the diaspora, in Europe, Canada, Australia, Asia, the Middle East, and Africa. The notion of home will become more entangled with those of the living.

NOTES

Preface

1. To this end, I am founder of the Diasporic Vietnamese Artists Network (DVAN), an organization dedicated to the promotion of Vietnamese artists in the diaspora (http://dvanonline.org).

Introduction

1. Related ideas have been discussed in depth by David Palumbo-Liu in "Civilization and Dissent," 151–152. See also Lowe, *Immigrant Acts*, 86.

2. *Catfish and Mandala* may be the Vietnamese American text most taught in Asian American studies classes. Andrew Pham's book received the Kiriyama Award for nonfiction, the Quality Paperback Book Club Nonfiction Prize, the Oregon Literary Arts Fellowship, and was a New York Times Notable Book of the Year. It earned its author a Whiting Fellowship. *Catfish and Mandala* was also a finalist for the Guardian Prize for First Book. It was translated into French and German.

3. Lan Cao's *Monkey Bridge* was the first Vietnamese American text to be reviewed in the *New York Times* (as an immigrant text and not as a foreign one).

4. Said, *Representations of the Intellectual*, 221.

1 / History

1. Bush also said: "In Vietnam, former allies of the United States and government workers and intellectuals and businessmen were sent off to prison camps, where tens of thousands perished. Hundreds of thousands more

fled the country on rickety boats, many of them going to their graves in the South China Sea." From "President Bush Attends Veterans and Foreign Wars National Convention, Discusses War on Terror." Kansas City Convention and Entertainment Center, Kansas City, Missouri, Office of the Press Secretary, August 22, 2007.

2. Thom Shanker, "Historians Question Bush's Reading of Lessons of Vietnam War for Iraq," *New York Times*, August 23, 2007. For my reasons for referring to Viet Nam instead of Vietnam, see chapter 2, note 26 below.

3. Note that President Bush's sudden recall of a segment of overlooked history defines Vietnamese Americans as refugees only.

4. Said, *Culture and Imperialism*, 8: "classical nineteenth- and early twentieth-century European imperialism still casts a considerable shadow over our own times. Hardly any North American, African, European, Latin American, Indian, Caribbean, Australian individual—the list is very long—who is alive today has not been touched by the empires of the past. Britain and France between them controlled immense territories: Canada, Australia, New Zealand, the colonies in North and South America and the Caribbean, large swatches of Africa, the Middle East, the Far East (Britain will hold Hong Kong as a colony until 1997), and the Indian subcontinent in its entirety—all these fell under the sway of and in time were liberated from British and French rule; in addition, the United States, Russia, and several lesser European countries, to say nothing of Japan and Turkey, were also imperial powers for some or all of the nineteenth century. This pattern of dominions or possessions laid the groundwork for what is in effect now a fully global world. . . . .Consider that in 1800 Western powers claimed 55 percent but actually held approximately 35 percent of the earth's surface, and that by 1878 the proportion was 67 percent, a rate of increase of 83,000 square miles per year. By 1914, the annual rate had risen to an astonishing 240,000 square miles, and Europe held a grand total of roughly 85 percent of the earth as colonies, protectorates, dependencies, dominions, and commonwealths."

Countries and regions experiencing American intervention after 1945 include China (1945–1949), the Philippines (1945–1953), South Korea (1945–1953), Indonesia (1957–58; 1965), Vietnam (1950–1975), Cambodia (1955–1975), Italy (1947–1948), Greece (1947–1949; 1964–1974), Albania (1949–1953), Germany (1950s), Iran (1953), Guatemala (1953–1990s), the Middle East (1956–1958), British Guiana/Guyana (1953–1964), Congo/Zaire (1960–1965), Brazil (1961–1964), the Dominican Republic (1963–1966), Cuba (1959 on), Chile (1964–1973), East Timor (1975–), Nicaragua (1978–1989), Grenada (1979–1984), Libya (1981–1989), Panama (1989), Iraq (1990s, 2000s), Afghanistan (1979–1992), El Salvador (1980–1992), Haiti (1987–1994), and Yugoslavia (1999). http://www.thirdworldtraveler.com/Blum/US_Interventions_WBlumZ.html.

5. The United States has risen to preeminence as a superpower over the past century. To maintain its status, it searched for new markets and engaged

in direct competition with other superpowers such as Britain and France, which were investing heavily in Asia. In 1898, the United States achieved a firm economic hold in the Southwest Pacific with the acquisition of Hawaii and the Philippines, and promoted an economic "open-door" policy with China. By the end of World War II, the United States claimed that Viet Nam was significant to its global interests. Southeast Asia provided close to 90 percent of America's crude rubber and 75 percent of its tin needed for car production. Although the U.S. government, in an effort to distance itself from colonial powers, initially opposed the return of Southeast Asian colonies to France after the Japanese occupation ended in 1945, it changed its position because of economic interests coupled with concerns about greater instability in the region, increasing fear of the Soviet Union as a competing superpower, and the communist victory in China. Not only did the U.S. government stop condemning colonialism it also deployed resources to support France in maintaining its colonies. After France lost its century-long hold on Viet Nam in 1954, the U.S. government announced that economic stagnation and political instability in Viet Nam caused by the departure of the French could provoke a communist takeover in Viet Nam that would spread across Asia. See Herring, *America's Longest War*, 8–17.

6. Pham, "Beyond and before Boat People." See also Rumbaut, "Vietnamese, Laotian, and Cambodian Americans," 240–241.

7. Some of these students came from affluent families and were self-funded or were funded by the U.S. government. They felt stigmatized as negative sentiments toward the Viet Nam War escalated in the United States (Pham, "Beyond and before Boat People," 25). They viewed themselves as outsiders and were mostly concerned with homeland politics and the situation in Viet Nam (ibid., 60).

8. Ibid., 20.

9. There are about 3 million people of Vietnamese descent living in the diaspora. According to Wikipedia, it is estimated that 160,000 live in Australia; 250,000 in France; 152,000 in Canada; 84,000 in Germany; and 55,000 in England. See http://en.wikipedia.org/wiki/Overseas_Vietnamese. I thank Quan Tran, who does research on Vietnamese memorials in Europe at Yale University, for this reference and for confirming the lack of precise demographic data about Vietnamese in the diaspora. For information about French Vietnamese, see Bousquet, *Behind the Bamboo Hedge*.

10. According to Wikipedia, 12,000 people of Vietnamese descent live in Sweden and 18,333 in Norway. For an article on Vietnamese immigration to Japan, see Ashley Carruthers, "Logics of the Multicultural and the Consumption of the Vietnamese Exotic in Japan," in *Positions: East Asia Cultures Critique* 12.2 (Fall 2004): 414.

11. According to E. F. Kunz, refugees are people who leave their countries because of a "well-founded" fear of persecution, "for reasons of race, religion, nationality, membership in a particular social group or politi-

cal opinion . . . and [are] unable, or owing to such fear, unwilling to avail [themselves] to the protection of that country." I thank Rebekah Collins for pointing out that not all South Vietnamese who worked with the American government during the war left Viet Nam, and that some chose to stay, thus complicating the notion of "forced" departure (conversation, December 2007).

12. After the victory of the North against the French at Dien Bien Phu, a treaty was signed in 1954 at the Geneva Conference. Although the Viet Minh dominated most of Viet Nam politically and militarily, it was pressured by the major powers present—namely, China, the Soviet Union, the United States, and France—to accept an armistice during which the country would be divided into two military zones. Troops of the Democratic Republic of Vietnam (the Viet Minh) would regroup north of the 17th parallel and the French Union forces would withdraw in the State of Vietnam in the South. This division was to be in place for two years until the general election by secret ballot in July 1956. Ngo Dinh Diem was selected to govern the South. Soon after, Diem, a Catholic, aided by Americans, welcomed and encouraged one million Catholics to move from the North to the South. In 1956, Diem refused to hold elections. See Young, *The Vietnam Wars*, 37–59.

13. From 111 B.C.E. to C.E. 939, Viet Nam was controlled by China, and then from the mid-nineteenth century to the mid-twentieth by the French. Vietnamese American writers occasionally use French words or make references to French culture because of the historical relationship of colonization by France for over a century. Colonization is an integral part of empire building, and the Vietnamese did not escape the "pattern of dominions and possessions" described by Edward Said. The logic of empire building combines capitalist enterprise with conquering the hearts and minds of the natives through language, education, and culture. In the nineteenth century, the French saw the colonization of Viet Nam as a moral right and duty—France's mission was to civilize the "native" Vietnamese. Moreover, as a capitalist country, France saw the colonies as "a source of raw materials, which, once turned into manufactured goods, could be distributed" on the French market. See Fanon, *The Wretches of the Earth*, 65.

14. Hein, "The New Communist Regimes in Southeast Asia," in *From Vietnam, Laos, and Cambodia*, 26–49.

15. Strand and Jones, *Indochinese Refugees in America*, 33.

16. See Haines, *Refugees in America in the 1990s*. See also "An Unfinished Journey," in Chan, ed., *The Vietnamese American 1.5 Generation*, 198–206.

17. Refugees initially had to stay in military camps (Camp Pendleton in southern California, Fort Chaffee in Arkansas, Fort Indiantown Gap in Pennsylvania, and Eglin Air Force Base in Florida). They had to register with one of the nine voluntary agencies that were contracted with the federal government in order to resettle. They were not allowed to leave the camp until they found a sponsor who promised to provide them with food, clothing,

and shelter until they became independent (some sponsors received $500 for each refugee they aided). The amount the refugees received from the federal government dwindled over the years.

18. See film documentary *Saigon USA*, produced and directed by Lindsey Jang and Robert C. Winn, KOCE-TV, 2002.

19. Vietnamese American activists argued during the Oakland Museum exhibit controversy that the correlation of ethnic Chinese and boat people overshadows the experiences of non-ethnic Chinese who also left by boat.

20. Anti-Chinese resentment was exacerbated by colonization, when ethnic Chinese were often used as middlemen by the French.

21. "The first migration [of ethnic Chinese] occurred at the end of 1977, after the political dispute between China and Vietnam started. The Communist government of Viet Nam ordered a sweeping campaign against all business merchants. Many lost their homes and were sent to farms. An estimated 30,000 Southern Chinese Vietnamese merchants and 150,000 dependent family members were affected. The Chinese Vietnamese remaining in the cities were denied government-controlled jobs and their children were denied admission to universities. At the same time, all young men were drafted to fight the war against the Khmer Rouge in Cambodia. The chaotic and somewhat discriminatory policies against the Chinese Vietnamese from 1977 to 1980 led to a mass exodus of Chinese Vietnamese estimated between 400,000 to 500,00 seeking freedom in neighboring countries . . . [and] in the United States." Chung Hoan Chuong and Minh Hoa Ta, "Overcoming the Past and Building a Future," in Lai and Arguelles, eds., *The New Face of Asian Pacific America*, 70.

22. See Duc Nguyen's documentary film *Bolinao 52*, ITVS, 2007. See also Freeman, *Changing Identities*.

23. According to the 2000 census, there were 24,473 Vietnamese Americans in Westminster, Orange Country, Cal.; 82,834 in San Jose, Cal.; 67,403 in Houston-Galveston-Brazoria, Texas; 49,698 in Dallas-Fort Worth, Texas; and 50,933 in Washington, D.C.

24. See Mayer-Rieckh, "Beyond Concrete and Steel."

25. See Freeman, *Hearts of Sorrow*, 346.

26. Slow to respond to the refugee crisis, the United Nations High Commissioner for Refugees (UNHCR) negotiated the Orderly Departure Program (ODP) with Viet Nam in 1979. Escapees were classified as either refugees under the Refugee Act of 1980 or as immigrants under the Immigrant and National Act. According to James Freeman, "Under the ODP, Vietnamese could enter the United States if they had close relatives living in the United States who applied to bring them over. These included spouses, sons, daughters, parents, grandparents, and unmarried grandchildren. Others who qualified were those who had been employed by Americans or American companies in Viet Nam, officials, soldiers, and their close relatives who had been associated with the United States. Finally, those who had

other ties to America might qualify such as students who had studied in the United States." See Freeman, *Changing Identities*, 35.

27. Freeman states that "in 1989, to discourage continued escapes from Viet Nam by asylum seekers, the UNHCR convened a multinational conference in Geneva. Seventy-eight nations signed and adopted a Comprehensive Plan of Action (CPA). Provisions within the CPA designated March 14, 1989 as the cutoff date for asylum seekers. Persons arriving in countries of first asylum before that date were automatically accepted as refugees. . . . By contrast, those arriving after the cutoff date had to prove they qualified for refugee status by going through a screening process. . . . Those screened out were told to repatriate" (ibid., 39).

28. Ibid., 36.

29. See Valverde, "From Dust to Gold," 144.

30. Ha, "Vietnam Refugees Find a Fresh Start." Those who married Filipinos were denied asylum. About five hundred eventually went to Australia and Canada. For more information, see Duc Nguyen's short documentary film *Stateless* about a forgotten group of Vietnamese refugees who spent over seventeen years in the Philippines waiting for resettlement; KTEH-TV, January 11, 2010.

31. Ha, "Vietnam Refugees Find a Fresh Start."

32. See Lai and Arguelles, eds., *The New Face of Asian Pacific America*, 67–72.

33. Kiang, "Checking Southeast Asian American Realities in Pan-Asian American Agendas." *AAPI Nexus*, 50. Kiang is referring to "the children of the U.S.-born children of first-wave professionals who escaped Vietnam in 1975." According to Kiang, "By 2020, the immigrant and refugee waves of the 1970s and 1980s will have matured as a generation of immigrant elders with third-generation grandchildren."

34. Even recent efforts by Vietnamese Americans to establish representations of Vietnamese Americans that differ from those of refugees of war only tend to emphasize Vietnamese American success stories; one example is the Smithsonian Vietnamese American Heritage Project, started in 2004 (http://vietnam.si.edu).

35. See Hing, *Making and Remaking Asian America through Immigration Policy*, 137: "Under the 1980 Refugee Act, refugees were given 36-month stipends of special refugee cash medical assistance programs, and other support services. But in 1982 amendments to the act reduced the stipends to 18 months to pressure refugees to become economically independent more quickly. These changes came during the entry of the poorer, less-educated, and more devastated second wave. After 1982 most programs stressed employment-enhancing services such as vocational, English-language, and job-development training. Most refugees were unable to acquire the skills that would qualify them for anything other than minimum wage jobs in 18 months. They were nonetheless constrained to take these positions in the

absence of continued public assistance. Restriction on federal assistance helped to account for increased Vietnamese American concentration in entry-level, minimum wage jobs requiring little formal education or mastery of English. For many refugees, in fact, these types of jobs and the poverty that results are unavoidable. Indeed, figures show that in 1979, a striking 35.1 percent of Vietnamese families were living below poverty level." See also Freeman's *Changing Identities*, 125: in 1995, "over one quarter of the Vietnamese in America live[d] under the poverty line. These people typically live in violent inner-city areas plagued with gangs, deteriorating schools, unemployment, and conflicts between themselves and other ethnic groups."

36. See Rutledge, *The Vietnamese Experience in America*, 107. For example, "in south Oklahoma City's area of lower income, . . . strong objections were made when Vietnamese refugees began to rent and purchase residences in the neighborhood." Interviews with persons in the area sparked comments such as:

"I bought myself a gun today. I don't think those damn Communists should be allowed to come over here and just take over." (Caucasian woman, thirty-four years old.)

"I don't like them people being in here. They have some strange beliefs and they can kill you with their feet. I don't let my kids play down there and I don't even walk down there after dark. Can't we do something about them?" (Caucasian woman, mother of five, twenty-six years old.)

"It ain't right. We need these housing for our people." (Black male, twenty-five years old.)

"I just don't like 'em. I don't know why. I just don't. I don't got to have a reason." (Black woman, forty-six years old.)

37. Espiritu, "Toward a Critical Refugee Study," 413. Espiritu gives the example of Christine Finnan's 1981 study of the occupational assimilation of Vietnamese in Santa Clara County, California. She writes: "In Finnan's account, the . . . exploitative electronics industry becomes a 'symbol of opportunity' in which Vietnamese technicians 'are eager to work as many hours of overtime as possible.' Even while praising the hardworking and enterprising Vietnamese, Finnan discursively distances them from normative American workers by reporting that 'occupations that may seem undesirable to *us* may be perfectly suited to [the refugees'] current needs' and that Vietnamese become technicians 'because they are patient and can memorize things easily.'" Finnan, "Occupational Adjustment of Refugees: The Vietnamese in the United States," *International Migration Review* 13.1 (1979), 26–27.

38. Freeman, *Changing Identities*, 43.

39. In a 1982 study reported by Alden Roberts, 77 percent of Americans surveyed "disapprove(d) of the marriage of Indo-Chinese refugees into their family," 65 percent did not want a refugee as a guest in their homes, and 11 percent wanted to exclude Indo-Chinese refugees from the United States altogether. Starr and Roberts, "Attitudes toward New Americans." See also

James W. Tollefson, "Covert Policy in the United States Refugee Program in Southeast Asia," *Language Problems and Language Planning* 12.1 (Spring 1988): 30–43. Tollefson states that many Americans continue to rely upon stereotypes formed during the war and its tragic aftermath. Renny Christopher also quotes Tollefson, stating: "During a generation of involvement with Indochina, Americans have seen Southeast Asians as creatures to be killed, pitied, or saved, but rarely as human beings"; *The Viet Nam War, the American War*, 152.

40. See *Anti-Asian Violence: Oversight Hearing*, 459.

41. See Dowers, *War without Mercy*, 9.

42. See "Slaughter in a School Yard," *Time Magazine* in partnership with CNN, 44; http://www.time.com/time/magazine/article/0,9171,151105,00. html. See also Chen, "Communication in Intercultural Relationships," 225.

43. Le, "Policy of a Community 'At-Risk,'" 179.

44. See Freeman, *Changing Identities*, 118. "In 1988, the Amerasian Homecoming Act paved the way to bring both Amerasian children and their immediate relatives to the United States, and through September 1994, nearly 20,300 Amerasians and 56,700 of their relatives had emigrated to America.... Vietnamese Amerasians who come to the U.S. face an exceptionally difficult period of adjustment. Some report that in Vietnam, they were mistreated or insulted and ridiculed at school by teachers or students who called them *half-Americans* or *half-breeds*. While many Amerasians were treated well most of the time, discrimination seems to have occurred most often if the child lived in an area controlled by Northerners or if the child's mother was considered to be lower class.... A number, however, were forced to become street children at the margins of society, scrounging for scraps of food. Many of these children were adopted by Vietnamese families and then mistreated. After passage of the Amerasian Immigration Act, adoptive families often used the Amerasian child to achieve immigration status. But once in the United States, these children were often abandoned."

45. These refugees included Hungarians in 1956, Chinese after 1949, and Cubans in 1959. According to Palumbo-Liu, "the influx of Indochinese refugees to the United States was part and parcel of a larger ideological effort to lean the balance of the Cold War toward the Free World"; *Asian/American*, 238–239.

46. See Hing, *Making and Remaking Asian America through Immigration Policy*, 121–132.

47. Ibid., 13. Also see commentaries by Ngo Vinh Long in Gettleman et al., eds., *Vietnam and America*, 355–372.

48. See Omatsu, *The State of Asian America*, 33.

49. Feagin, *Racial and Ethnic Relations*, 21.

50. See Cheng, "Remodeling the Minority," 26. According to the 2000 Census, more than 25,000 Vietnamese lived in Louisiana, nearly 6,000 in Mississippi, and about 5,000 in Alabama. Boat People S.O.S., a mutual as-

sistance association, played a major role in helping the evacuees in the Hong Kong IV Mall in Houston.

51. Some Vietnamese Americans had been displaced twice previously: during the 1954 flight from North to South Viet Nam and during their exodus to the United States. See "Hardboiled," *VietBAK*, November 2005. See also Phan, "Vietnamese Lose All," 1–2.

52. See "Vietnamese Fishermen's Association v. Knights of the Ku Klux Klan. Vietnamese Fishermen Case." http://www.splcenter.org/legal/docket/files.jsp?cdrID=40. See also *Monterey's Boat People*, documentary directed by Nakasako and DiGirolamo. The documentary looks at the 1982 controversies between Vietnamese and white fishermen in Monterey, California.

53. See Rutledge, *The Vietnamese Experience in America*, 43.

54. Mai Pham, "Grisly Account of Ly Killing Believed Penned by Suspect," *Los Angeles Times*, March 7, 1996.

55. Tran waved at the officer when she saw him approaching her house. According to police reports, she called the police because she had locked herself outside her apartment. The police department emphasized Tran's history of mental disorder. The killing outraged Vietnamese Americans everywhere and marches on City Hall and public vigils calling for justice were organized. See Victor Hwang, "Police Killing in San Jose Raises Questions," in *Asian American Bar Association of the Greater Bay Area Newsletter*, August 2003, 3–8. The Asian Law Alliance took the case and defended it as a race crime, which has contributed to increased self-identification by Vietnamese Americans as Asian American. See Cecilia Kang, "Stereotypes Cited in Police Slaying." See also http://www.indybay.org/newsitems/2004/07/19/22982.php.

56. Tran, Lam, and Nguyen, eds., *Once upon a Dream*, 184.

57. For a definition of transnationalism, see Shiller, Bash, and Blanc-Szanton, "Transnationalism: A New Analytical Framework for Understanding Migration," 1.

58. See Young, *The Vietnam Wars: 1945–1990*, 301–302: "The United States froze $150 million of Vietnamese assets and vetoed Vietnamese membership in the United Nations. . . . A Congressional amendment to the Foreign Assistance Appropriation Act of 1976 explicitly barred any aid whatsoever for Vietnam, Cambodia, or Laos. Vietnam's need for aid was extreme: in the South, 9,000 out of 15,000 hamlets, 25 million acres of farmland, 12 million acres of forest were destroyed, and 1.5 million farm animals had been killed; there were an estimated 200,000 prostitutes, 879,000 orphans, 181,000 disabled people, and 1 million widows. . . . North and south the land was cratered and plated with tons of unexploded ordinance, so that long after the war farmers and their families suffered serious injuries as they attempted to bring the fields back into cultivation. Nineteen million gallons of herbicide had been sprayed on the South during the war, and while the long-term effects were unknown in 1975 . . . severe birth defects and multiple miscarriages were apparent early on."

59. See "Viet Nam: Transition to the Market," in *The World Bank*, September 1993. Also, according to Bruce Franklin: "In early 1969, newly inaugurated president Richard Nixon and Dallas businessman H. Ross Perot secretly planned a media blitz to use US prisoners of war (POWs) and soldiers missing in action (MIAs) as a major issue to build public support for continuing the Vietnam War. By 1972, a significant number of Americans believed that the United States had gotten into the war to rescue the POWs. For more than two decades after US troops withdrew in 1973, the POW/MIA issue was the main official basis for continuing economic and political warfare against Vietnam. By the mid-1980s, Hollywood movies and the Reagan Administration had made belief in the existence of live POWs still held in Vietnam an article of popular faith." In Gettleman et al., eds., *Vietnam and America: A Documented History*, 500.

60. In the 1990s, American corporations were concerned that thirty-four countries were doing business in Viet Nam, the biggest investors being Taiwan, Hong Kong and France. See "Viet Nam: Transition to the Market," in *The World Bank*, September 1993.

61. These changes have created tensions between anti-communist "old timers," who adamantly condemn any contact with Viet Nam as abetting the communist regime, and those belonging to what Nguyen Qui Duc has called "the silent majority." In an op-ed letter published in the *Los Angeles Times*, Nguyen writes: "It is a majority that opposes censorship, both in the homeland and in America. . . . Now is the time for ending an intolerable silence among Vietnamese Americans." *Los Angeles Times*, Orange County edition, August 8, 1999, B9.

62. Takaki, *Strangers from a Different Shore*, 392–405.

63. Valverde, "Making Vietnamese Music Transnational"; Duong, "Desire and Design."

64. Phan, "Roots of Unrest."

65. The original name of the exhibit was "Next Stop, Vietnam," which was later changed to "What's Going On?" I thank Kathy Nguyen for pointing this out to me. The exhibit received $1.9 million in grants and took five years to be completed. At the end, it displayed more than 500 historical artifacts, photographs and documents, film clips, music, and oral histories.

66. Mimi Nguyen. "Memo to Oakland Museum Staff," October 17, 2003, unpublished document. According to Nguyen, the 4 million dead that she cited in her memo is based on Vietnamese sources. Mimi Nguyen, January 25, 2008, e-mail correspondence.

67. The petition and the signatures were sent to the Oakland Museum staff, and also to funders, senators, the mayor of Oakland, and assembly members of all the districts in the Bay Area. Nguyen writes, "When I expressed my ideas and input, I was dismissed and reprimanded for 'not listening and understanding the content.' Why should my different input from the staff's vision be a good reason for dismissal? This conflict over input

and interpretation became the basis for 'poor performance.'" Mimi Nguyen, "Timeline of Events," February 2004, unpublished document. .

The petition began: "We are writing to protest Mimi Nguyen's dismissal, and the content and direction of the *Next Stop Vietnam* exhibit that the Oakland Museum is organizing. As Vietnamese Americans, we find the Oakland Museum's vision for this exhibit to be narrow, biased, and unrepresentative of minorities and refugee history." Members of the petition publicly demanded that the museum "clear Mimi's name, retract any misleading or negative comments made against her, and reinstate her to her former position." They also requested that the exhibit be more inclusive of Vietnamese American experiences and voices and, in their words, be more historically "accurate." See Ngoc Nguyen, "Report on Petition," February 7, 2004, e-mail letter sent to delegation members.

68. See Joyce Nishioka, "Inclusive or Exclusive? Next Stop Exhibit Ire of Vietnamese Americans," *AsianWeek*, November 21, 2003. Vanessa Hua. "Oakland Museum Show Stirs Trouble. Vietnamese Angry over Firing of Staffer Who Criticized It," *San Francisco Chronicle*, December 19, 2003, A-1; Vanessa Hua, "Complaints about Oakland Museum's Vietnam Exhibit," *San Francisco Chronicle*, July 20, 2004; Pueng Vongs, "Vietnamese Slighted in Vietnam War Exhibit," *CaliToday* News Report, November 4, 2003; Carol Pogash, "In Imperfect Compromise, Exhibit Tells of Vietnam Era," *New York Times*, September 7, 2004.

69. J. H. Tompkins, "Extreme Measures: War Stories," *San Francisco Bay Guardian*, October 6, 2004, 48.

70. According to the 2000 U.S. census (SF3, Table PCT1), there are 484, 023 people of Vietnamese descent living in California.

71. After 1975, Vietnamese Americans insisted on remembering the new communist government's policy of collectivizing agriculture and nationalizing businesses, which resulted in economic and social failures. According to Jeremy Hein, between 90,000 and 500,000 people were sent to "reeducation camps" during the ten years that followed the fall of South Viet Nam; Hein, *From Vietnam, Laos, and Cambodia*, 26. In 1978, new economic policies led to the confiscation of businesses and private property, which disproportionately affected ethnic Chinese. The creation of "new economic zones" led urban dwellers to cultivate abandoned land without needed supplies and equipment. People suffered terribly, and those who sided with the Americans suffered the most. Their suffering was compounded by Viet Nam's wars and border clashes with Cambodia and China in 1978 and 1979, respectively. Without enough food to eat, hope for a better future for their families, access to higher education for their children, and above all because of the dehumanizing conditions in the reeducation camps, many risked their lives and fled to other countries in fragile boats, some even traveling on foot across Cambodia. See Ha, *Stormy Escape*.

2 / Overview

1. Janette, "Vietnamese American Literature in English, 1963–1994,"
276–277. Michelle Janette puts early Vietnamese American literature into
three categories: "Tales of Witness" (often autobiographical and with an
agenda linked to home politics); "Tales of Education" (aiming to educate the
American mainstream and future generations about Viet Nam and Vietnamese culture); and "Tales in America" (fully embracing America as the
land of opportunity but also exposing racism).

2. Kim, "Foreword," *Reading the Literature of Asian America*, xiii.

3. Dispersal policies combined with worries of integration and resettlement made life very difficult for many of the writers of the first generation. Men often had to change careers and acquire more practical skills
while women had to work to support their families.

4. Less widely distributed were *Nhan Van* (Humanities), *Van* (Literature), *Lang Van* (Literary Circle) and *Tan Van* (New Literature).

5. Cao, *Poetry by Cao Tan*.

6. Janette, "Vietnamese American Literature in English, 1963–1994," 271.

7. Ibid., 273.

8. See Tran Dieu Hang's *Mua dat la* (Ontario: Viet Publications, 1986)
and *Vu dieu cua loai cong* (Westminster, Cal.: Ngoc Lu, 1984). For a discussion of Tran Dieu Hang's writing, see Qui-Phiet Tran, "From Isolation to
Integration."

9. Janette, "Vietnamese American Literature in English," 273.

10. Neilson, *Warring Fictions*, 20, 25.

11. According to Michelle Janette, texts written in Vietnamese for a Vietnamese American audience display more overt anger than those written in
English. Janette, "Vietnamese American Literature in English," 271–272.

12. Nguyen-Vo, "Forking Paths: How Shall We Mourn the Dead?" 162.

13. In Cambodia, "the Khmer Rouge revolution aimed to reshape an
entire way of life, not merely the country's economy. . . . The Khmer Rouge
particularly targeted the approximately 65,000 monks who served in the
Buddhist temples that were the core of Khmer culture. Only about 3,000
survived. . . . From starvation, disease, and execution, about 2 million Cambodians died between 1975 and 1978, or one-quarter of the country's pre-
revolution population. The story of life under the Khmer Rouge is one of
the most tragic episodes of the twentieth century." In Laos, "the Hmong
and other highland ethnic groups that had been recruited by the American
military for its 'secret army' . . . were particularly vulnerable." Hein, *From
Vietnam, Laos, and Cambodia*, 27.

14. The book was adapted by Oliver Stone into a film called *Heaven and
Earth*.

15. Lam, "The Passing of Literary Traditions," 29.

16. Nguyen et al., *Fallen Leaves: Memoirs of a Vietnamese Woman*

from 1940 to 1975. This academic monograph did not receive wide distribution.

17. See Truong, "Vietnamese American Literature," 238.

18. Huynh, *South Wind Changing,* 260.

19. Ibid., 304.

20. Nguyen Qui Duc, "Light of Darkness," in his *Where the Ashes Are: The Odyssey of a Vietnamese Family.* The voice of the father was informed by memoirs and poems that Nguyen's own father had written in jail.

21. Ibid., 264.

22. Ibid., 265.

23. Said, "Intellectual Exile: Expatriates and Marginals," in *Grand Street* 12.3 (Fall 1993): 117.

24. Ibid., 114.

25. Ibid., 117. The narrator's mother was a French teacher. He speaks fluent French and has been exposed to French culture. His mother is a "member of President Thieu's Democratic party, head of the Vietnamese-American Friendship Association, the mother of children who had attended French schools and then gone off to American universities, wife of a former South Vietnamese government official." Nguyen Qui Duc, *Where the Ashes Are: The Odyssey of a Vietnamese Family,* 89.

26. Ibid., 264.

27. Traditionally, Vietnamese burn incense for ancestors in front of an altar. The belief is that the spirits of the dead affect the existence of the living and play an active role in their lives. Yet the act of bringing the ashes of his dead sister to San Francisco transgresses traditional beliefs that the spirits of the dead are connected to the land where they were born.

28. Larsen and Tran, *Shallow Graves: Two Women in Vietnam.* "Wendy Wilder Larsen, an American poet, spent 1970–71 with her husband, a journalist, in Saigon, South Vietnam, where she met Tran Thi Nga, the bookkeeper in her husband's office. 'Shallow Graves,' begun after the two women were reunited in the United States in 1975, tells Wendy Larsen's own story in her year as a teacher of English literature, as well as Tran Thi Nga's life story, beginning with her birth in China in 1927 and ending with her present life in Cos Cob, Conn., where she and her family maintain an uneasy relationship with American culture." Abram, "Vietnam, East and West."

29. Truong, "Vietnamese American Literature," 235.

30. Larsen and Tran, *Shallow Graves,* 32.

31. Translation work requires creativity and is an art form in itself. Walter Benjamin, for example, wrote that translation always implies change as it alters the relationship between content and language, and is an intellectual task that does not copy but echoes the original. Benjamin, *Illuminations,* 69–82.

32. Nguyen Qui Duc, "Translating Love," in Huu Thin, *The Time Tree,* xxxi.

33. George Evans, "The Black Duck Floats backwards off the River," in Huu, *The Time Tree*, xx. Huu Thinh is general director of the Writers Association of Viet Nam, editor-in-chief of *Van Nghe* (a literature and arts journal), ex-tank driver and lieutenant colonel in the North Vietnamese army. George Evans was a medical corpsman in the emergency unit at an Air Force hospital during the Viet Nam War. Reflecting on the war, he writes: "nothing will ever justify the unnecessary death and destruction rained upon the Vietnamese and my generation, or excuse the ruin we brought to the beautiful country of Viet Nam, or erase what was burned into my eyes and consciousness." Ibid., xix.

34. Nguyen, "Translating Love," xxviii. Nguyen explains that in April of 1995, he was invited to speak at U.C. Davis with other journalists, scholars, and writers to mark the twentieth anniversary of the end of the Viet Nam War. Nguyen deliberately invited protesters outside, who had been excluded, to join the conference. He writes in the introduction of *Time Tree* about this event: "About a hundred people protested outside, some dressed in military fatigues, waving the flag of the former South Viet Nam regime, shouting slogans and denouncing the participants as pro-communist. I was desperate to bring them inside to participate in an exchange that would raise their concerns, but their violent expression earned them little sympathy. Inside, I berated some of the participants for their exclusive interest in the North Vietnamese side, and [for] neglecting [the interests and perspectives of] those who had fought in the South. . . . I felt there was a need to recognize the validity of the experiences of the Southerners" (ibid., xxix). Nguyen says that he sees his work as one of reconciliation, to facilitate communication among former enemies. The cost, he says, is that many in the United States and in Viet Nam question his loyalty. In the United States he has been called a communist sympathizer by Vietnamese Americans, and in Viet Nam he was placed under house arrest for a week in 1992. Nguyen says his emotional loyalty goes to those who suffered in Viet Nam, that is, to the country itself. "The country needs a heart," he says. Nguyen Qui Duc, telephone interview, November 10, 2005.

35. "In the intense early years, five Vietnamese-American journalists were killed in the United States, apparently by a radical anti-communist group. Mr. Do chose not to visit his mother in Vietnam before she died, fearing reprisals from those who oppose any contact with the country they had fled." Mydans, "The Rough Drafts of Vietnamese-American History."

36. See Karlin et al., eds., *The Other Side of Heaven*, xiii.

37. Linh Dinh, telephone interview, February 5, 2001.

38. See Karlin et al., eds., *The Other Side of Heaven*; Lim and Chua, eds., *Tilting the Continent: Southeast Asian American Writing*; Stewart, Bowen, and Chung, eds., *Two Rivers: New Vietnamese Writing from America and Viet Nam*; Rebekah Linh Collins, ed., *Viet Nam: Beyond the Frame*.

39. The author of this piece asked that his name and the name of the

journal not be used. I have read the letter of rejection. No reason is given other than that the writing was "not Vietnamese enough."

40. Andrew Lam, e-mail correspondence, December 7, 2005.

41. See Tran et al., eds., *Once upon a Dream*, 1.

42. Tran et al., eds., *Watermark: Vietnamese American Poetry and Prose.*

43. Ibid., quoting Russell Leong, back cover.

44. Ibid., vi.

45. Ibid., vii.

46. See Norindr, *Phantasmatic Indochina.* According to Norindr, French literature offered prototypical figures of the French either as "heroic soldier," bold and enigmatic; "adventurer" who would be king; selfless man of science; or clergyman who dedicated his life to improving the fate of the natives. Other stories displayed the romance that naval officers experienced with native women (ibid., 3). These representations privileged the white man's struggle against an exotic, if not quite barbaric, Other.

47. American representations often dehumanized the Vietnamese, whose country only became of interest to the U.S. population as a theater of war. According to Renny Christopher, the Vietnamese were portrayed as "humble, passive, but also sneaky and treacherous" (Christopher, *The Vietnam War, the American War*, 177). Like their colonial predecessors, Americans considered the Vietnamese uncivilized (ibid., 181). Racist stereotypes were applied to all Vietnamese, even though half were nominal American allies. Christopher argues that many GIs, blinded by racism, simply did not see Vietnamese as equals.

48. Yen Le Espiritu argues that "the narrative of the 'good refugee' valorizes capitalism, equating 'freedom' with economic access and choice, upward social mobility, and free enterprise" in "Vietnamese Americans and U.S. Empire," xv. See also Le, "Policy for a Community 'At-Risk.'" Vietnamese Americans have often been portrayed in the media in terms of success or delinquency (Le 167).

49. A controversial tale of return to Viet Nam is depicted in a 1993 documentary by Tiana Thi Thanh Ngo titled *From Hollywood to Hanoi.* The filmmaker is the daughter of a former director of press and information in the South Vietnamese Thieu government and left Viet Nam with her family as a child in 1966. In the film, she goes back to Vietnam to retrace her family history, visits sites of war she had seen or heard of on television, and talks to people on the street and top government officials. Many Vietnamese Americans criticized her for giving voice to the North Vietnamese, while other Americans were simply not ready to reenter Viet Nam. The film did not attract national attention.

50. On the bookshelves of bookstores and libraries in American urban centers one can often find books filed under "Ethnic Literature" or "Asian American." In contrast, in France no distinction is made. The majority of French Vietnamese texts can be found on bookshelves under the rubric

"Asian literature" and therefore remain largely invisible, and the population voiceless. The popular books like those by Linda Le are, however, shelved in the French section.

51. Le, *Seattle-Post-Intelligencer*, March 6, 2000; and *San Francisco Examiner*, April 24, 2000. Lam, *San Francisco Examiner*, April 23, 2000.

52. Professor Hien Do was also hired as a narrator for the documentary *Viet Nam: At the Crossroads* (KTEH, San Francisco, 1994). It follows his trip shortly before the lifting of the embargo by President Clinton and examines the social, political, and cultural changes that have taken place there.

53. See Obayashi, "Mapping the Homeland Memories of 1.5 Generation Vietnamese Americans."

54. Mong-Lan also published *Why Is the Edge Always Windy* (2005) and *Love Poem to Tofy and Other Poems* (2007). Mong-Lan travels frequently and dances the tango, all of which are reflected in her poems.

55. Similar identity formation can be found in South Asian, Filipino/a and Korean American literature. See Srikanth, *The World Next Door*.

56. Nguyen, *The Unwanted: A Memoir*, 342–343.

57. Unlike the French, who arranged to bring Eurasian children to France after their departure, the Americans waited twelve years before allowing the repatriation of the children of their military men. In the meantime, these children were ostracized, neglected, and often abused by family members and communists in Viet Nam. See Valverde, "From Dust to Gold: The Amerasian Experience."

58. In this way, the text moves away from an American-centric and male-centered view of Viet Nam. The author conducted a considerable amount of research for this book. She did interviews with relatives, searched family records and archival documents, and read Vietnamese, French, and American historical documents (included in the bibliography).

59. In the preface, Duong Van Mai Elliott explains that the events she traces include "the French conquest of Vietnam, the war against French colonial rule, the brief years of peace, the socialist transformation of the North, the resumption of fighting in the South with American involvement until the communist victory in 1975, the evacuation of refugees from Saigon, and the effect of the communist victory on [her] relatives who remained in Vietnam" after 1975; Elliott, *The Sacred Willow*, xii.

60. In *The Sacred Willow*, Elliott writes: "My father had never thought the time would come when an Asian could strike down a Frenchman and get away with it" (103). Initial admiration of the Japanese soon turned into hatred for the brutal nature of the occupation. The narrator talks about the presence of "American planes" sent to defeat the Japanese during WWII (106). The allied bombing and the Japanese requisition of rice disrupted the supply of rice from the South to the North, and by the end of the war, led to famine in the North (107). The narrator's family managed to survive, but was deeply affected. The colonial regime "made no effort to deal with the famine.

The only group that was opposing the Japanese and dealing seriously with the famine was the Viet Minh" (112).

61. Christopher Benfey, "Ordering In," *New York Times Book Review,* April 6, 2003.

62. Truong, *The Book of Salt,* 250.

63. Truong, lecture at the University of California at Santa Cruz in Karen Yamashita's class, October 7, 2009.

64. See http://www.vacollective.com.

65. Danny Thanh Nguyen, "Monster Ballads, Fish Sauce, AND Us," *As Is,* The Vietnamese Artists Collective, 10–11.

66. They differ from a similar group formed in 1991 called *Ink and Blood,* of which I was a member. Like the Vietnamese Artists Collective, *Ink and Blood* organized and participated in readings in the Bay Area. Our work was much about the expression of the tormented soul, memory, and racism, but not overtly about sex.

67. Vietnamese Artists Collective Website: http://www.vacollective.org/members.php.

68. Danny Nguyen, interview with author, December 8, 2005.

69. See Bao Phi, "No Offense," *Refugeeography,* compact disc, 2005. See also http://www.baophi.com/poetry/p3.html and http://www.baophi.com/poetry.html.

3 / Hybridity

1. Peter Nien-chu Kiang notes that between 1995 and 2000, only eighty-five Vietnamese American scholars out of 2,162 presenters discussed their research at the annual meetings of the Association for Asian American Studies. Peter Nien-chu Kiang, "Checking Southeast Asian American Realities in Pan-Asian American Agendas," 54. At the 2000 conference held at U.C. Riverside entitled "30 Years beyond the War: Vietnamese, Southeast Asian and Asian/American Studies," out of forty-four speakers, only four came from Asian American studies and two from ethnic studies. And only one, myself, presented a paper on Vietnamese American literature. If Vietnamese American scholarship is slowly beginning to be integrated into Asian American studies and academia in general, this is mostly in the realm of the social sciences.

2. Peter Zinoman made this argument in his keynote address, "What's Going On?"

3. See Wong, "Denationalization Reconsidered," 3.

4. Chan, ed., *The Vietnamese American 1.5 Generation,* viii.

5. Vietnamese were forced to abandon rice farming and produce jute, castor oil, and other products needed to support the Japanese war effort. The Japanese destroyed wheat and rice fields to build railroads and electrical power plants, and prohibited the transport of rice surpluses from the South to the North.

6. It is important to note here that there were also Vietnamese students before 1975, many of whom were on the left and anti-war. See Gloria Emerson's *Winners and Losers* (New York: Random House, 1977) and Vu Pham's PhD dissertation ("Beyond and before Boat People: Vietnamese American History Before 1975"). I thank Viet Nguyen for these references.

7. When I entered graduate school in ethnic studies in 1993 at the University of California at Berkeley, I discovered that I was the first Vietnamese American literary studies scholar to be accepted into the program.

8. Kim, *Asian American Literature*, xi.

9. Wong, *Reading Asian American Literature*; Cheung, *Articulated Silences*; David Leiwei Li, *Imagining the Nation*. Leiwei Li extends Kim's definition by including South Asian literary texts.

10. Oscar Campomanes argues that the experiences of Filipino Americans must be contextualized within U.S. imperialist pursuits in order to fully understand Filipino American subjectivities. Frustrated by Filipino American invisibility in literature, Campomanes contrasted Filipino American literature with Asian American and other ethnic literatures. He states that "rather than the United States [serving] as the locus of claims or 'the promised land,' the Filipino case represents a reverse telos, an opposite movement." See Campomanes, "Filipinos in the United States and Their Literature of Exile," 51. Also see Srikanth, *The World Next Door*.

11. Campomanes, "Filipinos in the United States and Their Literature in Exile," 49, 51.

12. "These Filipinos and South Asian scholars include Deepika Bahri, Oscar Campomanes, Nazli Kibria, Susan Koshy, Vijay Prashad, E. San Juan, Jr., Lavina Dhingra Shankar, Rajini Srikanth, and Urvashi Vaid. Early reconsiderations of the limits of Asian American studies came from founders of the field such as Elaine Kim ("Beyond Railroads and Internment") and Michael Omi ("It Just Ain't the Sixties No More"). A growing number of Chinese and Japanese American scholars are also moving toward this reassessment of Asian American studies and its basis in panethnicity. These include Bill Ong Hing, Peter Kwong Li, Shirley Geok-lin Lim, Colleen Lye, Aihwa Ong (*Flexible Citizenship*), and Palumbo-Liu." Viet Thanh Nguyen, *Race and Resistance*, 174. Shelly Wong and David Eng in queer studies can also be added to this list.

13. Truong. "The Emergence of Voices"; this essay was reprinted with revisions three years later in Cheung, ed., *An Interethnic Companion to Asian American Literature*.

14. Lowe, *Immigrant Acts*, 58. The two girls are brought together as friends, mostly by their status as outcasts, one being Vietnamese American and the other being overweight. In school, Kelly denounces the bias of her teacher, who could not make the distinction between South Vietnamese allies and North Vietnamese enemies, nor among other Asians. Analyzing "Kelly," Lisa Lowe focused on the narrative's decentering role, mostly with

regard to its hybrid nature, and on autonomous notions of Western culture used in order to justify abuses of colonialism and neocolonization.

15. David Palumbo-Liu, "War, the Homeland, and the Traces of Memory," in *Asian/American*, 217–254. See also Truong, "Vietnamese American Literature," in *An Interethnic Companion to Asian American Literature*, edited by King-Kok Cheung.

16. Chan, *The Vietnamese American 1.5 Generation*.

17. President George H. W. Bush said of the first Iraq War victory: "The specter of Vietnam has been buried forever in the desert sands of the Arabian peninsula. . . . It's a proud day for America—and, by God, we've kicked the Vietnam syndrome once and for all." Norman Solomon, "Beyond the Vietnam Syndrome," http://www.inthesetimes.com/article/2296/beyond_the_vietnam_syndrome.

What is the Vietnam syndrome? After losing the Viet Nam War, national guilt, or "Vietnam syndrome," spread across America when the rationale behind the longest war in U.S. history proved untrue. The "loss" of Viet Nam did not result in a victory for the U.S.S.R. or China, nor did it lead to a communist Asia. During the conflict, America heavily bombed not only Viet Nam but also Cambodia and Laos. Two and a half years after the end of the Viet Nam War, 130,000 Vietnamese, 8,000 Laotians, and 6,000 Cambodians came to the United States as refugees. Although human rights violations by the Cambodian communist regime far surpassed those of the Vietnamese government, the discrepancy in the number of Vietnamese, Cambodian, and Laotian refugees stems from the "secret" nature of the U.S. war in Cambodia in contrast to the "televised war" in Viet Nam. The high visibility of the Viet Nam War explains the U.S. government's preferential treatment of Vietnamese refugees over Cambodians and Laotians, and also over Nicaraguans, Guatemalans, and Haitians who suffered human rights violations by dictatorial regimes supported by the American government. Refugee policies are not only about human rights concerns; they emerge from the contradictory desires of the United States to shift the balance of power towards the "free" world, America's concerns about the cost of resettlement, and nostalgia for ethnic purity.

18. See *Vietnamese Americans: Diaspora and Dimensions* 29.1 (2003); and *30 Years AfterWARd: Vietnamese Americans and U.S. Empire* 31.2 (2005).

19. Leong, "30 Years AfterWARd," xvi.

20. Lowe, *Immigrant Acts*, 82.

21. Donald A. Ranard, "Between Two Worlds: Refugee Youth," 6.22; Kim Zetter, "The Patriot Act Is Your Friend," *Wired*, April 2006.

23. Richard B. Schmitt, "Chief Architect of Patriot Act to Quit," *Los Angeles Times*, May 14, 2003, A16.

24. Eric Lishtblau, "Justice Dept. Lists Use of New Power to Fight Terror," *New York Times*, May 21, 2003.

25. *Los Angeles Times*, http://www.latimes.com/news/printedition/cali-

fornia/la-me-vietdems29feb29,0,5303050.story. A poll conducted by the *Orange County Register* in 2000 states that 71% of respondents ranked fighting communism as "top priority" or "very important". See Christian Collet's "Determinants of Vietnamese American Political Participation: Findings from the January 2000 Orange County Register Poll" (http://www1.doshisha.ac.jp/~AAAS%202000%20(Collet).pdf).

26. Tal, *Worlds of Hurt*, 17. I use the term "Viet Nam" instead of "Vietnam" here to mark what critic Lan Duong calls the violent history between Viet Nam and the West and to denote, in her words, a "particular construction of Viet Nam within the Western imaginary." Lan Duong, "Manufacturing Authenticity: The Feminine Ideal in Tony Bui's *Three Seasons*," in *Amerasia Journal* 31.2 (2005): 14.

27. My use of the concept of normative history is inspired by Judith Butler's *Gender Trouble*, xxi.

28. Right after the Viet Nam War ended, Hollywood was reluctant to make movies about it. Around the same time, Vietnamese American voices attracted disproportionate interest from medical, psychiatric, and legal researchers. See Tal, *Worlds of Hurt*.

29. For a discussion on American perceptions of the Viet Nam War, see Martin Andrew, *Reception of War: Vietnam in American Culture* (Norman: University of Oklahoma Press, 1993); Douglas Allen and Ngo Vinh Long, eds., *Coming to Terms: Indochina, the United States, and the War* (Boulder, CO.: Westview, 1991); John Carlos Rowe and Rick Berg, eds., *The Vietnam War and American Culture* (New York: Columbia University Press, 1991); Richard Morris and Peter Ehrenhaus, eds., *Cultural Legacies of Vietnam: Uses of the Past in the Present* (Norwood, N.J.: Ablex, 1990).

30. See Renny Christopher, *The Vietnam War, the American War*, 140.

31. See Espiritu, "Thirty Years AfterWARd: The Endings That Are Not Over," xiii.

32. Image of Thick Quang Duc, who burned himself to death in Saigon on June 11, 1963, to protest against the persecution of Buddhists by the Ngh Dinh Diem administration. Photo by Malcolm Browne (winner of a Pulitzer Prize for the photograph).

33. Image of Kim Phuc by Nick Ut (winner of the Pulitzer Prize for the photograph), 1972.

34. Image of commander of the South Vietnamese police General Nguyen Ngoc Loan and handcuffed prisoner Nguyen Van Lem, by Eddie Adams (February 1, 1968).

35. Photo by Hubert Van Es (some says that the photo was not taken from the embassy but on the roof of an apartment building in downtown Saigon where senior Central Intelligence Agencies were housed), April 29, 1975 (see http://www.mishalov.com/Vietnam_finalescape.html).

36. Sau-Ling Wong, "Denationalization Reconsidered," 1, 2.

37. Ibid., 12, 17.

38. Ibid., 13–15, 26, 18.

39. See Espiritu, "30 Years AfterWARd: The Endings That Are Not Over," xvi.

40. Lowe, *Immigrant Acts*, 83.

41. Chuh, *Imagine Otherwise*, 83, 96.

42. Nguyen, *Race and Resistance*, 4.

43. See power-conflict theorists Robert Blauner, *Racial Oppression in America* (1972); Mario Barrera, *Race and Class in the Southwest: A Theory of Racial Inequalities* (1979); Edna Bonacich, *Theory of Ethnic Antagonism: The Split Labor Market* (1972); and race-based theorists Yen Le Espiritu, *Asian American Panethnicity: Bridging Institutions and Identities* (1992); Andres Hacker, *Two Nations: Black and White, Separate, Hostile, Unequal* (2003); Derrick Bell, *Faces at the Bottom of the Well: The Permanence of Racism* (1992); Michael Omi and Howard Winant, *Racial Formation in the United States: From the 1960s to the 1980s* (1986, 1989); and Cornel West, *Race and Social Theory: Toward a Genealogical Materialist Analysis* (1987).

44. Chan, *In Defense of Asian American Studies*, 11.

45. See Omi and Winant, *Racial Formation in the United States*, 17–18.

46. Gordon, *Assimilation in American Life*.

47. See Allan Bloom, *The Closing of the American Mind: How Higher Education Has Failed Democracy and Impoverished the Souls of Today's Students* (New York: Simon and Schuster, 1987); and E. D. Hirsch, *Cultural Literacy: What Every American Needs to Know* (Boston: Houghton Mifflin, 1987).

48. See http://articles.latimes.com/2008/jan/23/opinion/oe-iweala23.

49. "The Chinese exclusion law specified Chinese by race and permitted entry to only a few, tightly defined exempt categories such as students, merchants, tourists, and diplomats. Chinese were not prohibited from entering altogether although the goal was to prevent their settlement. This priority is reiterated in the racial ban on naturalization for Asians." I thank historian Madeline Hsu for adding this comment (e-mail dated June 27, 2009).

50. Japanese could become naturalized citizens only after the passage of the Walter-McCarran Act of 1952. Harris, *Pattern of Race in the Americas*, 56. Asian Indians and Filipinos gained naturalization rights in 1946. I thank Madeline Hsu for this clarification.

51. They visited Texas, the District of Columbia, and California. See Ba Chung Nguyen, "The Long Road Home: Exile, Self-Recognition, and Reconstruction," *Manoa Journal* 14.1 (2002): 36.

52. Sau-Ling Wong makes a similar argument in *Reading Asian American Literature*, 15–16.

53. Danny Nguyen, "Introduction: Monster Ballads, Fish Sauce, and Us," in *As Is: A Collection of Visual and Literary Works by Vietnamese American Artists* (San Francisco: Vietnamese Artists Collective, 2006), 11.

54. Danny Nguyen, personal interview, June 10, 2006.

55. DuBois, "Construction Construed," 4–5.

56. Barbara Tran, "Viet Nam: Beyond the Frame," in *Michigan Quarterly Review* 18.4 (Fall 2004), 482.

57. Espiritu, "Toward a Critical Refugee Study," 420.

58. Ibid.

4 / Survival

1. According to Grace M. Cho, "the Korean War was both a launching point for an intensification of U.S. military dominance in Asia and a continuation of what had already been initiated by the Japanese colonizers"; *Haunting the Korean Diaspora* (Minneapolis: University of Minnesota Press, 2008), 51. In *Empire of Care*, Catherine Ceniza Choy argues that "legacies of empire and war continue to haunt Filipino Americans, most notably Filipino American war veterans who served under the U.S. Armed Forces of the Far East during World War II but continue to struggle for their veterans' benefits" (Durham: Duke University Press, 2003), 14. These observations were present at the beginning of Asian American studies. Victor Bascara reminds us in *Model-Minority Imperialism* that "the earlier formations of the Asian American movement made a more explicit connection to geopolitics, neocolonialism, and Third World consciousness" (Minneapolis: University of Minnesota Press, 2006), 10.

2. Vietnamese Americans have at times come together in protest, intermittently unified by memories of a traumatic past in Viet Nam, as in the fifty-two-day demonstration that ensued when Trung Van Tran displayed a photograph of Ho Chi Minh in his Orange County video store in 1999.

3. Ann Cvetkovich, *An Archive of Feelings* (Durham: Duke University Press, 2009), 18. This approach differs from the clinical psychology definition of trauma as post-traumatic stress disorder (PTSD). It does not, for instance, focus on symptoms (such as hyperarousal, numbing, repetition) that come from events "outside the range of usual human experience," or events that involve "actual or threatened death or serious injury, or other threat to one's physical integrity." For this kind of approach, see American Psychiatric Association, *Diagnostic and Statistical Manual of Mental Disorder*, 3d ed. (Washington, D.C.: American Psychiatric Association, 1987), 247, and *Diagnostic and Statistical Manual of Mental Disorders*, 4th ed. (Washington, D.C.: American Psychiatric Association, 1994), 424.

4. See, for instance, Michel Foucault's *Language, Counter-Memory, Practice.*

5. See Ann Svetkovich, *An Archive of Feelings*, 45.

6. For Native American studies, see Russell Thornton, ed., *Studying Native America: Problems and Prospects* (Madison: University of Wisconsin Press, 1998), and Gerald Vizenor, ed., *Survivance: Narratives of Native Presence* (Lincoln: University of Nebraska Press, 2008). For African American studies, see Toni Morrison, *Beloved* (New York: Knopf, 1987), and Russell Ferguson et al., eds., "Unspeakable Things Unspoken: The Afro-American

Presence in American Literature," *Michigan Quarterly Review* 28.1 (1989): 1–34. In regard to Holocaust studies, see Nadine Fresco, "Remembering the Unknown," *International Review of Psychoanalysis* 11 (1984): 417–427, and Efraim Sicher, "In the Shadow of History: Second Generation Writers and Artists and the Shaping of Holocaust Memory in Israel and America," *Judaism* 47.2 (1998): 169–185. In Japanese American studies, seé Donna Nagata, *Legacy of Injustice: Exploring the Cross-generational Impact of the Japanese American Internment* (New York: Plenum Press, 1993), and Nobu Miyoshi, "Identity Crisis of the Sansei and the Concentration Camp." Sansei Legacy Project (1994).

7. See Roger I. Simon, Sharon Rosenberg, and Claudia Eppert, *Between Hope and Despair*, 2.

8. Jacques Derrida, *Specters of Marx*, trans. Peggy Kamuf (New York: Routledge, 1994), xix.

9. Pham, *Catfish and Mandala*, 170. Hereafter in this section, pages in this book are given parenthetically in the text.

10. The French did not bring the opium trade to Viet Nam. But the French made the trade and the consumption of opium a state monopoly (that is, consumers could only purchase opium in outlets licensed by the state. Addicts could also smoke it in specially established dens, licensed by the state). See Truong, *Colonialism Experienced*.

11. As the only child allowed to stay with his parents during the war and the only one sent to a French school, he was expected to thrive in America.

12. See, for instance, Luis Chu's *Eat a Bowl of Tea* (1961), Maxine Hong Kingstons's *The Woman Warrior* (1975), Amy Tan's *The Joy Luck Club* (1980), and Fae Myenne Ng's *Bone* (1993).

13. The "model minority" thesis, "while invoking the American immigrant myth, assiduously searches traditional Asian cultures for clues to the Asian American success story." Wong, *Reading Asian American Literature*, 37.

14. According to Suzan Suleiman in "The 1.5 Generation: Thinking about Child Survivors and the Holocaust," "children under the age of eleven have a different way of understanding what is happening to them from those who are older; the older child possesses the capacity to think hypothetically, to use abstract words appropriately and with understanding, as well as vocabulary to name the experience that the younger child lacks" (282). According to Roberta Culbertson in "Embodied Memory, Transcendence, and Telling: Recounting Trauma," "to narrate a child's memory is not only to confront the confusion of violence in the mind/body, but to construct a culturally acceptable narrative unavailable to the child, to create in some sense then, a fiction, a story the child never knew, from a perspective that was not part of the original scene or experience" (9). See Obayashi, "Mapping the Homeland Memories of 1.5 Generation Vietnamese Americans." This author recognizes the difference between genocide and forced displacement, and does not mean to equate them. Yet she finds these particular studies

162 / NOTES

about traumatic memories and children helpful. They seem to fit with this particular narrative.

15. See Frank Chin and Jeffery Paul Chan, "Racist Love," in Kostelanetz, *Seeing through Shuck*, 65. They write: "For Fu Manchu and the Yellow Peril, there is Charlie Chan and his Number One Son. The unacceptable model is unacceptable because he cannot be controlled by whites. The acceptable model is acceptable because he is tractable. There is racist hate and racist love."

16. At other times, the narrator praises his father's courage and resilience; for example, 321–322.

17. Kim, *Asian American Literature*, 189. Unlike Chin, Pham seems aware of the contradictory space he inhabits, which increases his ambivalence.

18. About the impact of domestic violence among Southeast Asian women, Cheng Imm Tan writes: "In 1987 . . . over 20 Asian refugee and immigrant service workers and community activists, mostly Southeast Asians, gathered for the training on domestic violence. . . . Asian families, they said, were being torn apart by domestic violence. They had witnessed Asian refugee and immigrant women suffering in silence, not knowing what help was available. These women were afraid to tell their stories, afraid to seek outside help, afraid of being blamed, afraid of suffering more violence, and afraid of community censure. For some, the only way out was suicide." See Chen Imm Tan, "Building Shelter: Asian Women and Domestic Violence," in Shah, ed., *Dragon Ladies*, 110–111. Issues of domestic violence come up frequently in Vietnamese American literature. My Vietnamese American studies students always respond strongly to such passages in the text. When I ask them if they consider the father's way of disciplining his children as moderate or excessive, they tend to answer with the word "normal," and go on to talk about comparable beatings they have experienced. For more on the topic, see Nazli Kibria's *Family Tightrope*.

19. "'We didn't judge you so don't judge us,' sneered Aunt Huong. Mom shrieked: 'What do you mean judge? And did your father have a problem with borrowing from us?'"

20. He becomes terrified of ruining his family's plan. "I was too frightened about having told Hoa about our escape. . . .If she'd told anyone, we were all going to jail again," he recalls. "It was my fault she was hanging around the house every day," he added, expressing guilt and torment.

21. These observations coincide with Sigmund Freud's notion that memories are stored in the unconscious. Within this framework, masculinity is like the fantasy or "screen memory" that blocks certain memories. See Freud, *The Interpretation of Dreams*.

22. Bederman, *Manliness and Civilization*. Like race, masculinity is a construct, a historical and ideological process that keeps on changing.

23. Lowe, *Immigrant Acts*, 82.

24. Memmi, *The Colonizer and the Colonized*, 107.

25. Frank Chin, et al., eds. *Aiiieeeee!*, xxx.

26. Perhaps because he is more removed from the Vietnamese than from Vietnamese Americans and because he writes twenty years after Chin, Pham's attitude toward Vietnamese Americans may be more complex than Chin's views of Chinese Americans. Pham is aware of history and the cost it imposes on Vietnamese. He recalls, for instance, a story that a man he stays with one night tells him: "Mr. Ba tells me of how he had served the French, then the Japanese, then the Americans, a lifetime of servitude without rewards" (128).

27. I thank Rebekah Linh Collins for her observation about the narrator's heteronormativity.

28. Lowe, *Immigrant Acts*, 82.

29. I thank Rebekah Linh Collins for this observation.

30. The man adds: "You see, their pond is America. Here, in these hills, in this jungle, they are food. . . . The land took their spirit. I eat what grows out of this land and someday I will return all that I have taken from it. Here is my home, my birthland and my grave."

31. An uses, for instance, multiple voices and rhetorical stances. Although he appears to accept the role of representative of those he calls "his people," that referent constantly changes, depending on the situation. "We" occasionally and strategically refers to Vietnamese Americans, Vietnamese in general (7–8), South Vietnamese (68), the narrator's family, and Asian Americans (39). The pronoun "they" refers alternately to "the" Vietnamese or "the" Americans. And the pronoun "you" refers to those An would like to speak to: non-Vietnamese Americans in the United States and Vietnamese in Viet Nam (155).

32. Fanon, *Black Skin, White Masks*, 52, 66. Fanon gives the example of Jean Veneuse, a black man from the Antilles who attends a French school in France.

33. According to Sucheng Chan, "Children who grow up under the specter of racism suffer from a loss of self-esteem. Some find it difficult to become whole persons who can contribute productively to the progress of our communities. Adults who had repressed or oppressed childhoods tend to eschew the risks of self-expression lest the guts we place onstage for public scrutiny get thrown back at our face to taunt us." Chan, *In Defense of Asian American Studies*, 33.

34. Cao, *Monkey Bridge*, Hereafter in this section pages in this book will be given parenthetically in the text.

35. Du Bois, "Construction Construed."

36. This observation coincides with psychological research on trauma. See, for example, McCann and Pearlman, "Vicarious Traumatization."

37. Edward Said, *Reflections on Exile*, xxxv.

38. Mai criticizes American television reports on the end of the war, saying that it is as "if all of America were holding its breath, waiting for a

diseased body, ravaged and fatigued, and now all too demanding, to let go. Death must be nudged, hurried, if only it could be."

39. I borrow the term "bundle of silences" from Michel-Rolph Trouillot's *Silencing the Past, 27.*

40. I thank Kathy Nguyen for pointing this out to me. The French are often compared by Vietnamese to the Chinese, Japanese, and the Americans.

41. See Gordon, *Assimilation in American Life.*

41. Pham, *Catfish and Mandala,* 25

42. Nguyen-Vo, "Forking Paths: How Shall We Mourn the Dead?" 159.

43. Like a woman warrior, Mai remembers the day she had to fight a dangerous "tiger." She says: "Like the trained warrior that I was, I knew not to oppose an adversary head-on. I stepped to one side, and rather than block its powerful paw with my hand, I pulled it forward, deeper in the direction of its own motion. I used its own momentum to throw it off balance, and with one swift slash of my sword sliced its body in two."

44. De Certeau, *The Practice of Everyday Life,* xix

45. For discussions of America's representation of the Viet Nam War, see Martin Andrew, *Reception of War: Vietnam in American Culture*; Allen Douglas and Ngo Vinh Long, *Coming to Terms: Indochina, the United States, and the War*; John Carlos Rowe and Rick Berg, *The Vietnam War and American Culture*; Richard Morris and Peter Ehrenhaus, eds., *Cultural Legacies of Vietnam: Uses of the Past in the Present.*

46. De Certeau, *The Practice of Everyday Life,* xx.

47. Such practices were not uncommon under French colonialism, when the French granted large land concessions to French companies, colonists, and Vietnamese collaborators at the expense of the peasants. Colonialism strengthened private property rights and individual legal responsibility, disrupting the villages' economic and social structures. As a result, a large number of peasants became landless and women became vulnerable to abuses. For studies addressing the correlation between French colonialism and the strengthening of nationalist and communist forces, see John T. McAlister, *Vietnam: The Origins of Revolution* (1971); William J. Duiker, *The Rise of Nationalism in Vietnam* (1971); David Marr, *Vietnamese Anticolonialism* (1971) and *Vietnamese Tradition on Trial* (1982). Also see Buttinger, *Vietnam: The Unforgettable Tragedy.*

48. An does this by emulating a popular notion of manhood and Mai by mimicking stereotypes. For more discussion about issues of internal oppression, see Omi and Winant, *Racial Formation in the United States,* or Cudd, *Analyzing Oppression.*

49. These stories reproduce forgetting of their own. If Mai readily denounces America's erasure of South Vietnamese, never in her narrative does she address the losses of the North Vietnamese. In "Forking Paths: How Shall We Mourn the Dead?" Thu-Huong Nguyen-Vo writes that "for Vietnamese Americans, most of whom came from South Vietnam, the sources

of forgetting are many." She gives as an example Vietnamese Americans' silencing of "those who died fighting in the National Liberation Front or the People's Army of the Northern Democratic Republic of Vietnam" (159, 170).

5 / Hope and Despair

1. Bakhtin, *Creation of a Prosaics*, 140.
2. Ibid., 141.
3. Ibid.
4. Nam Le, *The Boat*, "Love and Honor and Pity and Pride and Compassion and Sacrifice" (New York: Knopf, 2008), 7. Hereafter in this section, pages in this book are given parenthetically in the text.
5. Tran, personal interview, September 10, 2004.
6. Ibid.
7. Lisa Lowe, *Immigrant Acts*, 83.
8. Tran, personal interview, September 10, 2004.
9. Said, "Reflections on Exile," 113.
10. This example was inspired by an interview with the author on September 10, 2004.
11. See, for example, Pierre Bourdieu, *In Other Words* (Stanford: Stanford University Press, 1990), 10–12. Habitus produces strategies that are not only rational, or based on reason.
12. Naficy, *The Making of Exile Cultures*, 153.
13. "To appease the self still finding comfort in of all things the gravity of words I'll refer to these ruptures as antipoem," the narrator explains (62).
14. The colors gray and blue were suggested by my students. These are the colors that came to their mind after reading *dust and conscience*.
15. My attempt to explain the text here goes against its spirit and intent.
16. *This Is All I Choose To Tell* does not wish to privilege one textual strategy over others but is interested in examining different literary approaches that shed light on the dialectical relationship between literary production and the audience.
17. Dinh, *Fake House*. Hereafter in this section, pages in this book are given parenthetically in the text. Dinh's publications also include *Drunkard Boxing* (1998) and *Blood and Soap* (2004). In 1996, Dinh translated and edited a collection of short stories called *Night, Again: Contemporary Fiction from Vietnam*, which includes works by Vietnamese writers in the diaspora.
18. Dinh, e-mail correspondence, December 7, 2000.
19. Thanks to an anonymous reviewer for related comments, May 16, 2005.
20. Cynthia Enloe writes: "Like sanitation and Christianity, feminine respectability was meant to convince both the colonizing and the colonized peoples that foreign conquest was right and necessary. . . . British colonial officers blamed the existing ideologies of masculinity in the colonized societies for women's degradation; if men's sense of manliness was such that it

didn't include reverence toward women, then they couldn't expect to be allowed to govern their own societies." Enloe, *Bananas, Beaches and Bases*, 48.

21. Chan, "Jackrabbit."

22. Kim, *Asian American Literature*, 190.

23. For a brief review of theories regarding racial and ethnic hierarchies in the United States, see Feagin, *Racial and Ethnic Relations*.

24. This story emerged from Dinh's return to Viet Nam. While in Viet Nam, he gave an interview to Leakthina Chau-Pech Ollier. Says Dinh, "People would ask me: 'You must know somebody, I have a beautiful daughter.' It's pitiful, but who can blame them? You hear the most horrible stories too: like the Taiwanese who come here to get married. There are these middlemen to hook them up. A Taiwanese pays a fee to a middleman, about $10,000, and the middleman goes to a village, finds a girl, then brings her back to Saigon." Winston and Ollier, eds., *Of Vietnam*, 163.

25. See Lowe and Lloyd, eds., *The Politics of Culture*, 27.

26. See Foucault, *Language, Counter-Memory, Practice*.

6 / Reception

1. *The Boat* by Nam Le garnered reviews in major newspapers across the country, including a review by lead critic Michiko Kakutani and an interview with the author in the *New York Times*. The *New York Times* book review and interview were published on two consecutive days on May 13 and May 14, 2008. The book was also reviewed on the front page of the *Datebook* section in the *San Francisco Chronicle* (see Michael McGaha, "'The Boat': Nam Le creates varied worlds," *San Francisco Chronicle*, May 18, 2008) and the *Los Angeles Times* (see Antoine Wilson, July 6, 2008, http://www.latimes.com/features/books/la-bk-namle6–2008jul06,0,7148269,print.story).

2. Nam Le in an interview with Patricia Cohen. Patricia Cohen, "Stories to Explore Someone Else's Skin," *New York Times*, May 14, 2008.

3. Le, *The Boat*, 9. Hereafter in this section, pages in this book are given parenthetically in the text.

4. Palumbo-Liu, *Asian/American*, 395.

5. Ibid., 396–397.

6. Cao, *Monkey Bridge*, 191.

7. De Certeau, *The Practice of Everyday Life*, xix.

8. Cao, *Monkey Bridge*, 38–39. More examples illustrating Mai's stance as a cultural guide can be found on pages 8, 34, 35, 141, 144, and 147.

9. Kim, *Asian American Literature*, 69.

10. See Kakutani, "The American Dream with a Vietnamese Twist."

11. The merits of a book were judged on the basis of what the book had to say or did not say about the evils of communism, and it was not considered an autobiography or an Asian American text. This argument is made in Renny Christopher's *Vietnam War*, 26.

12. J. Douglas and Allen Taylor, "Cycle of Life," *Metro: Silicon Valley's Weekly Newspaper,* October 14–October 20, 1999, 21.

13. Andrew Pham, personal interview, July 10, 2000.

14. Pham, *Catfish and Mandala,* 10.

15. Ibid., 9.

16. Ibid., 292.

17. Ibid., 329. Italics in original. In this passage, An discovers that Vietnamese feel the same ways about Viet Kieu as he feels about tall white men. Tourist guide Calvin says: "We look like monkeys because you make us look like monkeys just by your existence." Ibid., 330.

18. Lowell Weiss, "Voices from Vietnam," *Boston Globe,* February 27, 1994, A14.

19. Ibid.

20. She adds: "I have siblings in life and the girl does not have living siblings in the book." Thy Tran, "Modern Woman," 84.

21. Adair Lara, "A Girl's Flight to a Bright, Harsh Land," *San Francisco Chronicle,* May 18, 2003, M3.

22. le thi diem thúy, *The Gangster We Are All Looking For,* 99.

23. Kim, *Asian American Literature,* 18

24. Most popular Asian American texts emphasize mother-daughter relationships. Critic Lisa Lowe argued that the repetition of such stories "essentializes Asian American culture, obscuring the particularities and incommensurabilities of class, gender, and national diversities among Asians." Lowe, *Immigrant Acts,* 63.

25. Mehegan, "Refuge in Her Writing,"

26. Inside jacket of *The Sacred Willow.*

27. Monique T. D. Truong, personal interview, March 4, 2002.

28. Monique Truong, lecture at the University of California at Santa Cruz in Karen Yamashita's class, October 7, 2009.

29. Christopher Benfey, "'The Book of Salt': Alice B. Toklas's Cook's Book," *New York Times,* April 6, 2003. http://www.nytimes.com/2003/04/06/books/review/06BENFEYT.html?pagewanted=1, 1, 2, 4.30. Kingston, "Cultural Mis-reading by American Reviewers," 55–65.

31. Said, *Orientalism,* 49.

32. Joy Press, "The Hunger Artists: More Novels about Asians and Food," *Village Voice,* March 26–April 1, 2003. http://www.villagevoice.com/books/0313,press,42831,10.html.

33. Kim, "Asian Americans and American Popular Culture," 100.

34. See Roger Abrahams, "Equal Opportunity Eating: A Structural Excursus on Things of the Mouth," in Linda Keller Brown and Kay Mussell, eds., *Ethnic and Regional Foodways in the United States: The Performance of Group Identity* (Knoxville: University of Tennessee Press, 1984), 19–36.

35. Truong, *The Book of Salt,* 261.

36. See http://www.talawas.org/talaDB/showFile.php?res=4199&rb=0
102.

37. Dinh, *Fake House*, 105.

38. Ibid., 107.

39. Ibid., 144–145.

40. Ibid., 145.

41. Said, *The World, the Text, and the Critic*, 94.

42. For instance, Jade Ngoc Quang Huynh, author of *South Wind Changing*, says: "Listen to the publisher. First they tell me that my book is wonderful and then they tell me it will not sell. They told me to add more violence [from the Vietnam War]. If I say what I really want, I will never be published." Personal interview, June 24, 1994. Another example is Nguyen Qui Duc, author of *Where the Ashes Are*, who for years worked on a novel situated in Morocco. The main character of his story is an Englishman who tries to "go native." Nguyen's goal was to show the hypocrisy of this position. Nguyen's publisher successfully dissuaded him from writing the story, claiming it to be too psychological and not "Vietnamese" enough. Instead, Nguyen says he was hired to write a screenplay for Francis Ford Coppola about a GI returning to Viet Nam to face the consequences of his twenty-year-old love affair(s). Nguyen laments the fact that he can only write about Viet Nam: "After this movie will be over, no matter how good of a job I do, they may never hire me again. They will go on with other projects that have nothing to do with Viet Nam, and they won't think about me anymore. They can only see me as a Viet Nam specialist. . . . And meanwhile I still have to sell my soul." Personal interview, April 10, 1998.

43. Butler, public reading, Berkeley, CA, September 16, 1993.

44. Butler, *A Good Scent from A Strange Mountain*, 47–50.

45. Rivers, "Oriental Girls," 160.

46. Towers, "Far from Saigon."

47. Donna Seaman's full quote: "Dinh's painful stories feature tricky dialogue rife with pointedly racist misinformation, linguistic confusion, and dunning vulgarities, and evoke a skeptical yet tender vision of humanity, similar in spirit, if not in literary artistry, to that of Sherman Alexie and Aleksandar Hemon." Seaman, "Review of *Fake House*."

48. Monique T. D. Truong has made the same argument in "The Reception of Robert Olen Butler's *A Good Scent from a Strange Mountain*."

49. Dinh, *Fake House*, 108.

50. Ibid.

51. In an e-mail correspondence, Linh Dinh explains: "In this context, it's because she's younger than him, though in Vietnamese, he'd say 'em,' 'little sister.' No one would say 'chi,' 'bigger sister' to a prostitute. I used 'brother' to imply 'anh,' 'bigger brother,' because that's how a prostitute, or a woman in a romantic situation, would address a man. 'Sister' would sound

too formal in this case. A Vietnamese reader would think of 'chi,' which would make this passage unrealistic and even comic"; June 3, 2005.

52. Dinh, *Fake House*, 109.

53. Linh Dinh, e-mail correspondence, April 7, 2005.

54. Foucault, *Language, Counter-Memory, Practice*, 169.

Conclusion

1. I agree with Lisa Lowe when she writes: "The concept of 'strategic essentialism' suggests that it is possible to utilize specific signifiers or racialized ethnic identity, such as 'Asian American,' for the purpose of contesting and disrupting the discourses that exclude Asian Americans, while simultaneously revealing the internal contradictions and slippages of 'Asian American' so as to insure that such essentialism will not be reproduced and proliferated by the very apparatuses we seek to disempower." In *Immigrant Acts*, 82.

2. Andrew Lam (a member of the 1.5 generation) explains that in view of this back-and-forth movement between remembering and forgetting, the notion of home for him has "less to do with geography than imagination and memories." Lam, *Perfume Dreams*, 15.

3. Jinqi Ling, *Narrating Nationalism: Ideology and Form in Asian American Literature* (New York: Oxford University Press, 1998), 30.

4. Ibid., 482.

Bibliography

Abram, Linsey. "Vietnam, East and West." *New York Times*, June 15, 1986. http://query.nytimes.com/gst/fullpage.html?res=9A0DEFD8 1638F936A25755C0A960948260.

Anti-Asian Violence: Oversight Hearing before the Subcommittee on Civil and Constitutional Rights of the Committee on the Judiciary, House of Representatives, One Hundredth Congress, first session, Nov. 10, 1987.

Bakhtin, Mikhail. *Creation of a Prosaics.* Edited by Gary Saul Morson and Caryl Emerson. Stanford: Stanford University Press, 1990.

——. *The Dialogic Imagination: Four Essays.* Austin: University of Texas Press, 1981.

Balaban, John, and Nguyen Qui Duc, eds. *Vietnam: A Traveler's Literary Companion.* San Francisco: Whereabouts Press, 1996.

Barkan, Elazar, and Marie-Denise Shelton, eds. *Borders, Exiles, Diaspora.* Stanford: Stanford University Press, 1988.

Bates, Milton. *The Wars We Took to Vietnam: Cultural Conflict and Storytelling.* Berkeley: University of California Press, 1996.

Baudrillard, Jean. *Simulations\,.* translated by Paul Foss, Paul Patton, and Philip Beitchman. New York: Semiotext(e), 1983.

Bederman, Gail. *Manliness and Civilization: A Cultural History of Gender and Race in the United States, 1880–1917.* Chicago: University of Chicago Press, 1995.

Benfey, Christopher. "Ordering In," *New York Times Book Re-*

view, April 6, 2003. http://www.nytimes.com/2003/04/06/books/review/06BENFEYT.html?pagewanted=1.

Benjamin, Walter. *Illuminations: Essays and Reflections*, edited by Hannah Arendt, translated by Harry John. New York: Schocken Books, 1968.

———. "Paris, Capital of the Nineteenth Century." In *Reflections: Essays, Aphorisms, Autobiographical Writings*, edited by Peter Demetz, translated by Edmund Jephcott, 146–162. New York: Schocken Books, 1986.

Bhabha, Homi K. *The Location of Culture*. New York: Routledge, 1994.

———. "The Third Space: Interview with Homi Bhabha." In *Identity, Community, Culture, Difference*, edited by Jonathan Rutherford, 207–221. London: Lawrence & Wishart, 1990.

Blum, William. "A Brief History of U.S. Interventions: 1945 to the Present." *Z Magazine*, June 1999. http://www.thirdworldtraveler.com/Blum/US_Interventions_WBlumZ.html.

Bolinao 52. Documentary film directed by Duc Nguyen. ITVS, 2007. http://www.bolinao52.com.

Bong-Wright, Jackie. *Autumn Cloud: From Vietnamese War Widow to American Activist*. Sterling, Va.: Capital Books, 2002.

Bourdieu, Pierre. *Masculine Domination*. Stanford: Stanford University Press, 2001.

Bousquet, Gisele. *Behind the Bamboo Hedge: The Impact of Homeland Politics in the Parisian Vietnamese Community*. Ann Arbor: University of Michigan Press, 1991.

Brown, Wendy. *Regulating Aversion: Tolerance in the Age of Identity and Empire*. Princeton: Princeton University Press, 2006.

Bui, Diem and David Chanoff. *In the Jaws of History*. Boston: Houghton Mifflin, 1987.

Butler, Judith. *Gender Trouble: Feminism and the Subversion of Identity*. New York: Routledge, 2006.

Butler, Robert Olen. *A Good Scent from a Strange Mountain*. New York: Henry Holt, 1992.

———. Personal interview, September 16, 1993, Berkeley.

Buttinger, Joseph. *Vietnam: The Unforgettable Tragedy*. New York: Horizon Press, 1977.

Campomanes, Oscar V. "Filipinos in the United States and Their Literature in Exile." In *Reading the Literature of Asian America*, edited by Shirley Geok-lin Lim and Amy Ling, 62–124. Philadelphia: Temple University Press, 1992.

Cantrell, Nancy Tran. *Seeds of Hope.* Plymouth, Mass.: Five Corners Publications, 1999.

Cao, Lan. *Monkey Bridge.* New York: Viking, 1997.

Cao, Tan. *Poetry by Cao Tan.* Westminster: But Lua Publishing House, 1977.

Capps, Walter. *The Unfinished War: Vietnam and the American Conscience.* Boston: Beacon, 1990.

Caruth, Cathy. *Unclaimed Experience: Trauma, Narrative, and History.* Baltimore: Johns Hopkins University Press, 1996.

Cesaire, Aimé. *Cahier d'un retour au pays natal.* Paris: Présence Africaine, 1983.

Chambers, Iain. *Migrancy, Culture, Identity.* London: Routledge, 1994.

Chan, Jeffery Paul. "Jackrabbit." In *Yardbird Reader,* edited by Frank Chin and Shawn Hsu Wong, vol. 3, 217–238. Berkeley: Yardbird Publishing, 1974.

Chan, Sucheng. *In Defense of Asian American Studies: The Politics of Teaching and Program Building.* Urbana: University of Illinois Press, 2005.

———, ed. *The Vietnamese American 1.5 Generation: Stories of War, Revolution, Flight, and New Beginnings.* Philadelphia: Temple University Press, 2006.

Charter, Samuel, and Joe MacDonald. "I-Feel-Like-I'm-Fixin'-To-Die Rag." *I-Feel-Like-I'm-Fixin'-To-Die Rag.* Vanguard VSD 79266. Audiocassette. New York: Vanguard Studios Traditional Music, BMI. 1965.

Chen, Ling. "Communication in Intercultural Relationships." In *Cross-Cultural Intercultural Communication,* edited by William B. Gudykunst. 241–258. Thousand Oaks, Cal.: Sage, 2003.

Cheng, Wendy. "Remodeling the Minority." *Hyphen* 8 (Winter 2005): 26–29.

Cheung, King-Kok. *Articulated Silences.* Ithaca: Cornell University Press, 1993.

———. "Re-viewing Asian American Literary Studies." In *An Interethnic Companion to Asian American Literature,* 1–38. New York: Cambridge University Press, 1997.

———. "The Woman Warrior versus the Chinaman Pacific: Must a Chinese American Critic Choose between Feminism and Heroism?" In *Conflicts in Feminism,* edited by Marianne Hirsch and Evelyn Fox-Keller, 234–251. New York: Routledge, 1990.

Chin, Frank. "Food for All His Dead." In *Asian American Authors,* edited by Kai-Yu Hsu and Helen Paubinskas, 47–61. Boston: Houghton Mifflin, 1972.

Chin, Frank, et al., eds. *Aiiieeeee! An Anthology of Asian-American Writers*. New York: Anchor Books, 1975.

Christopher, Renny. "Blue Dragon, White Tiger: The Bicultural Stance of Vietnamese American Literature." In *Reading the Literatures of Asian America*, edited by Shirley Geok-Lin Lim and Amy Ling, 259–270. Philadelphia: Temple University Press, 1992.

———. *The Vietnam War, the American War: Images and Representations in Euro-American and Vietnamese Exile Narratives*. Amherst: University of Massachusetts Press, 1995.

Chuh, Kandice. *Imagine Otherwise: On Asian Americanist Critique*. Durham: Duke University Press, 2003.

Clifford, James, and George E. Marcus, eds. *Writing Culture: The Poetics and Politics of Ethnography*. Berkeley: University of California Press, 1986.

Cudd, Ann E. *Analyzing Oppression*. Oxford: Oxford University Press, 2006.

Culbertson, Roberta. "Embodied Memory, Transcendence, and Telling: Recounting Trauma." *New Literary History* 26.1 (1995): 169–195.

De Certeau, Michel. *The Practice of Everyday Life*, translated by Steven Rendall. Berkeley : University of California Press, 1984.

Deuleuze, Gilles, and Félix Guattari. *A Thousand Plateaus: Capitalism and Schizophrenia*, translated by Brian Massumi. Minneapolis: University of Minnesota Press, 1987.

Dinh, Linh. *Blood and Soap*. New York: Seven Stories Press, 2004.

———. *Drunkard Boxing*. Philadelphia: Singing Horse Press, 1998.

———. *Fake House*. New York: Seven Stories Press, 2000.

———, ed. *Night, Again: Contemporary Fiction from Vietnam*. New York: Seven Stories Press, 1996.

Dirlik, Arif. "Colonialism, Globalization and Culture: Reflections on September 11th." In *Asian Americans: On War and Peace*, edited by Russell Leong and Don Nakanishi. Los Angeles: UCLA Asian American Studies Center, (2002), 107–118.

Do, Hien Duc. *The Vietnamese Americans*. Westport, Conn.: Greenwood Press, 1999.

Douglas, Allen, and Ngo Vinh Long, eds. *Coming to Terms: Indochina, the United States, and the War*. Boulder: Westview, 1991.

Douglas, J., and Allen Taylor. "Cycle of Life." *Metro: Silicon Valley's Weekly Newspaper.* October 14– October 20, 1999, 21–28.

Dowers, John. *War without Mercy: Race and Power in the Pacific War.* New York: Pantheon, 1980.

Du Bois, W.E.B. "The Souls of Black Folk." In *Three Negro Classics,* 207–390. New York: Avon, 1965.

Dubois, Thomas A. "Construction Construed: The Representation of Southeast Asian Refugees in Academic, Popular, and Adolescent Discourse." *Amerasia Journal* 19.3 (1993): 1–25.

Duong Thu Huong. *Novel without a Name,* translated by Pham Huy Duong and Nina McPherson. New York: William Morrow, 1995.

———. *Paradise of the Blind,* translated by Phan Huy Duong and Nina McPherson. New York: William Morrow, 1991.

Duffy, Daniel, ed. "Editor's Note: What Is This Book?" In *Viet Nam Forum* 16, 7–10. New Haven: Yale University Council on Southeast Asia Studies, 1997.

Duiker, William J. *The Rise of Nationalism in Vietnam: 1900–1941.* Ithaca: Cornell University Press, 1976.

Duong, Lan. "Desire and Design: Technological Display in the Vietnamese American Café and Karaoke Bar." *Amerasia Journal* 29.1 (2003): 97–115.

Elliott Duong Van Mai. *The Sacred Willow: Four Generations in the Life of a Vietnamese Family.* New York: Oxford University Press, 1999.

Eng, David L., and Alice Y. Hom. *Q&A: Queer in Asian America.* Philadelphia: Temple University Press, 1998.

Enloe, Cynthia. *Bananas, Beaches & Bases: Making Feminist Sense of International Politics.* Berkeley: University of California Press, 1990.

Espiritu, Yen Le. *Asian American Women and Men: Labor, Laws and Love.* Thousand Oaks, Cal.: Sage, 1997.

———. "Toward a Critical Refugee Study: The Vietnamese Refugee Subject in US Scholarship." *Journal of Vietnamese Study* 1.1–2 (2006): 410–433.

———. "Thirty Years AfterWARd: The Endings That Are Not Over." *Amerasia Journal: 30 Years AfterWARd* 31.2 (2005): xiii–xxiii.

Fanon, Frantz. *Black Skin, White Masks.* London: MacGibbon and Kee, 1952.

———. *The Wretched of the Earth.* New York: Grove, 1963.

Feagin, Joe. *Racial and Ethnic Relations.* Englewood Cliffs, N.J.: Prentice Hall, 1989.

Ferguson, Russell. "Introduction: Invisible Center." In *Out There: Marginalization and Contemporary Culture,* edited by Russell Ferguson, Martha Gever, Trinh T. Minh-ha, and Cornel West, 9–17. New York: New Museum of Contemporary Art; Cambridge: MIT Press, 1990.

Fitzgerald, Frances. *Fire in the Lake: The Vietnamese and the Americans in Vietnam.* Boston: Little, Brown, 2002.

Foucault, Michel. "Film and Popular Memory: An Interview with Michel Foucault," translated by Martin Jordan. *Radical Philosophy* 11 (1975): 24–29.

———. *The History of Sexuality: An Introduction,* translated by Robert Hurley. New York: Vintage, 1990.

———. *Language, Counter-Memory, Practice: Selected Essays and Interviews,* edited by Donald Bouchard, translated by Donald Bouchard and Sherry Simon. Ithaca: Cornell University Press, 1977.

———. "Of Other Spaces.\," translated by Jay Miskowiec. *Diacritics* 16.1 (Spring 1986): 22–27.

Freeman, James M. *Changing Identities: Vietnamese Americans 1975–1995.* Boston: Allyn and Bacon, 1995.

———. *Hearts of Sorrow: Vietnamese American Lives.* Stanford: Stanford University Press, 1989.

Freud, Sigmund. *The Interpretation of Dreams.* New York: Avon Books, 1965.

From Hollywood to Hanoi. Documentary film directed by Tiana Thi Thanh Nha. Indochina Film Arts Foundation, 1993.

Fujitani, T., Geoffrey M. White, and Lisa Yoneyama, eds. *Perilous Memories: The Asia-Pacific War(s).* Durham: Duke University Press, 2001.

Gaiduk, Ilya. *Confronting Vietnam: Soviet Policy toward the Indochina Conflict, 1954–1963.* Stanford: Stanford University Press, 2003.

Gettleman, Marvin E., Jane Franklin, Marilyn B. Young, and H. Bruce Franklin, eds. *Vietnam and America: A Documented History.* New York: Grove Press, 1995.

Giroux, Henry. *Living Dangerously: Multiculturalism and the Politics of Difference.* New York: Peter Lang, 1993.

Gordon, Milton A. *Assimilation in American Life: The Role of Race, Religion, and National Origins.* New York: Oxford University Press, 1964.

Ha, Kim. Personal interview, July 9, 1999, Los Angeles.

———. *Stormy Escape: A Vietnamese Woman's Account of Her 1980 Flight through Cambodia to Thailand*. Jefferson, N.C.: McFarland, 1992.

Ha, Oanh K. "Vietnam Refugees Find a Fresh Start: Program Resettles Those Stranded in Legal Limbo." *San Jose Mercury News*, September 28, 2005, 17A.

Haines, David. *Refugees in America in the 1990s: A Reference Handbook*. Westport, Conn.: Greenwood Press, 1996.

———. *Refugees in the United States: A Reference Handbook*. Westport, Conn.: Greenwood Press, 1985.

Hall, Stuart. "Cultural Identity and Diaspora." In *Identity: Community, Cultural, Difference*, edited by Jonathan Rutherford, 222–237. London: Lawrence & Wishart, 1990.

Hardt, Michael, and Antonio Negri. *Empire*. Cambridge: Harvard University Press, 2000.

Hartman, Geoffrey. *Minor Prophecies: The Literary Essay in the Culture Wars*. Cambridge: Harvard University Press, 1991.

Hayslip, Le Ly, and James Wurts. *When Heaven and Earth Changed Places*. New York: Doubleday, 1989.

Harris, Marvin. *Pattern of Race in the Americas*. New York: Norton, 1964.

Harvey, David. *The Condition of Postmodernity*. Cambridge: Blackwell, 1990.

Hein, Jeremy. *From Vietnam, Laos, and Cambodia: A Refugee Experience in the United States*. New York: Twayne, 1995.

———. *States and International Migrants: The Incorporation of Indochinese Refugees in the United States and France*. Boulder: Westview, 1993.

Herring, George. *America's Longest War: The United States and Vietnam, 1950–1975*. New York: McGraw-Hill, 1996.

Hing, Bill O. *Making and Remaking Asian America through Immigration Policy, 1850–1990*. Stanford: Stanford University Press, 1993.

Ho, Anh Thai. *Behind the Red Mist: Short Fiction by Ho Anh Thai*, edited by Wayne Karlin, translated by Nguyen Qui Duc, Regina Abrami, Bac Hoai Tran, and Dana Sachs. Willimantic, Conn.: Curbstone Press, 1998.

Huu, Thinh. *The Time Tree: Poems by Huu Thin*. Translated by George Evans and Nguyen Qui Duc. Willimantic, Conn.: Curbstone Press, 2003.

Huynh, Jade Ngoc Quang. *South Wind Changing*. Saint Paul: Gray-wolf Press, 1994.

———. Telephone conversation with author, June 24, 1994.

Huyssen, Andreas. *Twilight Memories*. New York: Routledge, 1995.

Isaacs, Arnold. *Without Honor: Defeat in Vietnam and Cambodia*. Baltimore: Johns Hopkins University Press, 1983.

Jameson, Frederic. "Third-World Literature in the Era of Multinational Capitalism." *Social Text* 15 (1986): 65–88.

Janette, Michelle. "Vietnamese American Literature in English, 1963–1994." *Amerasia Journal* 29.1 (2003): 267–286.

Kahin, George T. *Intervention: How America Became Involved in Vietnam*. New York: Alfred A. Knopf, 1986.

Kakutani, Michiko. "The American Dream with a Vietnamese Twist." *New York Times*, August 19, 1997, C13.

Kang, Cecilia. "Stereotypes Cited in Police Slaying." *San Jose Mercury News*, October 17, 2003.

Karlin, Wayne, Le Minh Khue, and Truong Vu, eds. *The Other Side of Heaven: Postwar Fiction by Vietnamese and American Writers*. Willimantic, Conn.: Curbstone Press, 1995.

Kiang, Peter Nien-Chu. "Checking Southeast Asian American Realities in Pan-Asian American Agendas," *AAPI Nexus: Asian Americans and Pacific Islanders, Policy Practice and Community* 2.1 (Winter/Spring 2004): 48–76.

Kibria, Nazli. *Family Tightrope: The Changing Lives of Vietnamese Americans*. Princeton: Princeton University Press, 1993.

Kim, Daniel Young-Hoon. "Race, Writing and Manhood: Ambivalent Identifications and American Literary Identity in Frank Chin and Ralph Ellison." Unpublished essay. University of California, Berkeley, 1997.

Kim, Elaine. *Asian American Literature: An Introduction to the Writings and Their Social Context*. Philadelphia: Temple University Press, 1982.

———. "Asian Americans and American Popular Culture." In *Asian American History Dictionary*, edited by Robert H. Kim. New York: Greenwood Press, 1986: 99–114.

———. "Defining Asian American Realities through Literature." *Cultural Critique* 6 (1987): 87–112.

———. *Reading the Literature of Asian America*. Philadelphia: Temple University Press, 1992.

———. "Sex Tourism in Asia: A Reflection of Political and Economic

Inequality." In *Korean Women in Transition: At Home and Abroad.* Los Angeles: California State University, Los Angeles Center for Korean-American and Korean Studies, 1987.

Kingston, Maxine Hong. "Cultural Mis-readings by American Reviewers." In *Asian and Western Writers in Dialogue: New Cultural Identities,* edited by Guy Amirthayagam, 55–65. London: Macmillan, 1982.

———. *The Woman Warrior: Memoirs of a Girlhood among Ghosts.* New York: Vintage, 1977.

Kirkus Review. New York: Kirkus Service, November 15, 1993.

Kolko, Gabriel. *Anatomy of a War: Vietnam, the United States, and the Modern Historical Experience.* New York: Pantheon, 1985.

Kostelanetz, Richard. *Seeing through Shuck.* New York: Ballantine, 1972.

Kunz, E. F. "The Refugee in Flight: Kinetic Models and Forms of Displacement." *International Migration Review* 7.2 (1973): 125–146.

Lacy, Robert. "Author's War Experience Helps Form Collection of Stories 20 Years Later." *Minneapolis Star Tribune* [Metro edition], March 15, 1992, 11.F.

Lai, Eric, and Dennis Arguelles, eds. *The New Face of Asian Pacific America: Numbers, Diversity & Change in the 21st Century.* San Francisco: Asian Week and UCLA Asian American Studies Center, 1998.

Lam, Andrew. "A Child of Two Worlds." *San Francisco Examiner,* April 23, 2000.

———. *Perfume Dreams.* Berkeley: Heyday Books, 2005.

———. Personal e-mail, December 7, 2005.

———. Personal interview, June 4, 1994, San Francisco.

Lam, Mariam Beevi. "The Passing of Literary Traditions: The Figure of the Woman from Vietnamese Nationalism to Vietnamese American Transnationalism." *Amerasia Journal* 23.2 (1997): 27–53.

———. "Surfin' Vietnam: Trauma, Memory and Cultural Politics." Unpublished manuscript, 2008.

Langworthy, Christian Nguyen. *The Geography of War.* Oklahoma City: Cooper House, 1995.

Lara, Adair. "A Girl's Flight to a Bright, Harsh Land." *San Francisco Chronicle,* May 18, 2003, M3.

Larsen, Wendy Wilder, and Tran Thi Nga. *Shallow Graves: Two Women in Vietnam.* New York: Perennial Library, 1987.

Le, Minh Khue. *The Stars, the Earth, the River: Short Stories by Le*

Minh Khue, edited by Wayne Karlin, translated by Dana Sachs and Bac Hoai Tran. Willimantic, Conn.: Curbstone Press, 1997.

Le, Nam. *The Boat*. New York: Knopf, 2008.

Le, Ngoan. "Policy for a Community 'At-Risk.'" In *The State of Asian Pacific America: Policy Issues to the Year 2020*, 167–188. Los Angeles: LEAP Asian Pacific American Public Policy Institute and UCLA Asian American Studies Center, 1993.

Le, Samantha. *Little Sister Left Behind*. San Jose: Chusma House, 2007.

le, thi diem thúy. *The Gangster We Are All Looking For*. New York: Knopf, 2003.

Lee, Rachel. *The Americas of Asian American Literature: Gendered Fictions of Nation and Transnation*. Princeton: Princeton University Press, 1999.

Leiwei Li, David. *Imagining the Nation: Asian American Literature and Cultural Consent*. Stanford: Stanford University Press, 1998.

Leong, Russell C., Brandy Liên Worrall, Yen Lê Espiritu, and Nguyen-Vo Thu-Huong, eds. "'30 Years AfterWARd': Vietnamese Americans & U.S. Empire."*Amerasia Journal* 31.2.

Leong, Russell C., Brandy Liên Worrall, and Linda Trinh Vo, eds. "Vietnamese Americans: Diaspora and Dimensions." *Amerasia Journal* 29.1.

Lieberman, Kim-An. *Breaking the Map*. Yakima, Wash.: Blue Begonia Press, 2008.

Lim, Shirley Geok-Lin. "The Ambivalent American: Asian American Literature on the Cusp." In *Reading the Literature of Asian America*, 13–32. Philadelphia: Temple University Press, 1992.

Lim, Shirley Geok-Lin, and Cheng Lok Chua, eds. *Tilting the Continent: Southeast Asian American Writing*. Minneapolis: New Rivers Press, 2000.

Lim-Hing, Sharon, ed. *The Very Inside: An Anthology of Writings by Asia and Pacific Islander Lesbians and Bisexual Women*. Toronto: Sister Vision Press, 1994.

Ling, Amy. "Chinese American Women Writers: The Tradition behind Maxine Hong Kingston." In *Redefining American Literary History*, edited by A. LaVonne Brown Rouff and Jerry W. Ward Jr., 333–347. New York: Modern Language Association of America, 1990.

Lloyd, David. *Nationalism and Minor Literature: James Clarence Mangan and the Emergence of Irish Cultural Nationalism*. Berkeley: University of California Press, 1987.

Lowe, Lisa. *Immigrant Acts: On Asian American Cultural Politics.* Durham: Duke University Press, 1996.

———. "Literary Nomadics in Francophone Allegories of Postcolonialism: Pham Van Ky and Tahar Ben Jelloun." *Yale French Studies, Post/Colonial Conditions* 82.1.

Lowe, Lisa, and David Lloyd, eds. *The Politics of Culture in the Shadow of Capital.* Durham: Duke University Press, 1997.

Lowe, Peter, ed. *The Vietnam War.* New York: St. Martin's, 1998.

Lu, Van Thanh. *The Inviting Call of Wandering Souls: Memoir of an ARVN Liaison Officer to United States Forces in Vietnam Who Was Imprisoned in Communist Re-education Camps and Then Escaped.* Jefferson, N.C.: McFarland, 1997.

Marchetti, Gina. *Romance and the "Yellow Peril": Race, Sex, and Discursive Strategies in Hollywood Fiction.* Berkeley: University of California Press, 1993.

Marr, David. *Vietnamese Anticolonialism, 1885–1925.* Berkeley: University of California Press, 1971.

———. *Vietnamese Tradition on Trial.* Berkeley: University of California Press, 1981.

Martin, Andrew. *Receptions of War: Vietnam in American Culture.* Norman: University of Oklahoma Press, 1993.

Mayer-Rieckh, Elizabeth. "'Beyond Concrete and Steel': Power-Relations and Gender, The Case of Vietnamese Women in the Detention Centers in Hong Kong." Masters thesis, Institute of Social Studies, The Hague, 1993.

Mazumdar, Sucheta. "Asian American Studies and Asian Studies: Rethinking Roots." In *Asian Americans: Comparative and Global Perspectives,* edited by Shirley Hune, Hyung-Chan Kim, Stephen S. Fugita, and Amy Ling, 29–44. Pullman: Washington State University Press, 1991.

McCann, L., and L. Pearlman. "Vicarious Traumatization: A Framework for Understanding the Psychological Effects of Working with Victims." *Journal of Traumatic Stress* 3 (1990): 131–149.

Mehegan, David. "Refuge in Her Writing: Out of Her Family's Painful Emigration from Vietnam, le thi diem thuy Has Crafted a Quietly Powerful Novel." *Boston Globe,* June 2, 2003, B7.

Memmi, Albert. *The Colonizer and the Colonized.* New York: Orion Press, 1965.

———. *Portrait du colonisé.* Paris: Gallimard, 1985.

Min, Pyong Gap, ed. *Asian Americans: Contemporary Trends and Issues*. Thousand Oaks, Cal.: Sage, 1995.

Mohanty, Chandra Talpade. "Cartographies of Struggle: Third World Women and the Politics of Feminism." In *Third World Women and the Politics of Feminism*, edited by Chandra Talpade Mohanty, Ann Russo, and Lourdes Torres, 1–50. Bloomington: Indiana University Press, 1991.

Mong-Lan. *Song of the Cicadas*. Amherst: University of Massachusetts Press, 2001.

Monterey's Boat People. Documentary directed by Spencer Nakasako and Vincent DiGirolamo. NAATA, 1982.

Morokvasic, Miriana. "Women in Migration: Beyond the Reductionist Outlook." In *One Way Ticket: Migration and Female Labour*, edited by Annie Phizaklea. London: Routledge and Kegan Paul, 1983.

Morris, Richard, and Peter Ehrenhaus, eds. *Cultural Legacies of Vietnam: Uses of the Past in the Present*. Norwood: Ablex, 1990.

Mura, David. *Turning Japanese: Memoirs of a Sansei*. New York: Pantheon, 1991.

Mydans, Seth. "The Rough Drafts of Vietnamese-American History." *New York Times*, May 17, 2006. http://www.nytimes.com/2006/05/17/us/17yendo.html?n=Top/Reference/Times%20Topics/Subjects/I/Immigration%20and%20Refugees.

Naficy, Hamid. *The Making of Exile Cultures: Iranian Television in Los Angeles*. Minneapolis: University of Minnesota Press, 1993.

Neilson, Jim. *Warring Fictions: American Literary Culture and the Vietnam War Narrative*. Jackson: University Press of Mississippi, 1998.

Nguyen, Dinh Hoa. *From the City inside the Red River: A Cultural Memoir of Mid-Century Vietnam*. Jefferson, N.C.: McFarland, 1999.

Nguyen, Do, and Paul Hoover. *Black Dog, Black Night*. Minneapolis: Milkweed, 2008.

Nguyen, Huy Thiep. *The General Retires and Other Stories*, translated by Greg Lockhart. Singapore: Oxford University Press, 1992.

Nguyen, Kien. *The Tapestries: A Novel*. Boston: Little, Brown, 2002.

———. *The Unwanted: A Memoir*. Boston: Little, Brown, 2001.

Nguyen, Ngoc. Personal interview, November 19, 2005, Petaluma, Cal.

Nguyen, Ngoc Ngan, and E. E. Richey. *The Will of Heaven: One Vietnamese and the End of His World*. New York: E. P. Dutton, 1982.

Nguyen, Qui Duc. "Home Is Where You Hang Yourself: True Confessions of an Accidental Californian." In *Veterans of War, Veterans of*

Peace, edited by Maxine Hong Kingston, 393–394. Kihei, Hawai'i: Koa Books, 2006.

———. "Now Is the Time for the Majority to Speak up against the Vocal Clamor for Artistic Censorship at the Bowers Museum." *Los Angeles Times*, Orange County edition, August 8, 1999, B9.

———. Personal interview, April 10, 1998, San Francisco.

———. Personal interview, November 10, 2005, San Francisco.

———. *Where the Ashes Are: The Odyssey of a Vietnamese Family*. Reading, Mass.: Addison-Wesley, 1994.

Nguyen, Thi Thu-Lâm, Edith Kreisler, and Sandra Christenson. *Fallen Leaves: Memoirs of a Vietnamese Woman from 1940 to 1975*. New Haven: Southeast Asia Studies, Yale University, 1989.

Nguyen, Viet Thanh. "Book Reviews." *Amerasia Journal* 31.2 (2005): 190.

———. "A Destructive Obsession: Vietnamese-Americans Are Held Hostage by Fanatic Anti-communist Faction." *Orange County Register*, June 6, 2004.

———. *Race and Resistance: Literature and Politics in Asian America*. Oxford: Oxford University Press, 2002.

———. "Representing Reconciliation: Le Ly Hayslip and the Victimized Body." *Positions* 5.2 (1997): 605–642.

Nguyen-Vo, Thu-Huong. "Forking Paths: How Shall We Mourn the Dead?" In "'30 Years AfterWARd': Vietnamese Americans & U.S. Empire." *Amerasia Journal* 31.2 (2005): 157–175.

Ninh, Bao. *The Sorrow of War*, edited by Frank Palmos, translated by Vo Bang Thanh, Phan Thanh Hoa, and Katerina Pierce. London: Secker & Warburg, 1993.

Nora, Pierre. *Les lieux de mémoire*. Paris: Gallimard, 1984.

———. "Between Memory and History: Les lieux de mémoire." *Representations* 26 (Spring 1989): 7–24.

Norindr, Panivong. *Phantasmatic Indochina: French Colonial Ideology in Architecture, Film, and Literature*. Durham: Duke University Press, 1996.

Novich, Peter. *That Noble Dream: The "Objective Question" and the American Historical Profession*. New York: Cambridge University Press, 1988.

Obayashi, Yuki. "Mapping the Homeland Memories of 1.5 Generation Vietnamese Americans." Masters thesis. San Francisco State University, December 2007.

Ollier, Leakthina Chau-Pech. "Consuming Culture: Linda Le Autofiction." In Jane Bradley Winston and Leakthina Chau-Pech Ollier, *Of Vietnam: Identities in Dialogue*, 241–251. New York: Palgrave, 2001.

Olney, James. "Autobiography and the Cultural Moment: A Thematic, Historical, and Bibliographical Introduction." In *Autobiography: Essays Theoretical and Critical*, edited by James Olney, 3–27. Princeton: Princeton University Press, 1980.

Omatsu, Glen. *The State of Asian America*. Boston: South End Press, 1994.

Omi, Michael, and Howard Winant. *Racial Formation in the United States: From the 1960s to the 1980s*. New York: Routledge and Kegan Paul, 1986.

Ong, Paul, Edna Bonacich, and Lucie Cheng, eds. *The New Asian Immigration in Los Angeles and Global Restructuring*. Philadelphia: Temple University Press, 1994.

Osborne, Milton. "The Indochinese Refugees: Cause and Effects." *International Affairs* 56.1 (1980): 37–53.

Palumbo-Liu, David. *Asian/American: Historical Crossings of a Racial Frontier*. Stanford: Stanford University Press, 1999.

———. "Civilization and Dissent." In *Asian Americans: On War and Peace*, edited by Russel C. Leong and Don T. Nakanishi, 151–163. Los Angeles: UCLA Asian American Studies Center Press, 2002.

———. "Theory and the Subject of Asian America Studies." *Amerasia Journal* 21.1–2 (1995): 55–65.

Pelaud, Isabelle T. "The Plight of Vietnamese American Students at SFSU." *Nha Magazine*, July/August 2006, 118–120.

Pham, Andrew. *Catfish and Mandala: A Two-Wheeled Voyage through the Landscape and Memory of Vietnam*. New York: Farrar, Straus & Giroux, 1999.

———. Personal interview, June 10, 2000, Brisbane, Cal.

Pham, Vu Hong. "Beyond and before Boat People: Vietnamese American History before 1975." PhD dissertation, Cornell University, 2002.

Phan, Aimee. "Vietnamese Lose All, This Time to Katrina." Editorial, *USA Today*, September 15, 2005.

Phan, Hieu Tran. "Roots of Unrest: Understanding the Vietnamese Demonstrations in Orange County—The Story of a War that Will Not End." *Orange County Register*, June 13, 1999, sec. 2.

Portes, Jacques. *Les américains et la guerre du Vietnam*. Brussels: Éditions Complexe, 1993.

Ranard, Donald. "Between Two Worlds: Refugee Youth." *In America: Perspectives on Refugee Resettlement* 2 (January 1989): 6–8.

Rivers, Tony. "Oriental Girls: Tony Rivers Examines the Enduring Appeal of the Great Western Male Fantasy." *GQ British Edition*, October 1990, 160–162.

Ross, Andrew. *No Respect: Intellectuals and Popular Culture*. New York: Routledge, 1989.

Rotter, Andrew J. *The Path to Vietnam: Origins of the American Commitment to Southeast Asia*. Ithaca: Cornell University Press, 1987.

Rowe, John Carlos, and Rick Berg, eds. *The Vietnam War and American Culture*. New York: Columbia University Press, 1986.

Rubin, Merle. "Book Review; Tales of the World's 'Unchosen' Misfits; FAKE HOUSE and Other Stories by Linh Dinh." *Los Angeles Times*, October 2, 2000, 3.

Rumbaut, Ruben. "Vietnamese, Laotian, and Cambodian Americans." In *Asian Americans: Contemporary Trends and Issues*, edited by Pyong Gap Min, 262–291.Thousand Oaks, Cal.: Sage, 1995.

Rutledge, Paul. *The Vietnamese Experience in America*. Bloomington: Indiana University Press, 1992.

Said, Edward. *Culture and Imperialism*. New York: Vintage, 1993.

———. *Orientalism*. New York: Vintage, 1979.

———. *Reflections on Exile and Other Essays*. Cambridge: Harvard University Press, 2000.

———. "Reflections on Exile." In *Out There: Marginalization and Contemporary Cultures*, edited by Russell Ferguson, Martha Gever, Trinh T. Minh-ha, and Cornel West. New York: New Museum of Contemporary Art; Cambridge: MIT Press, 1990.

———. *Representations of the Intellectual*. New York: Vintage, 1994.

———. *The World, the Text, and the Critic*. Cambridge: Harvard University Press, 1983.

Saigon USA. Film documentary directed by Lindsey Jang and Robert C. Winn. KOCE-TV, 2002.

Seaman, Donna. "Review of *Fake House*." *Booklist*, September 15, 2000, 215–216.

Schiller, Nina Glick, Linda Bash, and Cristina Blanc-Szanton, eds. "Towards a Definition of Transnationalism: Introductory Remarks and Research Questions." In *Towards a Transnational Perspective on Migration: Race, Class, Ethnicity, and Nationalism Reconsid-*

ered, ix–xiv. New York: Annals of the New York Academy of Sciences, 1992.

Scott, George M. "Hmong Aspirations for a Separate State in Laos: The Effects of the Indo-China War." In *Secessionist Movements in Comparative Perspective*, edited by Ralph R. Premdas, S.W. R. de A. Samsarasinghe, and Alan B. Anderson, 111–125. New York: St. Martin's, 1990.

Shah, Sonia, ed. *Dragon Ladies: Asian American Feminists Breathe Fire*. Boston: South End Press, 1997.

Simon, Roger I., Sharon Rosenberg, and Claudia Eppert, eds. *Between Hope and Despair: Pedagogy and the Remembrance of Historical Trauma*. Lanham, Md.: Rowman and Littlefield, 2000.

Smith, Sidonie, and Gisela Brinker-Gabler. *Writing New Identities: Gender, Nation, and Immigration in Contemporary Europe*. Minneapolis: University of Minnesota Press, 1977.

Spivak, Ghayatri Chakravorty. "Can the Subaltern Speak?" *Wedge*, 7/8 (1985): 120–130.

———. *The Post-Colonial Critic: Interviews, Strategies, Dialogues*, edited by Sarah Harasym. New York: Routledge, 1990.

Srikanth, Rajini. *The World Next Door: South Asian American Literature and the Idea of America*. Philadelphia: Temple University Press, 2004.

Stam, Robert. "Bakhtin, Polyphony, and Ethnic/Racial Representation." In *Unspeakable Images: Ethnicity and the American Cinema*, edited by Lester D. Friedman, 251–276. Urbana: University of Illinois Press, 1991.

Starr, Paul D., and Alden E. Roberts. "Attitudes toward New Americans: Perceptions of Indo-Chinese in Nine Cities." *Research in Race and Ethnic Relations* 3 (1982), 165–186.

Stewart, Frank, Kevin Bowen, and Ba Chung Nguyen, eds. *Two Rivers: New Vietnamese Writing from America and Viet Nam*. Special issue of *Manoa Journal*. Honolulu: University of Hawaii Press, 2002.

Strand, Paul, and Woodrow Jones, Jr. *Indochinese Refugees in America: Problems of Adaptation and Assimilation*. Durham: Duke University Press, 1985.

Strom, Dao. *Grass Roof, Tin Roof*. Boston: Houghton Mifflin, 2003.

Sturken, Marita. "Absent Images of Memory: Remembering and Re-enacting the Japanese Internment." *Positions* 5.3 (1997): 687–778.

———. *Tangled Memories: The Vietnam War, the AIDS Epidemic, and the Politics of Remembering.* Berkeley: University of California Press, 1997.

Su, Lac. *I Love Yous Are for White People.* New York: Harper Perennial, 2009.

Suleiman, Suzan R. "The 1.5 Generation: Thinking about Child Survivors and the Holocaust." *American Imago* 59.3 (2002): 277–295.

Svetkovich, Ann. *An Archive of Feelings: Trauma, Sexuality, and Lesbian Public Cultures.* Durham: Duke University Press, 2003.

Takaki, Ronald. *Strangers from a Different Shore: A History of Asian Americans.* New York: Penguin Books, 1989.

Tal, Kali. *Worlds of Hurt: Reading the Literatures of Trauma.* Cambridge: Cambridge University Press, 1996.

Tang Truong Nhu, David Chanoff, and Doan Van Toai. *A Vietcong Memoir.* New York: Vintage, 1985.

Thach Hanh. "Gap Go." *Van Hoc* 95 (1994): 22–28.

The Vietnamese Artists Collective. *As Is: A Collection of Visual and Literary Works by Vietnamese American Artists.* San Francisco: Vietnamese Artists Collective, 2006.

Tollefson, James W. "Language Policy and Power: Yugoslavia, the Philippines, and Southeast Asian Refugees in the United States." *International Journal of Sociology of Language* 103 (1993): 57–72.

Tompkins, J. H. "Extreme Measures: War Stories." *San Francisco Bay Guardian,* October 6, 2004, 48.

Towers, Robert. "Far from Saigon." Review of *A Good Scent from a Strange Mountain* by Robert Olen Butler. *New York Review of Books* 40.14 (August 12, 1993): 249.

Tran, Barbara, and Rebekah Linh Collins, eds. *Viet Nam: Beyond the Frame,* special issue of *Michigan Quarterly Review* 1 (Fall 2004).

Tran, Barbara, Monique T. D. Truong, and Luu Truong Khoi, eds. *Watermark: Vietnamese American Poetry and Prose.* New York: Asian American Writers' Workshop, 1998.

Tran, De, Andrew Lam, and Hai Dai Nguyen, eds. *Once upon a Dream.* Kansas City: Andrews and McMeel, 1995.

Tran, Ky-Phong. "Nam Le Does Not Go Gently." *Asian American: Poetry and Writing.* http://www.aapw-la.org/interviews-namle.php.

Tran, Lan. "Lone Star." In *Falling Backwards: Stories of Fathers and Daughters,* edited by Gina Frangello, 117–125. Chicago: Hourglass Books, 2004.

Tran, Qui-Phiet, "From Isolation to Integration: Vietnamese Americans in Tran Dieu Hang's Fiction." In *Reading the Literature of*

Asian America, edited by Shirley Geok-Lim and Amy Ling, 271–284. Philadelphia: Temple University Press, 1992.

Tran, Thi. "Modern Woman: An Exclusive Interview with Novelist le thi diem thuy." *Nha Magazine*, September/October 2003.

Tran, Tri Vu. *Lost Years: My 1,632 Days in Vietnamese Reeducation Camps*. Berkeley: Institute of East Asian Studies, 1988.

Tran, Truong. *dust and conscience*. Berkeley: Apogee Press, 2002.

———. *Placing the Accents*. Berkeley: Apogee Press, 1999.

Tran, Truong, and Chung Hoang Chuong. *The Book of Perceptions*. San Francisco: Kearny Street Workshop, 1999.

Tran, Van Dinh. *Blue Dragon, White Tiger: A Tet Story*. Philadelphia: TriAm Press, 1983.

———. *No Passenger on the River*. New York: Vantage Press, 1965.

Trinh Minh Duc Hoai. *This Side, the Other Side*. Washington, D.C.: Occidental Press, 1985.

Trinh, Quang Do. *Saigon to San Diego: Memoirs of a Boy Who Escaped from Communist Vietnam*. Jefferson, N.C.: McFarland, 2004.

Trinh T. Minh-ha. *Woman Native Other: Writing Postcoloniality and Feminism*. Bloomington: Indiana University Press, 1989.

Trouillot, Michel-Rolph. *Silencing the Past: Power and the Production of History*. Boston: Beacon, 1995.

Truong, Buu Lam. *Colonialism Experienced: Vietnamese Writings on Colonialism, 1900–1931*. Ann Arbor: University of Michigan Press, 2000.

Truong, Monique. *The Book of Salt*. New York: Houghton Mifflin, 2003.

———. "The Emergence of Voices: Vietnamese American Literature 1975–1900." *Amerasia Journal* 19.3 (1993): 27–50.

———. "Kelly." *Amerasia Journal* 17.2 (1991): 41–48.

———. "The Reception of Robert Olen Butler's 'A Good Scent from a Strange Mountain': Ventriloquism and the Pulitzer Prize." *Viet Nam Forum* 16 (1997): 75–94.

———. "Vietnamese American Literature." In King-Kok Cheung, ed., *An Interethnic Companion to Asian American Literature*, 219–246. New York: Cambridge University Press, 1997.

Um, Khathary. Class lecture, University of California, Berkeley, Spring 1998.

———. "Southeast Asian Resettlement." Lecture, University of California, Berkeley, Spring 1997.

Valverde, Kieu Linh Caroline. "From Dust to Gold: The Amerasian

Experience." In *Racially Mixed People in America*, edited by P. P. Maria Root, 144–161. Newbury Park, Cal.: Sage, 1992.

———. "Making Vietnamese Music Transnational: Sounds of Home, Resistance and Change." *Amerasia Journal* 29.1 (2003): 29–49.

VietBAK. "Hardboiled." November 2005.

Vo, Nghia M. *The Bamboo Gulag: Political Imprisonment in Communist Vietnam*. Jefferson, N.C.: McFarland, 2004.

Weiss, Lowell. "Voices from Vietnam." *Boston Globe*, February 27, 1994, A14.

White, Hayden. *Tropics of Discourse: Essays in Cultural Criticism*. Baltimore: Johns Hopkins University Press, 1978.

Winston, Jane Bradley, and Leakthina Chau-Pech Ollier, eds. *Of Vietnam: Identities in Dialogue*. New York: Palgrave, 2001.

Wong, Sau-Ling Cynthia. "Denationalization Reconsidered: Asian American Cultural Criticism at a Theoretical Crossroads." *Amerasia Journal* 21.1–2 (1995): 1–27.

———. *Reading Asian American Literature: From Necessity to Extravagance*. Princeton: Princeton University Press, 1993.

———. "'Sugar Sisterhood': Situating the Amy Tan Phenomenon." In *The Ethnic Canon: Histories, Institutions, and Inventions*, edited by David Palumbo-Liu, 174–208. Minneapolis: University of Minnesota Press, 1995.

Yeager, Jack. *The Vietnamese Novel in French: A Literary Response to Colonialism*. Hanover, N.H.: University Press of New England, 1987.

Young, Marilyn B. *The Vietnam Wars: 1945–1990*. New York: Harper Perennial, 1991.

Yoneyama, Lisa. "Critical Warps: Facticity, Transformative Knowledge, and Postcolonialist Criticism in the Smithsonian Controversy." *Positions* 5.3 (1997): 779–809.

Zinoman, Peter. "What's Going On? The Oakland Museum's 'Vietnam War Exhibit' and the Fields of Vietnamese Studies." Keynote address delivered at the conference, "30 Years beyond the War: Vietnamese, Southeast Asian and Asian/American Studies," April 20, 2005, University of California, Riverside.

Zhai, Qiang. *China and the Vietnam Wars, 1950–1975*. Chapel Hill: University of North Carolina Press, 2000.

Zucker, Norman, and Naomi Flink Zucker. "The Uneasy Troika in U.S. Refugee Policy: Foreign Policy, Pressure Groups, and Resettlement Costs." *Journal of Refugee Studies* 2.3 (1989): 359–372.

Index

Cao, Lan, 3, 65, 104, 121; *Monkey Bridge*, 3, 36, 37, 65, 86–100, 139n3
Cao, Tan, 23, 24
Catfish and Mandala (Pham), 3, 36, 54, 65–85, 121–123; abandonment in, 67–68; anger in, 70–73, 76, 82–83; as creative nonfiction, 122; critical reception of, 123, 139n2; domestic violence in, 66–67, 70–71, 73–74, 162n18; exile in, 80; family in, 77; guilt in, 73–75, 76, 82–83; healing in, 82; heteronormativity in, 163n27; hybridity in, 100; identity formation in, 79, 81, 99, 163n31; as immigrant story, 122; intergenerational conflict in, 67, 78; internalized racism in, 78; masculinity in, 75–79, 81, 164n48; memory in, 80, 83; model minority myth in, 67, 72–73; and multiculturalism, 77; protagonist as cultural bridge, 122–123; racism in, 69–70, 73; reception of, 121; reeducation camps in, 74; survivor's guilt in, 75; trauma in, 68–69, 161n14; Viet Nam War in, 122
Chan, Jeffery Paul, 112, 162n15
Chan, Sucheng, 45, 48, 56, 163n33
Cheung, King-Kok, 47, 48
Chin, Frank, 71, 78–79, 162n15
Choy, Catherine Ceniza, 160n2
Chuh, Kandace, 55
Chung, Chuong, 46
civil rights movement, U.S., 18, 45
Cleveland Elementary School massacre (Stockton, CA), 14
Clinton, Bill, 17
Collier, Rebeka, 163n27
Collins, Rebekah, 142n11, 163n29
colonialism: and gender, 165n20; and hybridity, 49; and imperialism, 142n13; Memmi on, 77; psychic costs of, 130. *See also* colonialism, French.
colonialism, French, 142n13; opium policy, 161n10; role of education in, 93, 113, 131; sexual coercion under, 98–99, 164n47. *See also* Viet Nam

De Certeau, Michel, 98
Deer Hunter, The, 90–91
Derrida, Jacques, 65
diaspora, Vietnamese, xii, 32, 137; population demographics, 141n9
diaspora studies: and dehistoricization, 56; and depoliticization, 53, 56; and pan-Asian American coalition building, 53
Diasporic Vietnamese Artists Network (DVAN), 139n1
Dien Bien Phu, Battle of, 142n12
Dinh, Linh, 4, 128, 130, 165n17, 166n24; critics, response to, 131–132, 168n51; *Fake House*, 4, 111–117, 128–132; "555," 112–113, 128, 130; "Hope and Standard," 113–115, 128; *Night, Again*, 32–33; women, representation of, 128, 130
Do, Hien, 46, 154n52
Doi Moi, 31, 136
Duong, Lan, 158n26
dust and conscience (Truong Tran), 3, 36, 54, 102–111, 116–117; assimilation in, 110, 111; authenticity in, 110; betrayal in, 110; and exoticism, 109–110; exile in, 106; fluid identity in, 105; home in, 104–109; identity formation in, 107, 108; and identity politics, 103; narrative fragmentation of, 111; narrative ruptures in, 109–110; nationalism in, 110; reception of, 116–117; and representationality, 103, 116; role of nation in, 105; suspension of language in, 108

Eliot, T.S., 86
Elliott, Duong Van Mai, 38, 125, 154nn59, 60
Enloe, Cynthia, 165n20
Espiritu, Yen Le, 46, 48, 49, 59; on refugee narratives, 153n48

literature, Asian American;
literature Vietnamese American;
Vietnamese Americans

Tale of Kieu, The, 114
Tang, Truong Nhu, 26
Thao, Mai, 23–24
Thich Quang Duc, 52, 158n32
Time Tree, The (Huu), 31–32, 152n34
Tram, Dang Thuy, 33
Tran, Barbara, 59, 136
Tran, Cau Thi Bich, 16, 147n55
Tran Thi Nga, 30, 151n20
Tran, Truong, 3, 36, 102–104; *dust and conscience*, 3, 36, 54, 102–111, 116–117
trauma: historical, 64–65; and identity formation, 64; in Vietnamese American literature, 3, 54, 63, 68–69, 87–88, 98, 135, 161n14
Trung Trac, 96, 97, 120
Truong, Monique T.D., 30, 48, 48, 168n48; *Book of Salt, The*, 38–39, 125–127
Truong, Tran Van (video store controversy), 18, 160n2

United Nations: Comprehensive Plan of Action (CPA), 144n27; U.N. High Commissioner for Refugees (UNHCR), 143n26; and Vietnamese refugee status, 12
United States: Amerasian Homecoming Act (1987), 12, 146n44; anticommunism in, 8, 158n25; Chinese Exclusion Act (1882), 159n49; Japanese Americans, internment of, 18; Patriot Act (2001), 51; racial hierarchy in, 15–16, 166n23; Refugee Act (1980), 143n26, 144n35; refugee policies on, 12–13, 15, 142n17; Resettlement Opportunities for Vietnamese Returnees Program, 12–13; as superpower, 7, 50, 94, 140n5; Walter-McCarran Act (1952), 159n50

United States, foreign policy: Central Intelligence Agency, 8; and citizenship, 50, 159nn49, 50; and human rights, 7; in Korea, 160n1; and military intervention, 63, 140n4, 160n1; in Southeast Asia, 141n5; Viet Nam, economic embargo against, 17–18, 27, 32, 88, 136, 147n58, 154n52; Viet Nam, normalization of relations with, 36. *See also* United States, Viet Nam War
Unwanted, The (Kien Nguyen), 37–38

video store controversy (Westminster, CA), 18, 160n2
Vietcong Memoir, The (Tang), 26
Viet Kieu, 78; in *Catfish and Mandala*, 167n17; in *Fake House*, 113, 114, 115
Viet Minh, 142n12, 154n60. *See also* Viet Nam; Viet Nam War
Viet Nam: Amerasian experience in, 38, 146n44, 154n57; anti-Chinese resentment in, 11, 143nn19, 20; Cambodia, war with, 149n71; colonization of, 8, 9, 45; human rights in, 9, 23–24, 25–26, 105, 124; Japanese occupation of, 45–46, 154n60, 155n5; normative images of, 52–53; position of women in, 113–114; reeducation camps in, 9, 23, 27, 28, 63, 74, 103, 123, 149n71; relations with China, 149n71; repatriation to, 12; as term, 140n2, 158n26; U.S., normalization of relations with, 36; U.S. withdrawal from, 7. *See also* United States, foreign policy; Vietnamese; Vietnamese Americans; Viet Nam War
Viet Nam: At the Crossroads, 154n52
Vietnamese: representations of, 53, 92, 153n47; women, status of, 113–114. *See also* Viet Nam; Vietnamese Americans; Viet Nam War

About the Author

Isabelle Thuy Pelaud is an Associate Professor of Asian American Studies at San Francisco State University and founder of the Diasporic Vietnamese Artists Network (DVAN).

Josephine Lee, *Performing Asian America: Race and Ethnicity on the Contemporary Stage*

Deepika Bahri and Mary Vasudeva, eds., *Between the Lines: South Asians and Postcoloniality*

E. San Juan, Jr., *The Philippine Temptation: Dialectics of Philippines-U.S. Literary Relations*

Carlos Bulosan and E. San Juan, Jr., ed., *The Cry and the Dedication*

Carlos Bulosan and E. San Juan, Jr., ed., *On Becoming Filipino: Selected Writings of Carlos Bulosan*

Vicente L. Rafael, ed., *Discrepant Histories: Translocal Essays on Filipino Cultures*

Yen Le Espiritu, *Filipino American Lives*

Paul Ong, Edna Bonacich, and Lucie Cheng, eds., *The New Asian Immigration in Los Angeles and Global Restructuring*

Chris Friday, *Organizing Asian American Labor: The Pacific Coast Canned-Salmon Industry, 1870–1942*

Sucheng Chan, ed., *Hmong Means Free: Life in Laos and America*

Timothy P. Fong, *The First Suburban Chinatown: The Remarking of Monterey Park, California*

William Wei, *The Asian American Movement*

Yen Le Espiritu, *Asian American Panethnicity*

Velina Hasu Houston, ed., *The Politics of Life*

Renqiu Yu, *To Save China, To Save Ourselves: The Chinese Hand Laundry Alliance of New York*

Shirley Geok-lin Lim and Amy Ling, eds., *Reading the Literatures of Asian America*

Karen Isaksen Leonard, *Making Ethnic Choices: California's Punjabi Mexican Americans*

Gary Y. Okihiro, *Cane Fires: The Anti-Japanese Movement in Hawaii, 1865–1945*

Sucheng Chan, *Entry Denied: Exclusion and the Chinese Community in America, 1882–1943*